An illustrated survey of
Furniture Prices
at UK Auctions

2000-2004

2005 Edition

Editor: John Ainsley

An illustrated survey of

Furniture Prices at UK Auctions

2000-2004

2005 Edition

Editor: John Ainsley

First published in Great Britain 2004 by
Antiques Information Services Ltd. Wallsend House,
P O Box 93, Broadstairs, Kent CT10 3YR
Telephone: 01843 862069
Fax: 01843 862014
Email: john.ainsley@antiques-info.co.uk

Further details about the Publishers may be found on our website at
www.antiques-info.co.uk

ISBN: 0-9546479-1-2
Whilst every care has been exercised in the compilation of this guide,
neither the editor nor publishers accept any liability for any financial
or other loss incurred by reliance placed on the information contained
in *Furniture Prices at Auction*

Printed in the United Kingdom

Contents

Introduction

The Project

In December 2003 we published our pilot work *Pottery and Porcelain Prices at Auction.* This has proved so successful that we are now planning a series of books. *Furniture Prices at Auction* is the first in the new series and covers prices mainly from 2001-2004. This work will continue to address the needs of the professional user and the collector for the next two to three years, after which an updated edition will be published.

Price Guides in General

Previously, price guides have always followed the A-Z format, prices being based on the informed opinion of the author or experts from within the industry. This formula is not being challenged. It has a logic and such price guides play a significant role in providing information. However it is quite clear that they do not represent actual sales. *Furniture Prices at Auction* is unique. The provision of examples from all categories and from real sales is an extremely useful addition to existing price guide formats. Readers of *Pottery and Porcelain Prices at Auction*, even experts and dealers, tell us that they are frequently referring to this book.

A New Rationale

Here for the first time ever are actual furniture prices at auction from a mass of defined market situations representing the sales of over 3,030 lots. These have been placed in eleven price bands and in actual price order in the price range £240,000 down to only £20. The price bands are arbitrary but they provide a means of dividing the work into sections which not only aid the analysis but also provide a format which will help the reader keep their bearings. These illustrations have not only been chosen to represent the various price ranges but also to represent furniture from the last five hundred years with examples from the sixteenth to the twentieth centuries. The lots illustrated have been taken from sales occurring mainly between 2001 and 2004, a credible four years. In this period fashions and even prices have changed and the book represents these changes.

The rationale is the rationale of the market. This has been given priority. If you have tried to study the market from previous price guides you will be aware of the difficulties. The A-Z format is a weakness in itself bearing no relationship to the market which is a straightforward matter of when an item was sold, where it was sold and what it sold for! Here, in this work, the actual numeric price order, overseeing the price bands, representing the top to the bottom *is* the essential ingredient which aids a grasp of the fundamental elements which *are* the market. Here one can analyse the market in many ways. The reader can browse any price range. Or, using the comprehensive *Index*, it is possible to make, for example, a market study of a particular category such as dining tables or a particular style or a particular maker, such as Robert 'Mouseman' Thompson.

Each Section is preceded by an Editor's analysis and it is recommended that this be studied with the images and the captions themselves. This analysis is not definitive and is unobtrusive. The subject is not a science. Analyses may follow numerous paths at various levels. Hence, the Editor's analyses is personalised around the editor's interests and the editor's level of knowledge. A myriad of readers will each seek their own analyses based on their own knowledge and their own narrow or broad interests. For example, a specialist furniture dealer may take a broad interest in either checking out prices across the board or concentrate on furniture within his own price range. Alternatively a collector of say, early country furniture may concentrate on this area, at the same time familiarising themselves with the market. A collector or dealer specialising in Robert 'Mouseman' Thompson can study a whole range of categories of his work in the price range £9,000 to £210.

Auction Arithmetic

Most auctions in the UK publish only their hammer prices. The final price paid by the buyer is a matter of a private invoice which is not in the public domain.

Buying at auction

Auctions add on the following charges. Firstly there is a variable buyer's premium dependent on the hammer price. For example you may pay 15% on top of a hammer price of say £1,000 but only 10% on a hammer price of £30,000. In addition there is VAT to be paid on the premium and in some cases VAT may be due on the hammer price as well, depending on the age and origin of the lot. We advise you add 15% to the hammer prices to gauge the rough buying price. Auction catalogues will include the buyer's terms and conditions.

Selling at auction

The final cost to the vendor is private and is a matter of a final statement with a cheque for an item that has been sold. Again there is a premium to pay which on average will be at least 10-15% of the hammer price. Then there is the VAT and in addition there may be charges related to photographs, storage and even insurance. We would suggest that if you use this price guide to gauge how much you would receive if you were to sell an item, that this time you subtract about 15% from the hammer price. This is an important market statement. The real buying price and the real selling price will actually vary by at least 30%. Again the auction catalogue will always explain the terms and conditions relating to selling at auction. If the reader is in any doubt, auctions are always willing to explain their operations. And on viewing days, staff are usually on hand to offer information or advice on the lots themselves.

Auction Prices and the Market

Just as a fall in the housing or stock markets sends a shiver through the nation, so emerge the doom-mongers when antique furniture is experiencing a period of adjustment and re-appraisal. Yet this is hardly surprising following 30 years of quite astonishing growth when investing in antique furniture has out-performed houses and stocks. Let us see clearly from the very beginning what this adjustment really means. Regardless of those categories which have suffered, such as chaise longues, bureaux and much of the ordinary late Georgian and Victorian mahogany, that even here there is room for optimism. Almost any antique or second-hand furniture is still a better buy than brand new! Generally it is better made, is of higher quality materials and is certain to hold or maintain its value in the next, say 5-10 years. Today such furniture offers terrific value for money in terms of both function and investment. When you buy, primarily you must ensure, that your purchases have a clear use in the home and are in good condition. And in 'good condition' does not mean that all original surfaces have been destroyed and the piece over-restored. Carry out these simple rules and in a few years time if you have to or wish to sell you will soon find a buyer!

Having reviewed the worst scenario, let us now summarise the positives of recent years. The market for the higher quality, rarer items, of good colour and patination, is not only buoyant but is going through the roof! Early walnut, regardless of condition, is fetching a fortune and after a short lapse early country and oak has recovered and according to most reports is rising. Many auctioneers and dealers are judging that the market has 'bottomed out'. Decorative pieces are selling well and the unusual and the unique, or the quirky are in high demand. Arts and Crafts to Art Deco and the 1960s and 1970s are rising markets. In the meantime don't pass up a French farmhouse table at the right price but be more fussy about davenports, balloon-back chairs and chaise longues. 1970s Scandinavian rosewood is wildly collected and the twentieth century is on a high. Even 1930s utility oak is finding new homes as families realise the astonishing value of real wood compared to the futility of buying reproduction imitations or flat packs. Meanwhile, if you can find a good Victorian mahogany linen press (Georgian ones are more), or wardrobe for £400-£600 or a twin-pedestal sideboard for £300-£400, or even a good mahogany chest of drawers for £200-£300, don't hesitate! These prices might never be seen again. Also keep a look out for good dining room furniture such as large extending tables and long sets of chairs which continue in steady demand.

In summary it is simply not true that antique or old furniture has had its day and will never sell unless it is blue chip with an extensive provenance. Without doubt, minimalism, exchange rates and 9/11 have caused a re-appraisal following 30 years of astonishing growth. Undoubtedly, the glossies and the television have wooed potential buyers with their sleek laminate chipboard surfaces, silver appliances and halogen lighting. But the 'Ikea generation' is also a fashion and hardly likely to be as resilient as our history, our tradition and our heritage. However, many people have been prepared to borrow thousands of pounds against the enhanced values of their properties to purchase new furniture, some of which they have to fit together on the sitting room floor! As one auctioneer put it, "their dotcom wonderstock, which in a few years time they won't be able to give away".

Surely now one should consider that the depreciation in some sectors be viewed as a long-overdue correction. Therefore, now is precisely the time to buy from the huge resource of recycled furniture made from the very finest materials which represent our great heritage and which can bring huge pleasure and investment potential whilst having no adverse effect on the environment.

The Editor wishes to thank the dozens of auctioneers up and down the country who have spared some of their very precious time to comment on the furniture market.

How to use this Book

This book is an ideal browsing medium but it is recommended that both the full **Introduction** and the **Section Analyses** are read at an early stage. A significant part of this work are the descriptions to the images. These conclude with colour-coded market information, viz: *where the lot was sold, when the lot was sold* and *what the lot was sold for*. Hammer prices must be treated with caution. There are lots which have sold, say in 2001, which in 2004 are likely to fetch more or even less than they did then. The analyses may point up examples.

In addition whilst every effort has been made by the Editor to check out the attributions there exists the unlikely possibility of error. Auction cataloguing is a difficult task and even specialists cannot know everything. However, great care is usually taken and 'labelling' is in most cases very accurate. Incidentally, many auctions will rescind a sale within a set period of the purchase if the buyer can show inaccuracies in the catalogue description. Disputes usually revolve around marriages, damaged, restored or reproduction lots.

In some cases captions have been rationalised in order to solve editing requirements. Syntactical changes have been made and abbreviations used which did not occur in the original auction catalogue. And on occasions the Editor has used his discretion to omit descriptive detail which would be tedious and which would not materially influence the price. In all cases the Editor has ensured that changes in meaning have not occurred and that the content of a caption remains true to the original version. Foreign spellings also varied considerably in the original catalogues. These have been standardised to ensure the integrity of the Indexing system.

Finally, the reader's attention is drawn to the *Glossary of Terms* and the *Furniture Index*. These are integral parts of this work. The *Index* alone has approximately 7,500 cross-references to the main body of the book and is colour-coded to aid fast searches. **Editor**

Section I   £10,000 +

One of the most important market movements of recent years has been the remorseless rise in value of early walnut and the continuing price increases in general impacting at the top end of the market.

Some of the most important characteristics to be found in this price range are the exceptional quality and condition which will attach to most of the pieces. And frequently associated with these rarer attributes are a maker's name, or an association to a famous style, or to a famous person. Hence at **3** is a set of three Georgian Gainsborough chairs in the Chippendale manner which fetched on average over £50,000 each with added premium. It is worth skimming through this section to do some name-spotting. Here you will find for example, Johnstone and Jeanes, Martin, Hepplewhite, William Burgess, Jean-Francois Leleu, Thomas Hache, Norman Adams, Philip Webb, Gillows, Edwards and Roberts, Robert Mainwaring, and Morris & Co. In addition there are associations with famous people such as King George V and Oliver Cromwell.

One of the most important market movements of recent years has been the remorseless rise in value of early walnut which usually suggests furniture from the first half of the eighteenth century. Regardless of the fact that most woods are represented and particularly mahogany rather than oak, it is worth looking through the Section for walnut examples, in particular burr, oyster veneering and marquetry. Examples may be found at **23**, **30**, **34**, **45**, **52**, **54**, **65**, **67**, **76** and **93**, etc.

Here is the best of dining room furniture and particularly tables. The higher the seating capacity, the higher the price. Large dining tables can be found at **4**, **6**, **8**, **40**, **97** and **102**. These can seat often upwards of a dozen people. Other tables also fetch very large sums. Note the giltwood console table at **7**, the library drum at **9** and the pier at **10**. It is the same with chairs. As a guide a pair are valued at three times the single price, a set of four, six to seven times a single, a set of six, ten to twelve times and sets of eight over fifteen times the value of a single chair. Here there are even larger sets of fourteen, eighteen and even two sets of twenty chairs and they are rare and valuable. Follow from **17**, for a set of twelve Hepplewhite period mahogany shield-back dining chairs, which fetched £36,000 hammer in March 2003 to a set of eight early George III mahogany dining chairs in the style of Robert Mainwaring at £10,500. See **99**.

One is used to the ubiquitous fold-over card table at the lower end of the market but here at **28** is a George III rosewood version with a concertina action which fetched an amazing £22,500. See **28**. For further examples of side, card and console tables, see **56**, **66**, **80**, **91** and **98**. All of these examples contain marquetry.

The seventeenth and early eighteenth century is well represented with furniture ranging from the Jacobite period to William and Mary, Queen Anne and George I. The very best of cased furniture commences with the incredible £80,000 paid for a burr walnut chest of drawers at **5**. There are many other examples including a William and Mary walnut chest on stand with original brass, peardrop handles and engraved escutcheon plates which fetched £19,000 in June 2003 at Henry Duke & Son, Dorchester. See **34**.

The dining room is never far away. Whilst wine coolers are popular the £26,000 hammer is the best price in the book for such a small object. See **22**. On the same theme, note a wine bottle stand at **101**, which fetched £10,200. Country furniture can be found at **31** where an oak dresser fetched £20,000 hammer in October 2003 and a Montgomery oak dresser £17,000 at **47**. See also **51** and **63**. And dresser bases appear on page 11 with some really fine examples. Country chairs will not make an appearance until at least *Section 3*. See also two sixteenth century oak panel-back armchairs at £13,500 and £12,000 and a child's chair at an amazing £13,000. Other sales worthy of mention are the kettle-stand at **25** which reached £23,000 and the pair of occasional tables at **29** which fetched £22,500 - boulle, of course.

Other pieces which catch the eye are the display shelves at **36** which fetched £19,000, and a stool at **37** which reached the same figure. Several mirrors grace this Section with £190,000 paid for a pair of continental wall mirrors whilst a Regency giltwood convex reached £13,500. Note the early appearance of Irish furniture which can be followed through the *Index*. An eighteenth century stained pine console table and a pair of Waterford wall mirrors both appear on page 10 at £15,000 and £14,000 respectively. Seating furniture in this section is particularly appealing. Note the pair of early eighteenth century leather side chairs at **42** and the set of six dining chairs in petit-point at **92** with the set of eight dining chairs in the style of Robert Mainwaring at **99** in close contention.

1

Pair of George III mahogany benches made for William Beckford. (1760-1841) (Was a set of 6) *Hy. Duke & Son, Dorchester. Apr 03. £240,000.*

2

Pair 18thC Continental wall mirrors, Boulle style red, gilt verre eglomise border, 54cm. *Stride & Son, Chichester. July 03. £190,000.*

3

Three Georgian Gainsborough chairs in the Chippendale manner. *Stride & Son, Chichester. Oct 03. £145,000.*

4

Johnstone & Jeanes patent mahogany extending dining table, c1845, 2 sets of leaves, engraved brass boss, ht. 2ft 5in, dia's. 4ft 11.25in, 6ft 0.25in, 6ft 11.5in. *Gorringes, Bexhill. Nov 03. £135,000.*

5

George II burr walnut cross, feather banded chest, brushing slide, 30in x 19in. *Calcutt Maclean Standen, Cranbrook. Sep 03. £80,000.*

6

George III patent extending mahogany dining table, three leaves, brass plaque inscribed 'S Martin, Invenit et Fecit', 1.32m wide, 3.36m x 1.50m closed, 0.74m high. *Sworders, Stansted Mountfitchet. Sep 03. £63,000.*

7

Pair of George II giltwood console tables, original 'breche violette' marble top, 70in x 30in deep, 30in high. *Hy. Duke & Son, Dorchester. June 03. £60,000.*

8

George IV mahogany four pillar dining table. *Woolley & Wallis, Salisbury. Jan 01. £52,000.*

9

George IV pollard oak library drum table. *Hamptons, Godalming. July 00. £52,000.*

10

Chinoiserie decorated pier table and glass, table with moulded top above a frieze drawer supported on s-scroll legs, 96cm, mirror, arched cornice above a bevelled rectangular plate within a moulded frame, *Cheffins, Cambridge. Dec 01. £44,000.*

Hammer Prices £240,000-£29,000

11

George I burr walnut chest on stand, drawers with ebony and boxwood line inlaid fronts, 104cm wide. *Bristol Auction Rooms. June 02. £42,000.*

12

Queen Anne walnut bureau cabinet, 41in wide, 82in high. *Sworders, Stansted Mountfitchet. May 01. £42,000.*

13

Important Anglo-Japanese ebonised mahogany sideboard, by Dr Christopher Dresser, prob. Chubb & Co, 192cm wide. *Dreweatt Neate, Newbury. Nov 01. £40,000.*

14

19thC rosewood serpentine commode, panels of floral marquetry in sycamore and boxwood on a yew ground, 151cm wide. *Dreweatt Neate, Newbury. Apr 00. £38,000.*

15

Early 18thC walnut settee, Queen Anne vase splats, pink velvet seat, bird head terminal to arms on claw and ball feet, 140cm. *Stride & Son, Chichester. July 03. £36,000.*

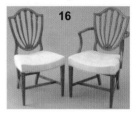

16

Fine set of 12 Hepplewhite period mahogany shield back dining chairs incl. two with arms. *Gorringes, Lewes. Mar 03. £36,000.*

17

Set of twenty Regency mahogany dining chairs. *Dreweatt Neate, Newbury. Apr 03. £36,000.*

18

George III mahogany secretaire bookcase, 33in wide. *Canterbury Auction Galleries, Kent. Apr 00. £29,000.*

Hammer Prices £28,000-£19,000

19

William Burgess painted chest. £28,000. Hogbens, Folkestone. July 03. £28,000.

20

Pair 18thC Italian specimen marble table tops, central chequered panels, guilloche borders, 3ft 3in x 1ft 10in, later underframes. Gorringes, Lewes. June 00. £27,000.

21

Sheraton period rosewood banded satinwood secretaire bookcase, 7ft 6in high x 3ft 1in wide. Gorringes, Lewes. Dec 00. £27,000.

22

Regency mahogany wine cooler of sarcophagus form, lion mask ring handles and ebonised mouldings, 28in high. Lots Road Auctions, Chelsea. July 01. £26,000.

23

William and Mary oyster veneered chest.
Clevedon Salesrooms, Bristol. Sep 00. £23,600.

24

Burr walnut feather-banded bureau bookcase, 18thC and later. Sotheby's, Billingshurst. Sep 00. £23,000.

25

George II mahogany kettle stand. Hy. Duke & Son, Dorchester. Apr 03. £23,000.

26

Louis XV kingwood/parquetry cartonnier by Jean-Francois Leleu, cavetto cornice over a long frieze drawer, 12 shelves, 38in wide, ht. 60in. Gorringes, Lewes. Oct 01. £23,000.

27

George II burr walnut bureau bookcase, 41in wide, ht. 81in. Sworders, Stansted Mountfitchet. May 01. £23,000.

28

George III rosewood fold over card table, concertina action, 36in wide. Sworders, Stansted Mountfitchet. May 01. £22,500.

> Prices quoted are hammer and exclude the buyer's premium. Adding 15% will give approx. buying price.

29

Pair of mid 19thC boulle occasional tables executed in premier and contra partie. Hamptons, Godalming. Sep 00. £22,500.

30

French marquetry commode chest, floral scroll panels in walnut, maple & olivewood, ivory chequer rim, gilt metal mask plaque to each side in manner of Thomas Hache of Grenoble, 130cm.
Stride & Son, Chichester. Oct 01. £22,000.

31

Early 18thC oak dresser, 52in x 77in. £20,000.
Ewbanks, Send, Surrey. Oct 03. £20,000.

32

Set of 18 Regency mahogany dining chairs, moulded square backs with reeded cresting, stuffover seats, including two elbow chairs. Woolley and Wallis, Salisbury. Jan 04. £20,000.

33

18thC mahogany double inverted block front commode having four graduated long drawers. Amersham Auction Rms, Bucks. May 01. £19,700.

34

William & Mary walnut chest on stand, original brass pear drop handles and engraved escutcheon plates, 41.24in wide, 62.5in high.
Hy. Duke & Son, Dorchester. June 03. £19,000.

George III mahogany tripod table. *Mellors & Kirk, Nottingham. Feb 03. £19,000.*

Pair of George III mahogany open front display shelves, 18in wide x 31in high. Some veneers missing to front and slight damage to frets. One drawer interior inscribed in ink 'Anne Pzott' 1799. *Canterbury Auc.Galleries, Kent. Aug 03. £19,000.*

Fine George II stool. *Woolley & Wallis, Salisbury. Jan 01. £19,000.*

Louis XV style giltwood suite, 20thC, three seat sofa, upholstered in 18thC style, 6 open armchairs, a three fold screen and fire screen. *Rosebery's, London. Dec 03. £19,000.*

George III inlaid satinwood and mahogany banded secretaire bookcase, c1790, 114cm wide. (later handles) *Sworders, Stansted Mountfitchet. Feb 04. £18,000.*

George III mahogany twin pedestal dining table, 8ft 4in long max x 4ft 4in wide. *Sworders, Stansted Mountfitchet. Mar 01. £17,500.*

3rd Empire library bookcase, 7ft 3in wide, 7ft 5in high. *Woolley & Wallis, Salisbury. Apr 00. £17,000.*

Pair of early 18thC French walnut side chairs, leather upholstered, acanthus carved cabriole legs and paw feet. *Dreweatt Neate, Newbury. Apr 00. £17,000.*

Hammer Prices £19,000-£16,000

Queen Anne walnut chest, c1710. *Sotheby's, London. Apr 02. £17,000.*

Regency rosewood dwarf bookcase, boxwood stringing, Greek Key brass gallery, two bevelled glazed silk lined doors, 4ft 2in. (Norman Adams label), *Gorringes, Lewes. Apr 01. £17,000.*

George I burr walnut tallboy, inlaid with 'sunburst' medallion in boxwood and ebony, 40.75in wide, 69.75in high. *Hy. Duke & Son, Dorchester. June 03. £17,000.*

Set of 12 Regency mahogany dining chairs, yoke backs, sabre uprights, Corinthian capitals, stuffover seats. *Lyon & Turnbull, Edinburgh. Mar 04. £17,000.*

18thC Montgomeryshire oak dresser. *Woolley & Wallis, Salisbury. Jan 01. £17,000.*

Set of 14 Regency mahogany dining chairs. (including two carvers) *Stride & Son, Chichester. Oct 02. £16,500.*

Mahogany, satinwood inlaid sideboard, 19thC. *Sotheby's, Billingshurst. July 00. £16,000.*

Set of ten Regency gilt brass inlaid and strung mahogany dining chairs. (2 with arms), *Gorringes, Lewes. Mar 01. £16,000.*

18thC Welsh oak dresser. *Gorringes, Bexhill. Feb 00. £16,000.*

Hammer Prices £16,000-£14,000

George II walnut tallboy, 45in wide. Hy. Duke & Son, Dorchester. June 03. £16,000.

Set 10 Regency mahog. dining chairs, incl. 2 arms. Cheffins, Cambridge. Mar 01. £15,550.

George I walnut settee, drop in seat in contemporary needle-work, 6ft wide. Hy. Duke & Son, Dorchester. June 03. £15,500.

George III mahogany breakfront bookcase, 234cm wide. Sworders, Stansted Mountfitchet. July 03. £15,500.

Pair of late Georgian inlaid demi-lune mahogany games tables. Garry M Emms, Great Yarmouth. June 00. £15,100.

18thC Irish stained pine console table, 60in, later walnut framed top inset with heavy white veined marble slab. Canterbury Auction Galleries, Kent. Dec 00. £15,000.

William & Mary oyster laburnum chest, c1700, 99cm wide. Sotheby's, Billingshurst. June 01. £15,000.

King George V dressing table off Royal Yacht 'Britannia'. On his death it was his wish that the yacht was sunk and this was done in the Solent. Shanklin Auction Rooms, Shanklin. June 00. £15,000.

Mid-late 18thC mahogany framed elbow chair. Amersham Auction Rooms, Bucks. May 01. £14,500.

Pair of George IV mahogany Bergère library armchairs, cane panelled back and arms, now upholstered fittings. Canterbury Auc. Galleries, Kent. Oct 01. £14,500.

Lunar atlas in oak case. Shanklin Auction Rooms, Shanklin. June 00. £14,500.

The numbering system acts as a reader reference as well as linking to the Analysis of each Section

George III oak dresser, 4ft 4in wide. Gorringes, Lewes. Sep 03. £14,000.

Pair of early 19thC Irish Waterford wall mirrors, original plates, alternating hob cut blue and clear glass raised button border, 41 x 30in. Dee, Atkinson & Harrison, Driffield. Sep 02. £14,000.

Set 8 antique Dutch marquetry dining chairs, floral tapestry seats. Stride & Son, Chichester. July 03. £14,000.

Pr. Vic. mahogany and satinwood/marquetry side tables, urns, festoons in boxwood, harewood and penwork, cross banded in partridge wood and rosewood, 75cm high, drawers stamped 4995/ 4996. Mellors & Kirk, Nottingham. June 03. £14,000.

Early 18thC feather banded walnut bureau bookcase, 3ft 2in. Gorringes, Lewes. Dec 00. £14,000.

Vic. mahogany Chippendale style breakfront bookcase, in Gothic manner, 254cm wide. Lyon & Turnbull, Edinburgh. Mar 04. £14,000.

10

69

Early 18thC walnut framed wing back armchair, cabriole legs. Cheffins, Cambridge. Apr 04. £14,000.

70

Morris & Co dark coloured walnut sideboard, c1890, by Philip Webb, 156cm wide, 52cm deep. Dreweatt Neate, Newbury. Apr 02. £13,800.

71

George II oak lowboy of good colour. Hamptons, Godalming. Nov 00. £13,500.

72

Oak panel back armchair, Anglo French, mid 16thC, brass plaque 'Herein sate Oliver Cromwell at Chequers Court Bucks'. Restorations. Sotheby's, Billingshurst. June 01. £13,500.

73

Regency giltwood convex mirror, 134cm dia. Hamptons, Godalming. July 01. £13,500.

74

Queen Anne walnut/feather-banded bureau bookcase, restorations, 3 parts, 7ft 1in by 3ft 3in. Sotheby's, Billingshurst. Jan 01. £13,200.

75

Early 19thC satinwood occasional table, probably 'Gillows', 29in high, 24in wide. Hamptons, Godalming. Sep 01. £13,000.

76

Walnut and marquetry chest of drawers, William & Mary, c1690. Sotheby's, Billingshurst. Apr 00. £13,000.

77

Late 17thC child's oak high chair, seat 21.5in high, 38.5in overall. Dreweatt Neate, Newbury. Apr 00. £13,000.

Hammer Prices £14,000-£12,000

78

William III oak dresser base, boarded top above 12 twin moulded drawers, 87cm high. Mellors & Kirk, Nottingham. June 03. £13,000.

79

Early 18thC oak low dresser, three mahogany crossbanded and boxwood, ebony strung drawers, 70.5cm high x 204cm wide. Dreweatt Neate, Newbury. Apr 00. £12,500.

80

Pair of satinwood/marquetry console tables, neo classical style, 89.5cm high, 124cm wide. Dreweatt Neate, Newbury. July 02. £12,500.

81

Regency rosewood and brass inlaid breakfast table. af. Lots Road Auctions, Chelsea. May 01. £12,500.

82

19thC gilt 4/5 seat settee, 95in, thought to be by Gillows. Canterbury Auction Galleries, Kent. Apr 03. £12,500.

83

George III wall mirror in rococo gilt wood frame, with scrolls and foliage, 55in high. Sworders, Stansted Mountfitchet. Feb 02. £12,200.

84

George III mahogany library bookcase with later cornice over 4 glazed doors, 7ft 1in wide, 8ft 1in high. Gorringes, Lewes. Dec 00. £12,000.

85

Small carved mahogany wall mirror bracket, George III, c1760. Sothebys, Billingshurst. Sep 00. £12,000.

86

Oak & panel back armchair, Charles II, second half 17thC. Sotheby's, Billingshurst. Sep 00. £12,000.

Hammer Prices £12,000-£10,000

William & Mary oyster olive-wood chest of drawers, sides with lozenge shaped panels containing circles on an 'oyster' ground, 37.5in wide, Hy. Duke & Son, Dorchester. June 03. £12,000.

Set of 6 George III mahogany framed dining chairs,19thC, in petit point figural and animal scenes. Rosebery's, London. Dec 03. £11,000.

Charles II oyster-olive and floral marquetry side table, single frieze drawer, spirally turned legs, X over stretcher, later turned feet, 37.5in wide, 25in deep. Hy. Duke & Son, Dorchester. June 03. £11,000.

George III mahogany straight front library bookcase, 101in high, 98in wide. Amersham Auction Rooms, Bucks. Apr 02. £10,200.

Small carved mahogany wall mirror bracket, George III, c1760. Sothebys, Billingshurst. Sep 00. £12,000.

William & Mary oyster walnut chest, cross banded, boxwood inlaid circles, scrolls, hearts & quatrefoils, 37.5in. (repairs, modifications), Gorringes, Bexhill. Oct 02. £11,000.

19thC mahog. dining table, seven extra leaves, original leaf cabinet, Cope & Collinson, 192in fully extended x 57.5in wide. Tayler & Fletcher with Humberts, Bourton on the Water, Glos. Feb 04. £11,000.

George III mahogany oval wine bottle stand, 28in wide. Sworders, Stansted Mountfitchet. Jul 01. £10,200.

The illustrations are in descending price order. The price range is indicated at the top of each page.

19thC Continental carved pine console table, Greek key frieze, lion mask boss, replacement olivewood top, 121cm wide. Sworders, Stansted Mountfitchet. Feb 03. £11,500.

William IV mahogany dining table, moulded rounded rectangular top with three leaf insertions, 499cm long. Cheffins, Cambridge. Oct 00. £10,000.

George IV figured mahogany library bookcase, 184cm wide. Bristol Auction Rooms. June 02. £11,000.

Set of 8 Regency dining chairs, c1815. Hamptons, Godalming. May 00. £11,500.

Pair of marquetry inlaid console tables, label for M. Butler Ltd Collector and Restorer of 'Chippendale, Adam & Sheraton Furniture, etc' Upper Abbey St, Dublin, 4ft 6in. Woolley & Wallis, Salisbury. Jan 04. £10,500,

George IV giltwood rectangular stool, attributed to Gillows with padded seat, 202cm long x 66cm wide x 46cm. Dreweatt Neate, Newbury. Apr 00. £10,000.

Pair of Edwards and Roberts satinwood/marquetry card tables, 3ft. Gorringes, Lewes. Apr 00. £11,000.

George IV mahogany drum top table, tooled leather inset 4 drawers, 4 false, gilt metal handles and a nulled border, 111cm dia. Dreweatt Neate, Newbury. May 02. £11,000.

Set of eight early George III mahogany dining chairs in the style of Robert Mainwaring. Hamptons, Godalming. Mar 00. £10,500.

A matching pair of William IV mahogany D-end cutlery and plate stands, 26in high, 13in wide. Amersham Auction Rooms, Bucks. Nov 02. £10,000.

Section II   <£10,000 to £5,000

The twentieth century accounts for only eight examples in this price range, but boasts the top lot when an Edwardian mahogany display cabinet reached £9,800 hammer at Canterbury Auction Galleries in 2001.

It was noted in the ***Introduction*** that the Sections have no rationale other than the convenience of using rounded numbers and of course the organisational requirement to divide the work into sections which aid useage. Therefore, as prices dip under £10,000 for the first time the changes will not be that obvious and will tend to be quite subtle. Hopefully, we can track the content as a continuation as well as point up changes.

Mahogany furniture again dominates this Section followed very closely by walnut. There are about ninety lots alone in these two favoured woods, although early oak and country furniture is beginning to appear more frequently, but with only one elm example. Here also are eight rosewood examples and four of satinwood. Several other native and exotic woods can be found such as yew, beech, chestnut, olive wood, cedar and kingwood. Note also several lacquered and ebonised lots in this Section. Names of manufacturers or associations with styles are perhaps less obvious than in ***Section I***, but one can still find references such as Gillows, Morant, Mainwaring, etc. Also such terms as Derbyshire, Welsh, Irish, North Country etc add credibility to certain lots and are also evident. One new name appearing for the first time is that of Robert 'Mouseman' Thompson from the twentieth century. See **117**. There are about twenty examples altogether of Thompson's work in the price range £9,000 down to a mere £210 for a stool in poor condition. This shows how the ***Index*** may be used to make a particular study of one furniture maker. The 'Mouseman' will be studied in ***Section IV*** where more appropriately, hammer prices drop below £4,000. Here the £9,000 hammer bought a great deal, including an adzed oak trestle table and ten chairs with cowhide seats, including two carvers.

As one should expect, this Section is dominated by the Georgian period including the Regency. Equally the seventeenth century and the Victorian period offer about twenty examples each. The twentieth century accounts for eight examples in this price range but boasts the top lot at **105** when an Edwardian mahogany display cabinet reached £9,800 hammer at Canterbury in 2001. One of the most remarkable lots in this Section is surely at **111**. Here is the magic of the Chinese Chippendale style. Two carver chairs, only two, fetching £9,200! By our chair 'ready-reckoner' which appeared in ***Section I*** this suggests that if only one chair were available it would

have cost at least £3,000! Now would you have been able to pick the quality of the two Victorian burr walnut side cabinets at **123** which fetched £8,800 in 2002 at Dreweatt Neate, Newbury? And whilst on page 15, clearly the George II card table at **125** screams quality but would you have thought that the Victorian reformed Gothic occasional table, **133**, would have reached £8,500 at Mellors & Kirk in Nottingham in 2003?

On page 16 a pair of nineteenth century Chippendale design 'Gainsborough' armchairs appear at **155**, fetching £7,500. The values of these particular chairs can be followed through the ***Index***. On the same page it is not clear why, what looks like an ordinary linen fold coffer should fetch £7,500 even though one suspects that it must be sixteenth century. See **157**. There are at least thirty examples of coffers in this book and interested readers can easily study the market from this selection.

Sheraton Revival furniture is very fashionable at the moment and will usually find a buyer. The display cabinet at **159** found £7,200 at Gorringes, Lewes in 2002, and at **176** an oak back-stool high chair achieved £6,600 in April 2004. Remember the high chair which fetched £13,000 on page 11? Conversely davenports are apparently out of favour. There are about twenty examples in these pages. Their market status achieved over the last few years may be checked out here, starting with the incredible olive wood example on page 18.

Turning to page 19 and the first image, **194**. Our apologies for the clutter in the photograph but it was the only picture the auction had available. One recalls the controversy in April 2004 relating to the pedigree of these six Charles II Derbyshire chairs which fetched £6,000. Is it ever possible for the furniture trade or experts to definitively and categorically say that every part of this set is original? Meanwhile at **196** one single eighteenth century splat-back sold at Bearnes in Exeter a month earlier for the same amount! Staying on chairs, now at **213**, how many of us would pass up this pair of (probably beech) carvers in poor condition, if they were a few hundred pounds, let alone £5,800. Why did they fetch so much? Finally in our sample analysis of ***Section II***, it is worth pointing up more firsts, namely the Art Deco cabinet at **229** which weighed in at £5,400 and the aesthetic movement cabinet which made £5,000 in December 2001 at Cheffins, Cambridge. See **242**.

Hammer Prices £9,800-£9,000

105

Edwardian mahogany display cabinet, 60in wide, 96in high. (Three spade toes missing) *Canterbury Auction Galleries, Kent. May 01. £9,800.*

106

18thC oak dresser, banded, crossbanded in mahogany, 185cm wide. *Dockree's, Manchester. June 01. £9,750.*

107

Two of a set of 12 mahogany Hepplewhite style dining chairs c1930. *Stride & Son, Chichester. May 01. £9,600.*

108

George II walnut lowboy, quarter veneering inlaid with herring-bone bandings/cross-banded, 29.5 x 19 x 29in high. *Canterbury Auction Galleries, Kent. Apr 02. £9,600.*

109

Late George III mahogany and crossbanded serpentine chest, c1820, drawers with lozenge ivory escutcheons and brass knop handles, 102cm high, 104cm wide. *Wintertons Ltd, Lichfield. July 02. £9,500.*

110

Pair Regency rosewood and ebonised tripod tables, each with a crossbanded canted top, 75cm high, 49.5cm wide. *Sotheby's, Billingshurst. Apr 01. £9,200.*

111

Pair of Georgian period Chinese Chippendale style armchairs, drop in seats, square chamfered legs, with front open brackets, some later repair and restoration. *Tring Market Auctions, Herts. Mar 02. £9,200.*

112

George III mahogany, serpentine front commode, 37in high, 48in wide. *Amersham Auction Rooms, Bucks. Nov 03. £9,200.*

113

Pair early mahogany 19thC Irish hall benches, fluted scroll crested backs, scroll arms, solid seats, turned and fluted tapered legs, 5ft. *Gorringes, Lewes. Feb 00. £9,000.*

114

Regency mahogany bow fronted linen press. *Sworders, Stansted Mountfitchet. Feb 00. £9,000.*

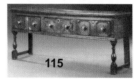

115

Oak dresser base, Charles II, last quarter 17thC, 183cm wide. *Sotheby's, Billings-hurst. Nov 00. £9,000.*

116

Regency mahogany library table, leather inset top, 122 x 80cm. *Henry Adams, Chichester. July 02. £9,000.*

117

Adzed oak dining table,108in, plus 10 chairs incl. 2 elbows, panelled backs and cow hide seats, by Robert 'Mouseman' Thompson. *Andrew Hartley, Ilkley. June 02. £9,000.*

118

George III mahogany bachelors chest, folding top and brushing slide, 2ft 5in. *Gorringes, Lewes. Apr 01. £9,000.*

119

George III crossbanded oak dresser. *Halls Fine Art, Shrewsbury. July 03. £9,000.*

120

William IV figured mahogany secretaire bookcase, 43in wide, 98in high. *Canterbury Auction Galleries, Kent. Aug 01. £9,000.*

121

Mahogany three pillar dining table, having a later top on Georgian pillars, 8ft 2in long, 4ft 6in. *Sworders, Stansted Mountfitchet. Dec 01. £9,000.*

122

Late 17th/early 18thC cedar-wood dining table, 120cm long. *R. Toovey, Washington, Sussex. Dec 03. £9,000.*

123

Pair of Victorian burr walnut serpentine side cabinets, gilt metal borders and mounts, 107cm high, 100cm wide. *Dreweatt Neate, Newbury. July 02. £8,800.*

124

Regency mahogany telescopic extending dining table, four leaves, 330 x 136cm extended, later leaf cabinet. *Bristol Auction Rooms. Jan 03. £8,800.*

125

George II mahogany foldover card table, 82cm. *Stride & Son, Chichester. July 03. £8,800.*

126

Late 17th/early 18thC yew wood side table, moulded plank top, engraved back plate, 2ft 5.5in. *Gorringes, Lewes. Sep 03. £8,800.*

127

18thC oak gateleg table, barleytwist legs, 4ft 9in x 5ft 8in. *Gorringes, Lewes. Oct 00. £8,600.*

128

George III cabinet bookcase, mahogany veneered, satin wood inlay, secretaire drawer. *Amersham Auction Rooms, Bucks. Mar 01. £8,600.*

129

Late Regency mahogany drum table, crossbanded and leather lined top, 54in dia, 30in high. *Hamptons, Godalming. Sep 01. £8,600.*

130

Early 18thC walnut bureau. *Canterbury Auc. Galleries, Kent. Aug 02. £8,600.*

131

Charles II oak dresser, planked top, fitted later brass plate and swing handles, 6ft 9in wide. *Woolley & Wallis, Salisbury. Jan 04. £8,600.*

132

Fine George IV mahogany five section library bookcase, 241cm wide. *Bristol Auction Rooms. June 02. £8,500.*

133

Victorian reformed gothic inlaid oak table. m *Mellors & Kirk, Nottingham. Feb 03. £8,500.*

134

Regency design flame mahogany extending dining table, David Linley workshop, 3 spare leaves, 13ft 1in x 4ft 4in, together with Linley ink and watercolour table design drawing. *Gorringes, Lewes. Oct 01. £8,400.*

> Prices quoted are hammer and exclude the buyer's premium. Adding 15% will give approx. buying price.

135

Large Regency convex wall mirror, ebonised reeded surround, gilt ball ornament on a green ground, 122cm. *Sworders, Stansted Mountfitchet. Mar 04. £8,400.*

136

Set 6 Regency mahogany hall chairs attributed to Gillows, scallop carved backs, painted armorial crests. *Cheffins, Cambridge. Nov 01. £8,250.*

137

Pair of George IV giltwood sofas, attributed to Gillows, 42.5 x 92 x 35.5in. *Dreweatt Neate, Newbury. Apr 02. £8,200.*

138

Walnut gateleg table, William & Mary, late 17thC, restorations, 69cm x 81cm open. *Sotheby's, Billingshurst. Feb 01. £8,200.*

139

12 Regency mahogany dining chairs, two with arms. *Lots Road Auctions, Chelsea. June 01. £8,200.*

140

Late George III mahogany breakfront bookcase, 110in wide. *Canterbury Auction Galleries, Kent. Aug 02. £8,200.*

141

19thC mahogany breakfront bookcase, glazed doors, 230cm wide. *Cheffins, Cambridge. Feb 04. £8,000.*

Hammer Prices £8,000-£7,200

142

Early 18thC oak dresser base, mahog. barbers pole strung drawers, 91in. Gorringes, Lewes. Dec 01. £8,000.

143

William & Mary walnut chest on stand, c1685, oyster veneer, holly banded, later feet, (stand poss. later) 36.5in wide. Gorringes, Bexhill. Nov 03. £8,000.

144

George III mahogany secretaire bookcase, 203cm high x 84cm wide. Wintertons Ltd, Lichfield. May 01. £8,000.

145

George I walnut bureau bookcase, glazed doors (formerly mirrored), candle slides, ht. 81.5in, 33.5in wide. (restoration/modification). Gorringes, Bexhill. Nov 03. £8,000.

146

Early 19thC Dutch walnut marquetry chest, 103cm wide. Cheffins, Cambridge. Mar 01. £7,800.

147

George III mahogany bureau bookcase. Hamptons, Godalming. Mar 01. £7,800.

148

Early George III bachelor's mahogany chest, 28.5in wide, 30in high. Canterbury Auction Galleries, Kent. Apr 01. £7,800.

149

George IV rosewood pedestal library desk, blind Gothic tracery to the canted corners, each side with open bookshelf with two simulated rosewood adjustable shelves, 147cm wide, 78.5in high. Sworders, Stansted Mountfitchet. Mar 04. £7,800.

150

Lacquered chinoiserie bureau bookcase, mirrored doors, 98cm wide. (possibly 18thC and later decorated) Sworders, Stansted Mountfitchet. Feb 04. £7,700.

151

Late 19thC French kingwood and ormolu display cabinet, top set breccia marble, parquetry panels, 4ft 8in wide. Gorringes, Lewes. June 03. £7,600.

152

George III strung padouk wood bureau bookcase, astragal glazed doors, 96cm wide. Sworders, Stansted Mountfitchet. Feb 03. £7,600.

153

Regency mahogany ebony strung sideboard, 2 drawers, bow cupboard and cellaret drawer, 90in. Gorringes, Lewes. Jan 02. £7,500.

154

Regency rosewood library table, inset with foliate scroll brass banding, 4ft. Gorringes, Lewes. June 02. £7,500.

155

Pair of 19thC Chippendale design 'Gainsborough' armchairs, silk brocade. Gorringes, Lewes. Dec 03. £7,500.

156

Early 18thC walnut bureau, fitted interior, 92cm wide. Cheffins, Cambridge. Feb 04. £7,500.

157

Oak coffer, linenfold carved, tripanelled front and hinged planked top, 45in wide. Amersham Auction Rooms, Bucks. Feb 04. £7,200.

158

Early 18thC oak enclosed dresser, 170cm wide Peter Wilson, Nantwich. Apr 00. £7,200.

159

Sheraton Revival ebony strung inlaid satinwood display cabinet, astragal glazed, 4ft 3in, 6ft 3in high. Gorringes, Lewes. Mar 02. £7,200.

160

Fourteen 19thC Sheraton design mahogany dining chairs. Gorringes, Bexhill. Feb 00. £7,000.

161

17thC elm coffer, carved 'THE 24 MAI ANO 1646 JAMES GRIFFIN'. Clevedon Sale-rooms, Bristol. Mar 01. £7,000.

162

Irish George III mahogany kneehole desk, c1770. Rosebery's, London. Mar 01. £7,000.

163

Set of ten late 19thC dining chairs in the style of Robert Mainwaring, incl. 2 armchairs leaf capped scroll terminals. Canterbury Auction Galleries, Kent. Feb 02. £7,000.

164

Mahogany breakfront book-case, 2nd qtr 19thC, 9ft 7in x 9ft 5in. Lots Road Auctions, Chelsea. Nov 01. £7,000.

165

Early Victorian burr maple breakfast table, inscribed brass plaque, 43.5in dia. Gorringes, Bexhill. Sep 03. £7,000.

166

George I walnut tallboy, 40in wide, in need of restoration. Canterbury Auc. Galleries, Kent. May 01. £7,000.

167

George III serpentine chest of drawers, 105cm wide. (some fading). Dreweatt Neate, Newbury. Nov 02. £6,900.

168

Early 18thC English oak 3 drawer dresser base, later unexposed timbers, 70.5in wide. Tring Market Auctions, Herts. Nov 03. £6,800.

Hammer Prices £7,200-£6,600

169

William & Mary walnut and oyster veneered chest, 36.5in wide. Sworders Stansted Mountfitchet. July 01. £6,800.

170

Set of 4 Regency ebonised and gilt carver open armchairs having cane seat, lattice back, Greek key top rail on legs. Stride & Son, Chichester. Oct 01. £6,800.

> The numbering system acts as a reader reference as well as linking to the Analysis of each Section

171

c1840 mahogany three leaf pull out dining table in original condition. Richard Wintertons, Burton on Trent. Apr 02. £6,800.

172

Mid Victorian mahogany D-end extending dining table, 10ft fully extended. Sworders, Stansted Mountfitchet. Mar 01. £6,700.

173

17thC 3 drawer oak dresser base. Richard Williams, Pershore. June 00. £6,700.

174

Small walnut bureau with feather banding, fall front enclosing fitted interior, 18thC and later, 27in wide. Andrew Hartley, Ilkley. Feb 04. £6,600.

175

William and Mary walnut and oyster veneered side table, top inlaid with concentric bands of oyster wood, dummy drawer to front, 31in wide. Canterbury Auc.Galleries, Kent. May 01. £6,600.

176

Oak backstool high chair, late Stuart, arched rested back, solid seat, 115cm high, 36cm wide. (slight losses and restoration) Richard Wintertons, Burton on Trent. Apr 04. £6,600.

Hammer Prices £6,600-£6,200

177

George III mahogany serpentine dressing chest, 36.75in wide, 23.5in deep, 31.5in high. Hamptons, Godalming. Nov 01. £6,600.

178

Early 19thC late Empire rosewood glazed cabinet on stand, stepped pediment supported by Mona Scagliola marble columns, 46in wide. Tring Market Auctions, Herts. Mar 03. £6,600.

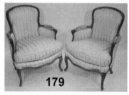

179

Pair of Louis XV Bergere armchairs, beechwood frames, inventory mark of the Chateau de Chanteleup. Ewbank Auctioneers, Send, Surrey. Oct 03. £6,600.

180

Pair of Edwardian satinwood display cabinets in Georgian manner, each 41in wide x 69in high. Canterbury Auction Galleries, Kent. Apr 01. £6,600.

181

Mid 18thC Dutch banded walnut serpentine chest of drawers, 2ft 7in. Gorringes, Lewes. Apr 01. £6,500.

182

Set of 12 Georgian revival mahogany chairs. Lots Road Auctions, Chelsea. Dec 02. £6,500.

183

Geo. III mahogany standing corner cabinet, 47.25 x 99in. D. Duggleby, Scarborough. July 01. £6,400.

184

Oak and stained pine dresser, mid 19thC, probably North Wales, 7ft high, 5ft 1in wide. Sworders, Stansted Mountfitchet. May 02. £6,400.

185

Regency chinoiserie double sided screen. Mellors & Kirk, Nottingham. Feb 03. £6,400.

186

Oak press cupboard, William and Mary, late 17thC/early 18thC, fluted frieze with twin pendants and date 1701. £6,200. Sotheby's, Billingshurst. May 00. £6,200.

187

George III mahogany breakfast table, 143cm. Cheffins, Cambridge. Dec 01. £6,200.

188

Mid Georgian walnut serving table with a dished tray top, moulded frieze, cabriole legs with bold pad feet, 30in wide. Tring Market Auctions, Herts. May 02. £6,200.

189

George II Cuban mahogany chest, c1750, brushing slide, 80 x 76cm. Rosebery's, London. June 03. £6,200.

190

Late 19thC olive wood davenport, writing slope with a parquetry band and painted Jerusalem, panelled doors to sides enclosing 6 drawers, back veneered, 105cm high, 72cm wide. Dreweatt Neate, Newbury. July 02. £6,200.

191

Victorian inlaid figured walnut credenza. Bristol Auction Rooms. Nov 02. £6,200.

192

Pr. Victorian mahogany boxwood strung, inlaid cutlery urns on pedestal bases. Halls Fine Art Auctions, Shrewsbury. July 03. £6,200.

193

Early 18thC oyster veneered and fruitwood inlaid chest, on replacement 19thC elm veneered bracket feet, 87cm wide, 86cm high. (replacement handles). Sworders, Stansted Mountfitchet. Feb 04. £6,200.

Set 6 Charles II Derbyshire oak dining chairs, bobbin legs, bobbin/rectangular section stretchers, sunken seats, with acorn finials and carved decoration. *Clarke Gammon, Guildford. Apr 04. £6,000.*

George III mahogany secretaire bookcase, astragal glazed, secretaire drawer, 43in wide, 97in high. *Ewbank Auctioneers, Send, Surrey. Mar 04. £6,000.*

18thC mahogany armchair, carved back, 'paperscroll' solid vase splat, drop in seat, some restoration. *Bearne's, Exeter. Mar 04. £6,000.*

19thC rosewood breakfront open library bookcase, 22 adjustable shelves, 19ft wide x 6ft high. *Clevedon Salerooms, Bristol. Nov 00. £6,000.*

18thC Maltese olivewood and marquetry bureau, cabriole legs with 'hoof' feet, 3ft 2in. *Gorringes, Lewes. Feb 01. £6,000.*

Late 17thC Italian walnut and marquetry centre table. inlaid with a battle scene, mother of pearl cherubs and flowers, 61in x 31in. (some later timbers). *Gorringes, Lewes. Dec 01. £6,000.*

> The illustrations are in descending price order. The price range is indicated at the top of each page.

George III design mahogany breakfront bookcase, four gothic arched astragal glazed doors, 8ft 8in. *Gorringes, Lewes. July 01. £6,000.*

Early 19thC rio rosewood bookcase, 37 x16.5 x 80.5in. *Hamptons, Godalming. Mar 02. £6,000.*

George II walnut 4 chair back settee, shaped top rail, intertwined splats, carved arms and knees, claw and ball feet. *Sworders, Stansted Mountfitchet. May 02. £6,000.*

19thC commode, satinwood with rosewood and exotic wood crossbanding and inlays, 120cm wide. af. *Lots Road Auctions, Chelsea. Sep 02. £6,000.*

George I walnut and featherbanded kneehole desk, 81cm high. *Mellors & Kirk, Nottingham. June 03. £6,000.*

Queen Anne feather banded walnut escritoire, cushion drawer, fall-front enclosing a cupboard, drawers and pigeon holes, 2 short and 2 graduated long drawers, later bracket feet, 3ft 5in. *Gorringes, Lewes. Sep 00. £6,000.*

Geo. III oak dresser, boarded top, 3 beaded drawers, pot board and stretchers, 170cm wide. *Mellors & Kirk, Nottingham. Sep 03. £6,000.*

Cedar wood and ebonised panelled secretaire by Welles Bosworth, 64in wide, 65in high. *Andrew Hartley, Ilkley. Apr 02. £6,000.*

Victorian telescopic action extending mahogany dining table by James Winter of London. *Hamptons, Godalming. July 00. £5,900.*

Walnut and inlaid commode, Milanese c1790, later feet, 50in wide. *Sotheby's, Billingshurst. Apr 01. £5,800.*

Victorian walnut credenza inlaid floral decoration, 64.5in wide. *Clarke Gammon, Guildford. Feb 02. £5,800.*

19

Hammer Prices £5,800-£5,400

211

Carved oak tester bed, Charles II and later. Sotheby's, Billingshurst. Feb 00. £5,800.

212

Late George II / early George III oak dresser base, 181cm wide, also an associated rack of near contemporary date. Hamptons, Godalming. May 02. £5,800.

213

Pair of Regency ebonised simulated bamboo carver chairs, top rail detached from one and paintwork in poor condition. Stride & Son, Chichester. Oct 03. £5,800.

214

George I walnut escritoire, overhung moulded cornice, contemporary but associated drawer base, 42in. Gorringes, Lewes. Dec 03. £5,800.

215

Geo. III mahogany serpentine commode, c1780. Rosebery's, London. June 03. £5,800.

216

Pair of Regency upholstered armchairs with simulated rosewood legs, later upholstery. Tring Market Auctions, Herts. Jan 03. £5,700.

217

Set of 10 William IV rosewood dining chairs, curved cresting rails and spars and drop-in seats. Gorringes, Lewes. Sep 00. £5,600.

218

William & Mary walnut chest on stand, feather banding, 109cm. D M Nesbit & Co., Southsea. Mar 03. £5,600.

219

Queen Anne pine chest, on possibly associated stand) 2ft 8.5in. Gorringes, Lewes. Jan 04. £5,600.

220

Late Victorian roll top desk, mahogany/tulipwood banded, stamped Morant & Co, 91 New Bond St, London, 42in wide. Lots Road Auctions, Chelsea. Feb 02. £5,600.

221

Regency mahogany bow front serving table. Stride & Son, Chichester. Nov 00. £5,500.

222

19thC carved walnut cassone. Rosebery's, London. Mar 01. £5,500.

223

Harlequin set of 4 walnut and 2 oak chairs by E W Pugin, attributed to C and R Light of Shoreditch, c1880. Cheffins, Cambridge. Mar 01. £5,500.

224

19thC Italian walnut/kingwood banded commode, 46in wide, losses, wear. Wintertons Ltd, Lichfield. Feb 02. £5,500.

225

Rosewood love seat by Stuart Devlin, (b1931) c1978, typical of the Devlin filigree, green dralon seats. Hamptons, Godalming. Mar 02. £5,500.

226

George I walnut miniature chest, 13in high, 16in wide, 9in deep. Clarke Gammon, Guildford. June 02. £5,500.

227

Louis XIV dated oak bed. Mellors & Kirk, Nottingham. Feb 03. £5,500.

228

Late 18thC chestnut double sided library table with tan skiver, 57in x 32in. Gorringes, Lewes. Mar 03. £5,500.

229

Anon., a French ebonised Art Deco cabinet, c1920, vellum doors with a circular metal lock plate depicting a naked female archer, blonde wood interior, plinth with gilt metal border, 58.5in x 78.5in. Sotheby's, Billingshurst. Mar 01. £5,400.

18thC & later walnut oyster veneered chest on stand, parquetry inlaid top, 96cm wide. *Cheffins, Cambridge. Feb 04. £5,200.*

19thC canvas five fold screen, painted decoration of Eastern court scene. *Clevedon Salerooms, Bristol. Mar 01. £5,200.*

George III oak/mahogany crossbanded dresser, width 183cm. *Wintertons Ltd, Lichfield. Mar 04. £5,200.*

Set of six mahogany dining chairs, stamped 'Gillows, Lancaster', c1825, *Hamptons, Godalming. Sep 01. £5,200.*

Housekeepers cupboard, oak banded in mahogany, c1820, upper 4 doors enclosing shelves and small drawers, on base of 8 short drawers, 85in long. *Peter Wilson, Nantwich. Feb 02. £5,200.*

Gothic revival walnut ebonised and fruitwood marquetry cylinder breakfront secretaire bookcase, stamped 'Holden & Co., Liverpool'. *Dreweatt Neate, Newbury. May 02. £5,200.*

George III mahogany library armchair and a similar later armchair. *Clarke Gammon, Guildford. Dec 02. £5,200.*

Writing table bearing stamp of Gillows, Lancaster in 2 places. *Lots Road Auctions, Chelsea. Sep 03. £5,200.*

17thC Italian walnut cassone, carved foliate motifs, putti, mythical beasts, gadrooned top and lions paw feet, 6ft long, 2ft height. *Gorringes, Lewes. Dec 00. £5,000.*

George I walnut lowboy with canted top, 2 over 3 short drawers, 2ft 8in. *Gorringes, Lewes. June 02. £5,000.*

George II feather banded burr walnut chest on chest, 3ft 7in. *Gorringes, Lewes. Sep 02. £5,000.*

Unrestored walnut bureau, desirable interior, secret drawers, 32in. *Stride & Son, Chichester. Mar 03. £5,000.*

Victorian aesthetic movement ebony inlaid satinwood side cabinet. *Cheffins, Cambridge. Dec 01. £5,000.*

George II North Country oak linen press, 2 shelves over 3 small drawers, base with 3 drawers, c1740-1760, 49in wide. *Byrne's, Chester. Mar 04. £5,000.*

Hammer Prices £5,200-£5,000

Regency mahogany sofa table, 65in wide. *Hamptons, Godalming. Sep 01. £5,000.*

Queen Anne walnut escritoire, 106cm. *Locke & England, Leamington Spa. Jan 03. £5,000.*

Queen Anne walnut escritoire, cushion frieze drawer, ratcheted writing surface, replacement oak bun feet, 110cm wide. *Sworders, Stansted Mountfitchet. Mar 04. £5,000.*

Sheraton period mahogany bowfront sideboard, c1790, 79.5 x 32.5 x 36in. *Hamptons, Godalming. Mar 02. £5,000.*

Early 18thC walnut lowboy. *Locke & England, Leamington Spa. Sep 02. £5,000.*

Section III <£5,000 to £4,000

Throughout the eighteenth and early nineteenth centuries all kinds of designs attempted to solve the problems of multiple seating but frequently they imposed the table legs in positions which compromised diners.

Less lots fall between £4,000 and £5,000 than in any other price range. This could be a quirk. Yet even when we have asked, few auctions provided examples and we have been asking for five years? Here mahogany is the most frequent wood. Walnut and oak provide only about half as many entries each. Unaccountably the seventeenth century has fallen away. Now the nineteenth century provides about 70% more lots than the eighteenth. The twentieth century is poorly represented.

Image **250** offers some scope for analysis. With only a few examples of satinwood in this Section and only four in the previous, satinwood is very difficult to come by except for Revival examples and other twentieth century pieces. The worry must be that might we not mistake a Georgian example for a much later Revival piece, which could be a costly error? This simple George III fold-over demi-lune table, even with later marquetry, found £4,900 at Gorringes, Bexhill in June 2002. Note the Regency bow-front sideboards at **251** and again at **257** and **263**, all achieving the best part of £5,000. Also the bergère armchairs at **252** point up the considerable value attaching to the name, the quality and the period. There are plenty of examples to enable readers to study these chairs. The final example in this book at **2712** on page 164 is a rather quirky Art Deco walnut bergère which fetched £300 in 2001. I doubt whether you could buy at such a low price today!

Whilst we have seen some fine examples of the larger pieces of case furniture, there are at **261** and **262**, two fine quality Victorian examples of library bookcases. The first is in the standard mahogany but unusually **262** is in a brown oak. Both reached £4,800. And on page 24, a smaller rosewood example fetched £4,750 at Lambert & Foster in Tenterden, Kent. There are other bookcases and cabinets in this price range and the *Index* points up literally dozens of other examples throughout this book.

There are about half a dozen examples of dining tables in this price range and there are four sets of dining chairs. At **296** is a serving table, a much rarer item, which I am sure would fetch more than £4,400 if it were to come back on the market today. Dining tables can present problems. Throughout the eighteenth and early nineteenth centuries all kinds of designs attempted to solve the problems of multiple seating but frequently they imposed the table legs in positions which compro-

mised seating and presented men and women (trousers or dresses) with restricted choice! **739** on page 51 offers a different dilemma where wider Georgian chairs will not fit into the smaller gaps between the legs on the 'D' ends. During the nineteenth century, the substantially legged wind-outs began to solve the problem. The Editor strongly advises readers to buy antique, but check that all of the seating alternatives match your entertainment needs without compromising your guests! Incidentally, readers should note the fine walnut dining suite, c1920 which fetched £4,400 at Rosebery's in London in September 2002 or the alternatives presented by the nineteenth century examples at **294** or **303**.

On page 26 is a fine oak court cupboard, dated 1680 which sold at Gorringes in Lewes for £4,200 in 2004. But was it bought by the trade, or privately? Note also on this page, two Edwardian mahogany inlaid display cabinets at £4,200. However a far less easier object for judging value is **319**, a simple seventeenth century cricket table which fetched a small fortune in December 2002 at Kivell and Sons in Bude. More on this subject in a later Section. Linen presses were discussed briefly in the *Introduction* and there are over forty examples in the book which should give the reader a good feel for the market. **325** is a particularly fine example at £4,100 but there is a linen press in *Section I* which reached £9,000.

The first whatnot appears at **332**. You can check out this category right down to a Victorian three tier rosewood example on page 162 which fetched only £320 in March 2003. Why was the price so low for what appears to be a delightful piece of furniture? At **340** is a set of ten reproduction Chippendale style chairs, c1900 which fetched £4,000. Many eighteenth and early nineteenth century Georgian styles have been continuously reproduced. This book is full of examples in all categories. In many cases the quality is superb, often being produced by very reputable makers. As time goes by the value difference between original examples and later reproductions is becoming blurred and quality rather than age is the dominant criterion on which to judge value.

On page 28, what a pity the James I oak refectory table has had its corners rounded at a later date. At 174 inches its value has been compromised at only £4,000 in 2003. And how much would the matching set of five George II walnut chairs have fetched if there had been a sixth?

249

Early 18thC oak dresser. John Taylors, Louth. Feb 00. £4,900.

250

George III satinwood demi-lune folding-top card table, cross-banded in kingwood and later inlaid with urns, swags, scrolls and other motifs, 3ft 2in. Gorringes, Bexhill. June 02. £4,900.

251

Regency period mahogany bow front sideboard of substantial form, 79in wide. Tring Market Auctions, Herts. Mar 03. £4,900.

252

Regency mahogany library bergere armchairs, curved top rails, scroll arms, turned and fluted tapered legs, fitted brass castors. Gorringes, Lewes. Feb 00. £4,800.

253

18thC oak dresser base, 82.5in wide. Wintertons Ltd, Lichfield. Nov 00. £4,800.

254

Pair 19thC ebonised amboyna strung and marquetry pier cabinets, 44.5in high, 30.5in wide. Wintertons Ltd, Lichfield. Mar 01. £4,800.

255

19thC mahogany extending dining table with rounded rectangular top, four leaves, 10ft x 4ft 4in. Gorringes, Lewes. June 01. £4,800.

256

George I oak dresser, 65in wide, 81in high. Sworders, Stansted Mountfitchet. July 01. £4,800.

257

Late Regency mahogany bow front sideboard, 74in wide, 29in high. Tring Market Auctions, Herts. Nov 02. £4,800.

258

Victorian burr walnut and inlaid credenza, c1850-1860, two convex glazed doors, two velvet lined shelves, 75in wide, 42.5in high. Byrne's, Chester. Mar 04. £4,800

259

George III mahogany serpentine front commode, 33in high x 41in wide. Amersham Auction Rooms, Bucks. June 01. £4,800.

260

19thC mahogany twin pillar dining table, 83.5in long, 42in wide. Andrew Hartley, Ilkley. Feb 01. £4,800.

261

Victorian mahogany break-front bookcase, 84in wide, 88in high. Andrew Hartley, Ilkley. Aug 01. £4,800

262

Fine Victorian brown oak library bookcase, 101.5in high, 123in wide, 17in deep. Clarke Gammon, Guildford. Feb 03. £4,800

263

Geo III bowfront mahogany sideboard, rosewood/chevron banding, 5ft 4in. Gorringes, Lewes. Mar 02. £4,800

Hammer Prices £4,900-£4,800

264

18thC burrwood hanging corner cupboard, applied moulded walnut veneered arched cornice, William and Mary style walnut framed mirror insert, 21in x 36.5in high. Tring Market Auctions, Herts. Mar 02. £4,800

265

Late 17thC oak dresser base, 95cm wide, 54cm deep, 83cm high. Hamptons, Godalming. July 01. £4,800.

266

Late 19thC French kingwood and ormolu mounted vitrine in the Louis XVI style, marble top, 147cm high, 70cm wide. Sworders, Stansted Mountfitchet. June 03. £4,800

267

Geo III mahogany serpentine chest, rosewood and boxwood banded top, 4 graduated long drawers, 3ft 6in. Gorringes, Lewes. Mar 01. £4,800

Hammer Prices £4,750-£4,500

268

19thC rosewood bookcase. *Lambert & Foster, Tenterden. May 02. £4,750.*

270

William IV mahogany and figured walnut library table, c1835, qtr. cut leather insert, 4 drawers, plates stamped 'Cope & Collinson', 47.5in dia. *Halls Fine Art, Shrewsbury. Mar 04. £4,600.*

269

South German cross-banded walnut bureau-cabinet. *Mervyn Carey, Tenterden. Feb 03. £4,700.*

271

William IV pollard oak sarcophagus wine cooler, of octagonal form with lion paw feet, 2ft 6in. *Gorringes, Lewes. Feb 00. £4,600.*

272

Pair of yew windsor armchairs by John Gabbitass, Worksop. *Andrew Hartley, Ilkley. June 01. £4,600.*

273

George III mahogany bookcase, 51in wide. af. *Lots Road Auctions, Chelsea. Apr 01. £4,600.*

Prices quoted are hammer and exclude the buyer's premium. Adding 15% will give approx. buying price.

274

George II mahogany bureau cabinet c1740, 43.75in wide, 90.25in high. *Hamptons, Godalming. July 00. £4,600.*

275

Lacewood, plane and walnut mule chest, 18th/19thC. *Hamptons, Godalming. Jan 00. £4,600.*

276

Late Regency rosewood card table, amboyna crossbanded top, baize lined interior, 39 x 19 x 28.5in. *Hamptons, Godalming. Sep 01. £4,600.*

277

Late 18th/early 19thC oak dresser, 65in x 82in high. *Canterbury Auc. Galleries, Kent. Oct 01. £4,600.*

278

Early Victorian mahogany library table, 6 frieze drawers, carved reeded legs, stamped 'A Solomon 59 Gt Queen St', 8ft long. *Sworders, Stansted Mountfitchet. Apr 01. £4,600.*

279

George II North Wales oak dresser, 4ft 8.5in. *Gorringes, Bexhill. Oct 02. £4,600.*

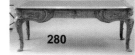

280

Louis XVI design bronze and kingwood bureau plat, leather top, 90in x 38in. *Gorringes, Lewes. June 02. £4,600.*

281

George IV mahogany library armchair. *Sworders, Stansted Mountfitchet. Dec 02. £4,600.*

282

French Regence rosewood bow front commode, c1730, 83cm high, 120cm wide. *Wintertons Ltd, Lichfield. May 03. £4,600.*

283

Set of 8 (2 arm) Chippendale design mahogany dining chairs, upholstered drop in seats. *Gorringes, Lewes. Sep 00. £4,500.*

284

Regency carved giltwood console table, marble top, 54.5in wide. *Clarke Gammon, Guildford. June 02. £4,500.*

285

Art Nouveau mahogany dresser, probably Glaswegian School, fitted arrangement of panel doors and four lead and opaque glass panel doors, 282cm long. *Ambrose, Loughton. Feb 02. £4,500.*

286

19thC Dutch marquetry and walnut display cabinet, 160cm wide x 220cm high. *Sworders, Stansted Mountfitchet. Oct 02. £4,500.*

287

Geo IV mahogany extending dining table, provision for 4 leaves, total length 264 x 136cm. *Locke & England. Leamington Spa. Sep 02. £4,500.*

288

Carved oak bible box on stand, with moulded edged plank lid, 25in wide, 31.5in high. *Andrew Hartley, Ilkley. Feb 00. £4,400.*

289

Set of 12 adzed oak chairs by Robert 'Mouseman' Thompson including two elbow chairs. *Andrew Hartley, Ilkley. Feb 01. £4,400.*

290

William IV mahogany dining table, 3 extra leaves, 9ft 2in extended. *Lots Road Auctions, Chelsea. Mar 01. £4,400.*

291

Early 19thC Dutch walnut birds eye maple, marquetry bonheur du jour, 2ft 10in. *Gorringes, Lewes. Oct 00. £4,400.*

292

Burr walnut dining suite, c1920, comprising: oval extending dining table plus one leaf, 8 chairs incl. 2 armchairs, serpentine sideboard and side cabinet. *Rosebery's, London. Sep 02. £4,400.*

293

Set of 8 Regency mahogany dining chairs. *Clevedon Salerooms, Bristol. Nov 01. £4,400.*

294

Victorian mahogany extending dining table with 3 leaves, 3.19 x 1.35m max. *Sworders, Stansted Mountfitchet. Oct 02. £4,400.*

Hammer Prices £4,500-£4,200

295

Pair of rosewood bookcases in gothic taste, 19thC, 100.5in high, 51in wide. *Andrew Hartley, Ilkley. Apr 03. £4,400.*

296

Geo III mahogany, boxwood strung serving table, c1800, 81cm high, 275cm wide, 92cm deep. *Wintertons Ltd, Lichfield. Nov 02. £4,400.*

297

Geo III mahogany secretaire bookcase, lancet glazing bars, 130cm. *Rosebery's, London. Sep 00. £4,300.*

298

Early George III mahogany reading table, 73cm high. *Dreweatt Neate, Newbury. May 02. £4,300.*

299

Set of eight Sheraton period mahogany dining chairs. *Mervyn Carey, Tenterden. Nov 00. £4,300.*

300

19thC Continental carved walnut specimen cabinet, 97in high, 46in wide. *Andrew Hartley, Ilkley. Feb 00. £4,200.*

301

George IV mahogany dining table, 60.75in dia. *Clarke Gammon, Guildford. Apr 00. £4,200.*

302

Oak dresser base, George II, mid 18thC, North Wales, 92cm x 154cm wide. *Sotheby's, Billingshurst. May 00. £4,200.*

303

Pull out extending dining table, 57in wide x 72in unextended. *Dockree's, Manchester. Feb 00. £4,200.*

Hammer Prices £4,200-£4,100

Late 17thC oak court cupboard, dated 1680, 5ft 1in wide, 5ft 11in. Gorringes, Lewes. Jan 04. £4,200.

George III mahogany pembroke table. Ambrose, Loughton. Dec 00. £4,200.

Set 8+ 2 late 19thC mahogany shieldback dining chairs of Hepplewhite design. Canterbury Auction Galleries, Kent. May 01. £4,200.

George III mahogany Pembroke table. Ambrose, Loughton. Dec 00. £4,200.

Louis XIV design walnut centre table, later green marble top, 4ft 2in x 2ft 8in. Gorringes, Lewes. Apr 00. £4,200.

Early 19thC mahogany serpentine sideboard, manner of Gillows, 2 metres 12cm wide x 57cm deep. Hamptons, Godalming. July 01. £4,200.

Regency mahogany pedestal sideboard, three quarter gallery, 84.5in wide. Andrew Hartley, Ilkley. Feb 01. £4,200.

Edwardian inlaid mahogany serpentine display cabinet. Sworders, Stansted Mountfitchet. Sep 01. £4,200.

Paul Sormani, French ormolu mounted mahogany envelope card table, lock stamped P Sormani, 10 rue Charlot, Paris, the drawer with an S H Jewell label, 23in. Gorringes, Lewes. Oct 00. £4,200.

Victorian mahogany extending dining table. W & H Peacock, Bedford. Dec 02. £4,200.

William IV mahogany writing table. John Taylors, Louth. Apr 00. £4,200.

18thC mahogany supper table, 33in wide. Sworders, Stansted Mountfitchet. Feb 02. £4,200.

Regency rosewood sofa table, boxwood strung, D flaps, 2 drawers, 3ft. Gorringes, Lewes. June 02. £4,200.

Edwardian marquetry inlaid and strung mahogany glazed serpentine front display cabinet, 150cm. D M Nesbit, Southsea. Apr 03. £4,200.

George III oak dresser base, single short plate rack tier, 3 short drawers, 36 x 70.5 x 17.5in. Wintertons Ltd, Lichfield. Mar 02. £4,200.

17thC elm cricket table, 30 in dia. Kivell & Sons, Bude. Dec 02. £4,200.

Set 14 Geo III mahog. dining chairs, 2 arms, in brown hide. (later repairs, restorations and iron straps to many legs). Canterbury Auc. Galleries, Kent. Aug 03. £4,200.

Victorian birds eye maple Wellington chest, single locking bar, 2ft 2in. Gorringes, Lewes. July 00. £4,200.

Geo II lady's walnut kneehole dressing table, inlaid herringbone, crossbanded, 33in wide. Canterbury Auc. Galleries. Feb 04. £4,100

Set of 8 George IV mahogany dining chairs. D. Duggleby, Scarborough. July 01. £4,100.

324

William IV mahogany dining table, 2 leaves, on turned and leaf capped legs, bold carved paterae to top of legs, brass castors, 102 x 48in extended. Canterbury Auc. Galleries, Kent. Feb 02. £4,100.

325

Geo III mahog. linen press, 51in wide. Clevedon Salerooms, Bristol. Nov 01. £4,100.

326

18thC oak dresser, fielded panel cupboard flanked by 2 flights of crossbanded lipped drawers, 209cm. Dockree's, Manchester. June 01. £4,100

327

Regency rosewood library table. Ambrose, Loughton. Dec 00. £4,000.

328

Mid 18thC oak Shropshire dresser, 78in wide. P. Wilson, Nantwich. Apr 00. £4,000.

329

George III inlaid mahogany secretaire bookcase. Dee, Atkinson & Harrison, Driffield. Apr 01. £4,000.

330

Regency inlaid mahogany & rosewood bowfront sideboard, 2 drawers, a cellaret & cupboard, 54in. Gorringes, Lewes. Apr 00. £4,000.

331

Set of eight Regency rosewood chairs on reeded sabre legs, caned seats, curved rail and rope twist features, possibly by Gillows. Clarke Gammon, Guildford. Dec 00. £4,000.

332

Regency rosewood three tier whatnot, sloping ratcheted top. Sworders, Stansted Mountfitchet. Sep 01. £4,000.

Hammer Prices £4,100-£4,000

333

Set of 6 + 2 Regency mahog. dining chairs. Stride & Son, Chichester. July 01. £4,000.

334

Brass bound leather studded chest, with the Royal cypher believed to be of Katherine of Braganza, 98cm. Cheffins, Cambridge. Dec 01. £4,000.

> The numbering system acts as a reader reference as well as linking to the Analysis of each Section

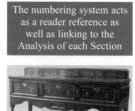

335

A mid 18thC oak dresser with 5 spice, 3 long drawers and shaped apron with a further drawer, 6ft 2in. Gorringes, Lewes. Oct 00. £4,000.

336

Early 19thC mahogany breakfast table. Hamptons, Godalming. May 01. £4,000.

337

Sofa table, rosewood veneer, satinwood/kingwood banding, 3ft 1.5in. Woolley & Wallis, Salisbury. Apr 00. £4,000.

338

George III oak dresser, 75.5in wide, 76.5in high. A. Hartley, Ilkley. Feb 01. £4,000.

339

Regency style mahogany pedestal dining table. Lots Road Auctions, Chelsea. July 00. £4,000.

340

Set of ten Chippendale style mahogany side chairs, c1900. Dockree's, Manchester. Nov 00. £4,000.

341

Regency mahogany sofa table. Dee, Atkinson & Harrison, Driffield. Mar 00. £4,000.

342

William & Mary marquetry chest of drawers. G W Finn, Canterbury. July 01. £4,000.

Hammer Price £4,000

343

Mid 19thC French walnut inlaid centre table in Louis Quinze style, 163 x 106cm. Hamptons, Godalming. May 02. £4,000.

344

Burr walnut large hall table, c1870, carved leaf rim, 147cm long. Peter Wilson. Nantwich. July 02. £4,000.

345

Edwardian satinwood and mahogany lady's writing desk, 2ft 6.5in. Gorringes, Lewes. Mar 03. £4,000.

346

Victorian mahogany windout dining table, 3 leaves, two later, extending to 10ft x 4ft wide. Sworders, Stansted Mountfitchet. July 01. £4,000.

347

19thC French ormolu & burr walnut bureau plat, 48 x 31in. Gorringes, Lewes. Oct 02. £4,000.

28

348

George III Irish mahogany serving table, 5ft. Gorringes, Lewes. Oct 02. £4,000.

349

George III satinwood demi-lune fold over card table. Wintertons Ltd. Bakewell. Sep 02. £4,000.

> The illustrations are in descending price order. The price range is indicated at the top of each page.

350

Joined oak refectory table, James I and later, single plank top, later rounded corners on a plain frieze, cup and cover legs, 174in long, 31.5in wide, 34in high. Halls Fine Art, Shrewsbury. Oct 03. £4,000.

351

Late George III mahogany and ebony strung secretaire book case, c1820, 230cm high, 102cm wide. Wintertons Ltd, Lichfield. Nov 02. £4,000.

352

Oak cupboard. Dreweatt Neate, Newbury. Apr 03. £4,000.

353

Mid 19thC walnut/kingwood credenza with Sévre style porcelain panels. Locke & England, Leamington Spa. Sep 02. £4,000.

354

Walnut wing armchair with needlepoint upholstery. Eastbourne Auction Rooms, Sussex. July 02. £4,000.

355

Victorian mahogany library bookcase, 238cm high, 203cm wide. Mellors & Kirk, Nottingham. Sep 03. £4,000.

357

William and Mary walnut oyster veneered and seaweed marquetry chest, later barley twist stand, 3ft 1in. Gorringes, Lewes. Dec 03. £4,000.

358

Wm. IV mahogany extending dining table, 4 leaves, 310cm extended. Sworders, Stansted Mountfitchet. Mar 03. £4,000.

359

George I design walnut bachelors chest, hinged baize lined top, 2ft 4.5in. Gorringes, Lewes. Jan 04. £4,000.

360

George III mahogany and inlaid secretaire bookcase, 45in wide, 92.5in high. Dee, Atkinson & Harrison, Driffield. Apr 01. £4,000.

356

Matched set of five George II walnut and upholstered salon chairs, c1745. Wintertons Ltd, Lichfield. May 03. £4,000.

Section IV   <£4,000 to £3,000

Robert Thompson, the 'Mouseman of Kilburn' was born in 1876 in this tiny Yorkshire village. By the beginning of the twentieth century, with the country embracing the machine age, he turned in the opposite direction.

Between £3,000 and £4,000 is a price range which now begins to offer a much wider appeal although one can pay much, much more for items of new furniture! Brand new seventeenth/eighteenth century top quality reproduction oak is typically in this price range but, of course like anything new seriously depreciates on purchase. The original is at this time in late 2004, exceptionally good value with added investment potential. Readers are reminded to check the *Introduction* for a current market survey. In this Section, whilst the ubiquitous mahogany continues to appear, oak and walnut are not far behind with about forty lots each to study. Satinwood examples remain scarce which is why the simple demi-lune fold-over card table at **349** fetched £4,000! There are only three examples in this Section.

Once again the Georgian period dominates, although there is a large amount from the 1800-1835 period. The seventeenth century is now less well represented with only half a dozen examples. In fact, the oldest item in the Section is a sixteenth century Italian carved walnut collector's cabinet on a later stand at **379** which fetched £3,800 at Gorringes in Lewes in 2004. Indeed, Continental furniture abounds throughout this work and thematically presents its own potential study area. Here one can check out Spanish, Italian, Irish, Dutch, German, American, Welsh, Russian and particularly French furniture, which has about sixty examples.

As previously outlined, *Section IV* offers an excellent opportunity to study Robert 'Mouseman' Thompson, the 'Mouseman of Kilburn'. Born in 1876, in this tiny Yorkshire village, by the beginning of the twentieth century, when the country was embracing the machine age, he turned in the opposite direction, not only replicating the style of Medieval wood carvers but also their methods of production. Each piece of his work is signed, usually in an inconspicuous place, with a carved mouse. His work was to appear in great cathedrals, in public buildings and grand homes. Here you can check out his work at **361**, **386**, **399**, **448**, **522** and **539** and of course in other Sections. Whilst his furniture can appear, as here, in auctions around the country, many examples are auctioned at Andrew Hartley in Ilkley, as were four in this Section. Readers wanting more information should study, *The Tale of the Mouse*, by Patricia Lennon, published by Great Northern Books in 2001. ISBN 0-906899-88-5, £8.99.

At **362** is an eighteenth century oak dresser showing its full 'blue and white' display potential, including the pot board below. It is beyond belief that someone will pay as much for a 'cinema system' which in a few years time they won't able to give away! The sadder story of bureaux will be tackled later but their decline does not seem to have affected the hammer price of this burr walnut specimen at **366** which fetched the same £3,900 as the oak dresser. On the subject of walnut, notice also the Spanish side table at **375**. Only 81 inches long it was snapped up for £3,800. It could be worth more today. An oak refectory table at **380**, nine feet long, seventeenth century and later fetched the same price as did a rare North Italian neo-classical marquetry commode in walnut and olive wood at **389**.

There are dozens of examples of dressers and dresser bases in these pages. Check out the *Index* on page 189. In this price range, see also the Charles II oak livery cupboard at **446** and the unusual carved pine hall bench at **440**. This is not only unusual but almost quirky. It will always sell because where will you find another? On the subject of pine, this is the only example in this Section and I believe you could count on the fingers of one hand the number of pieces of pine furniture in the first four Sections. More on pine later.

Check image **459** on page 35, the Regency mahogany extending dining table, manner of Gillow, plus four leaves which fetched £3,400. On a one off basis it is very difficult to study prices from only one small photograph. One would need to know about condition, patina and colour and much more. At the time of the sale the piece could have been examined in detail and the auctioneer will always help. Here it is only possible to look at many tables to assess an average market value for this category as this specimen has fetched a lower than average hammer price for its type. Several beds appear in this Section and throughout this book. Here for example at **464**, **478** and **544**. Beds rarely appear at auction except those where there is space enough for their display such as Gorringes in Lewes or Lots Road Auctions, Chelsea.

Finally, as a statement piece for the hall of a traditional home, how about the William and Mary oak side table, single frieze drawer, **545**, which fetched a mere £3,000 at Sworders, Stansted Mountfichet in Essex, only two years ago.

Hammer Prices £3,900-£3,800

361

Robert 'Mouseman' Thompson, 1930s adzed oak dresser, 68in wide. Andrew Hartley, Ilkley. Feb 01. £3,900.

362

18thC oak dresser, 70.5in wide, 77.5in high. Andrew Hartley, Ilkley. Apr 00. £3,900.

363

Queen Anne style walnut bureau bookcase, 230 x 89cm. Sworders, Stansted Mountfitchet. Dec 02. £3,900.

364

George III mahogany whatnot, 31 x 31 x 123cm. Hamptons, Godalming. July 01. £3,900.

365

George III satinwood demi-lune fold-over card table. Rupert Toovey, Washington, Sussex. Jan 03. £3,900.

366

George I burr walnut bureau, 96cm wide. Rupert Toovey, Washington. Dec 03. £3,900.

367

Pair of narrow 86cm mahogany astragal glazed bookcases. Sworders, Stansted Mountfitchet. Dec 03. £3,900.

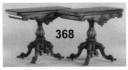

368

Pair of Victorian mahogany card tables, 'D' shape, 92cm. Phillips, Bath. May 00. £3,900.

369

George III mahogany architect's desk, adjustable top, 2 slides, gilt metal pulls, 92cm wide, 71cm high. Wintertons Ltd, Lichfield. July 00. £3,800.

370

19thC burr walnut, ebonised bonheur du jour, 53.25in wide. Andrew Hartley, Ilkley. Feb 00. £3,800.

371

Pair of French serpentine card tables veneered in burr yew and figured walnut, 32.25in. Woolley & Wallis, Salisbury. Aug 00. £3,800.

372

19thC Italian carved giltwood mirror, 'jewelled' frame, 4 portraits of Raphael, 41 x 36in. Halls Fine Art Auctions, Shrewsbury. Oct 03. £3,800.

373

Aesthetic movement ebonised and amboyna pier cabinet, 28in wide, stamped Gillow & Co 12244. Andrew Hartley, Ilkley. Apr 01. £3,800.

374

Geo III mahogany sideboard with breakfront top, 84in wide. Dee, Atkinson & Harrison, Driffield. Feb 00. £3,800.

375

18thC Spanish walnut side table, 2 drawers geometric carved fronts, 81in. Gorringes, Lewes. Sep 00. £3,800.

376

Victorian burr walnut Wellington chest. Ambrose, Loughton. Jan 01. £3,800.

377

Pair early 19thC mahogany tea tables, 35.5 x 35.75in maximum. David Duggleby, Scarborough. July 01. £3,800.

378

Victorian walnut breakfront bookcase, bevelled glass, 10 collectors drawers, 72in wide. Canterbury Auction Galleries. Feb 04. £3,800.

379

16thC Italian carved walnut collectors cabinet, later stand, 1ft 11in. Gorringes, Lewes. Jan 04. £3,800.

380

Oak refectory table, 17thC & later, 108 x 34in. Andrew Hartley, Ilkley. Aug 01. £3,800.

381

George II walnut tea table, 3 drawers and folding top, 30.5in dia. Clarke Gammon, Guildford. Apr 02. £3,800.

382

Set 8 mid 19thC Hepplewhite design, mahogany dining chairs. Amersham Auction Rooms, Bucks. Apr 02. £3,800.

383

Victorian olivewood and inlaid davenport, c1870, slope inscribed Jerusalem, 70cm wide. Wintertons Ltd, Lichfield. May 02. £3,800.

384

18thC marquetry occasional table, hinged top inlaid, 69cm wide. Sworders, Stansted Mountfitchet. Feb 04. £3,800.

385

Sheraton Revival Irish mahogany/satinwood display cabinet, stamped 'Butler, W', 126cm wide. Thos Mawer & Son, Lincoln. Nov 02. £3,800.

386

Oak sideboard, Robert 'Mouseman' Thompson, 152cm long. Richard Wintertons, Burton on Trent. Oct 03. £3,800.

387

Dutch walnut and marquetry display cabinet, c1800, 43in wide, 6ft 9in high. Gorringes, Bexhill. Mar 03. £3,800.

388

George III oak dresser and shelves. Louis Taylor, Stoke on Trent. Dec 02. £3,800.

Hammer Prices £3,800-£3,700

389

North Italian neo classical marquetry commode in walnut and olivewood, 87cm high, c1780. Mellors & Kirk, Nottingham. June 03. £3,800.

390

Regency rosewood low bookcase, boxwood inlaid, 25in wide. Gorringes, Bexhill. Nov 03. £3,800.

Prices quoted are hammer and exclude the buyer's premium. Adding 15% will give approx. buying price.

391

19thC French inlaid Kingwood bureau plat, gilt metal mounts. Sworders, Stansted Mountfitchet. Sep 01. £3,750.

392

George III oak dresser, 68.5in wide, 74in high. A. Hartley, Ilkley. June 01. £3,750.

393

George III oak standing dresser of golden patina. Richard Wintertons, Burton on Trent. Nov 01. £3,700.

394

George III mahogany dresser, c1785, 97cm high, 198cm wide. Wintertons Ltd. Lichfield. May 03. £3,700.

395

19thC Dutch display cabinet, walnut and floral marquetry. Lots Road Auctions, Chelsea. May 02. £3,700.

396

Liberty walnut and parcel gilt draw leaf table, stamped Liberty, top 120.5 x 318cm extended. Dreweatt Neate, Newbury. Nov 02. £3,700.

397

Georgian oak and elm Welsh potboard dresser, 123cm. D M Nesbit, Southsea. Jan 03. £3,700.

Hammer Prices £3,700-£3,600

Set of 8 Queen Anne design walnut dining chairs, 2 arms, tapestry seats. Gorringes, Lewes. July 03. £3,700.

Oak dining room suite, Robert 'Mouseman' Thompson, 2nd qtr. 20thC, sideboard and a set of 4 chairs. Sotheby's, Billingshurst. Mar 00. £3,600.

Early 19thC rosewood scroll end settee, overstuffed seat, 223cm wide. Cheffins, Cambridge. Feb 04. £3,600.

George III oak dresser, 72.5in high. Andrew Hartley, Ilkley. Feb 00. £3,600.

George III mahogany chest, brushing slide, 84cm. Sworders, Stansted Mountfitchet. Feb 04. £3,600.

Set 8 (6+2) Edwardian mahogany Hepplewhite design dining chairs. Gorringes, Lewes. Mar 02. £3,600.

Oak dresser, George III, late 18thC, 196cm high x 188cm wide. Sotheby's, Billingshurst. May 00. £3,600.

Set of 10 (8 + 2) Chippendale style mahogany dining chairs. Sworders, Stansted Mountfitchet. Apr 01. £3,600.

Set of 9 William IV mahogany dining chairs, acanthus scroll curved top rails. Gorringes, Lewes. Mar 01. £3,600.

George I walnut chest with figured veneers & patination. Lots Road Auctions, Chelsea. July 00. £3,600.

Late 17thC oak chest, shaped apron and later bun feet, 35.5 x 36.5in. Andrew Hartley, Ilkley. Feb 00. £3,600.

Early George III mahogany kneehole desk, 32in wide. Andrew Hartley, Ilkley. Apr 02. £3,600.

George III mahogany tray top commode, ceramic liner, 21in. Gorringes, Lewes. Mar 01. £3,600.

19thC walnut wing armchair, upholstered in modern red chenille. Lots Road Auctions, Chelsea. Feb 02. £3,600.

George III mahogany Pembroke table. Rosebery's, London. Mar 01. £3,600.

17thC Flemish boullework cabinet. Lots Road Auctions, Chelsea. Oct 00. £3,600.

George IV mahogany sideboard, bow front crossbanded in satinwood, boxwood strung, 54 x 35in. David Duggleby, Scarborough. July 01. £3,600.

Edwardian George III design inlaid mahogany breakfront library bookcase, 8ft 8in height 7ft 11in. Gorringes, Lewes. Oct 00. £3,600.

Geo III style mahogany 4 pedestal dining table c1900, 3 leaves, 594cm long (19ft 6in). Rosebery's, London. Sep 00. £3,600.

417

Montgomeryshire oak Welsh dresser, early 19thC, 196cm high. *Hamptons, Godalming. May 02. £3,600.*

418

19thC burr oak Davenport. *Rupert Toovey, Washington, Sussex. May 03. £3,600.*

419

Pair of antique Continental walnut pedestal cupboards, crossbanded tops, probably Dutch, 47cm. *Stride & Son, Chichester. Jul 03. £3,600.*

420

Dutch walnut 'Amsterdam' cabinet, c1800, 8ft 4in high, 6ft 6in wide. *Gorringes, Bexhill. Oct 02. £3,600.*

421

18thC oak dresser. *W & H Peacock, Bedford. Aug 02. £3,600.*

422

18thC oak dresser, 5ft 1in. *Gorringes, Lewes. Apr 01. £3,600.*

423

George II mahogany fold over, triple top games table. *Rupert Toovey, Washington, Sussex. Oct 03. £3,600.*

424

19thC library table, mahogany, later leather lined top, 140 x 82cm. *Lots Road Auctions, Chelsea. Nov 03. £3,600.*

425

Geo III mahog. linen press, 5 sliding trays over 2 short, one long drawer, 1.34m wide. *Sworders, Stansted Mountfitchet. Feb 04. £3,500.*

Hammer Prices £3,600-£3,500

426

George III mahogany bow-front sideboard, 4ft 9in wide. *Lots Road Auctions, Chelsea. Mar 00. £3,500.*

427

William IV rosewood centre table, 2 drawers, 2 dummy, 114 x 71cm. *Wintertons Ltd, Lichfield. Mar 00. £3,500.*

> The numbering system acts as a reader reference as well as linking to the Analysis of each Section

428

Geo III mahogany/satinwood banded serpentine sideboard. *Lots Road Auctions, Chelsea. Sep 01. £3,500.*

429

Regency rosewood dwarf bookcase with beaded frieze above a pair of panel doors flanked by fleur-de-lys, 76in wide. *Lots Road Auctions, Chelsea. Aug 01. £3,500.*

430

Victorian walnut credenza, on plinth, 63in wide, 15.25in deep. *Andrew Hartley, Ilkley. Apr 01. £3,500.*

431

19thC mahogany Georgian style pedestal dining table, 2 matching 'D' ends, 102in extended by 48in. *P. Wilson, Nantwich. Nov 00. £3,500.*

432

Inlaid yew marquetry foldover games table. *Stride & Son, Chichester. Feb 01. £3,500.*

433

Set 8 (6 + 2) George III mahogany dining chairs. *Hamptons, Godalming. Jul 00. £3,500.*

434

Regency mahogany telescopic action extending dining table, with only 2 of its 3 leaves. *Bristol Auction Rooms, Bristol. Sep 01. £3,500.*

435

19thC mahogany bookcase, stamped T Wilson, Great Queen Street, London, c1850, length 187cm. *Ambrose, Loughton. May 00. £3,500.*

Hammer Prices £3,500-£3,400

436

18thC, south German walnut, crossbanded, inlaid bureau, 111cm. *Lots Road Auctions, Chelsea. Mar 02. £3,500.*

437

George IV mahogany dining table, 301cm extended. *Lots Road Auctions, Chelsea. Mar 02. £3,500.*

438

Oak dresser, c1790, 201cm high, 155cm wide. *Wintertons Ltd, Lichfield. July 02. £3,500.*

439

Pair of Russian Karelian birch bergeres, early 19thC. *Clarke Gammon, Guildford. Dec 03. £3,500.*

440

Continental carved pine hall bench. *Sworders, Stansted Mountfitchet. May 00. £3,400.*

441

Pair 19thC French mahogany 35in wide console tables. *Lots Road Auctions, Chelsea. Apr 00. £3,400.*

442

Regency gilt frame convex wall mirror, 23in. *Gorringes, Bexhill. Feb 01. £3,400.*

443

18thC Dutch walnut/marquetry commode, 34.75in wide. *Canterbury Auc. Galleries, Kent. June 00. £3,400.*

444

Mid Victorian dining table, 3 leaves. *Rosebery's, London. Sep 00. £3,400.*

445

Early 18thC feather banded walnut kneehole desk, quarter veneered top, 32in. *Gorringes, Lewes. Oct 00. £3,400.*

446

Oak livery cupboard, Charles II and later, faults, 122cm high x 119cm wide. *Sotheby's, Billingshurst. May 00. £3,400.*

447

George III mahogany bureau bookcase, 46.5in. *A. Hartley, Ilkley. Dec 00. £3,400.*

448

Adzed oak wardrobe, Robert 'Mouseman' Thompson, 48in wide, 73in high. *A. Hartley, Ilkley. Feb 01. £3,400.*

449

Wellington chest, birds eye maple, rosewood banding, secretaire 2 dummy drawers, 25in wide. *Andrew Hartley, Ilkley. Aug 01. £3,400.*

450

Set 6 + 2 Regency simulated rosewood dining chairs, imp'd. numbers to seat rails, one stamped RR and GT. (repairs) *Sworders, Stansted Mountfitchet. July 01. £3,400.*

451

Oak low dresser, mahogany cross banding, basically 18thC, 72in wide. *A. Hartley, Ilkley. Aug 01. £3,400.*

452

Geo. III mahog. wine cooler, 18in. (af) *Lots Road Auctions, Chelsea. Feb 02. £3,400.*

453

Small Regency writing table, c1820, tiered leather inset top over 4 frieze drawers, 70 x 100cm. *Rosebery's, London. Sep 02. £3,400.*

454

Georgian mahogany cellaret, fitted interior, 45cm. *Ambrose, Loughton. June 02. £3,400.*

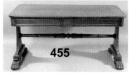

455

William IV pollard oak refectory library table, 2 opposing drawers, 2 dummy drawers, 60in. *Tring Market Auctions, Herts. Nov 02. £3,400.*

456

Vic. mahog. extending circular dining table, extra leaf, 194cm. *Locke & England, Leamington Spa. May 03. £3,400.*

457

William IV mahogany library table, 180 x 123cm. (one caster loose). *D M Nesbit & Co, Southsea. Dec 03. £3,400.*

458

Irish Geo. mahog. bow front sideboard, 90in. *Denhams, Warnham. Dec 03. £3,400.*

459

Regency mahogany extending dining table, manner of Gillow, plus 4 leaves, pull-out action, 12ft long. *A. Hartley, Ilkley. Dec 03. £3,400.*

460

William III oak chest, c1700, 95cm wide. *Wintertons Ltd, Lichfield. July 02. £3,300.*

461

Set 6 + 2 19thC Chippendale style ladderback chairs. *Hamptons, Godalming. Nov 01. £3,300.*

462

Victorian mahog. extending dining table, 3 leaves, 3.02m x 1.27m. *Sworders, Stansted Mountfitchet. Dec 02. £3,300.*

463

18th/early 19thC Continental carved giltwood/gesso centre table, 110cm long, 70cm wide. *R. Toovey, Washington, Sussex. Jan 04. £3,300.*

The illustrations are in descending price order. The price range is indicated at the top of each page.

464

James I design oak tester bedstead, carved headboard and footboard, (part 17thC) 5ft wide, 6ft 9in long. *Gorringes, Lewes. Mar 04. £3,250.*

465

George III mahog. sofa table, line inlaid, 30in deep, 62in extended. *Lots Road Auctions, Chelsea. Apr 01. £3,200.*

466

George III mahogany secretaire chest on chest, c1770, 46in wide. *Peter Wilson, Nantwich. Apr 00. £3,200.*

467

18thC oak dresser base. *Phillips, Bath. May 00. £3,200.*

468

Pr. Empire design ormolu gueridons, (tables) green marble tops, stylised swan columns, 2ft 1in. *Gorringes, Lewes. Feb 00. £3,200.*

469

George III Sheraton style sideboard. *Clarke Gammon, Guildford. Sep 01. £3,200.*

470

Satin banded, string inlaid Edwardian mahogany lady's writing desk by Maple & Co, 33in wide, 42in high. *Dee, Atkinson & Harrison, Driffield. Dec 00. £3,200.*

471

18thC oak dresser base (back legs reduced) 97in wide. *Sworders, Stansted Mountfitchet. Oct 01. £3,200.*

472

George III mahog. drop leaf dining table, 137 x 172cm. *Hamptons, Godalming. July 01. £3,200.*

473

Queen Anne period walnut stool with drop in upholstered seat. *Mervyn Carey, Tenterden. Feb 04. £3,200.*

474

19thC French kingwood parquetry writing table, 101 x 66.5cm. *Dreweatt Neate, Newbury. Apr 00. £3,200.*

475

Late 18thC carved giltwood mirror, 42.5in high. *Andrew Hartley, Ilkley. Oct 00. £3,200.*

Hammer Price £3,200

476

Regency simulated rosewood settee, 89.5in long. (lacks castors). *Diamond Mills, Felixstowe. Oct 01. £3,200.*

477

Fine inlaid camphorwood two part campaign secretaire chest, c1840. *Bristol Auction Rooms. Sep 01. £3,200.*

478

Kingsize mahog. lit en bateau, incl. new Harrod's mattresses. *Lots Road Auctions, Chelsea. Feb 2002. £3,200.*

479

Pair of mahogany folding tea tables, reeded edged swivel top, 36in wide. *A. Hartley, Ilkley. Feb 03. £3,200.*

480

Edwardian mahogany library table from Bank of England, pair to the desk currently used by Sir Eddie George, tooled leather top, each side one real drawer with Bramah locks, 68in x 64in. *Sworders, Stansted Mountfitchet. July 01. £3,200.*

481

18thC ash/elm seated Windsor armchair of primitive form. (seat wormed and split). *Canterbury Auction Galleries, Kent. Apr 02. £3,200.*

482

Geo. III mahog. 4-tier what-not, lectern top, candle slides, mid-tier drawer, 1ft 6in, height 4ft 1in. *Gorringes, Lewes. Mar 01. £3,200.*

483

Geo. III mahogany chest on chest, 112cm wide. *Hamptons, Godalming. May 02. £3,200.*

484

Sheraton Revival mahogany and painted wardrobe by Walker & Edwards, London, 19thC, 74in wide. *A. Hartley, Ilkley. Oct 01. £3,200.*

485

Vict. mahog. serving table, 72in long. *Andrew Hartley, Ilkley. Aug 01. £3,200.*

486

George III mahog. standing corner cabinet, 4ft 1in wide, 6ft 8in high. *Gorringes, Lewes. Mar 03. £3,200.*

487

Geo. mahog. wall hanging shelf, 95 x 46cm. *Rosebery's, London. Dec 03. £3,200.*

488

Set 8 early Vic. mahogany dining chairs. *Rosebery's, London. Jan 00. £3,200.*

489

Victorian oak dresser base, 19thC, Carolean style, 4 drawers above an apron suspended with ball finials, six rope twist legs, 135in long, 22.5in deep, 32in high. *Halls Fine Art Auctions, Shrewsbury. Oct 03. £3,200.*

490

Early 18thC oak dresser base, moulded planked top, 5ft 8in. *Gorringes, Lewes. Dec 00. £3,200.*

491

Regency mahogany two tier etagere, c1820, marble shelves. *Rosebery's, London. June 03. £3,200.*

492

Regency mahog. washstand by Gillows. *Mellors & Kirk, Nottingham. Feb 03. £3,200.*

493

Geo. III, Hepplewhite style, mahogany dining chairs, 3 standards and 2 carvers. *Amersham Auction Rooms, Bucks. May 03. £3,200.*

494

Edwardian mahog. marquetry display cabinet, astragal glazed, 47in. *Andrew Hartley, Ilkley. Feb 04. £3,200.*

499

Ebonised corner cabinet, satinwood inlaid animals in the style of C. Dresser. *Academy Auctioneers, Ealing. Jan 00. £3,100.*

Hammer Prices £3,200-£3,000

503

George III mahogany linen press, 49in wide. *A. Hartley, Ilkley. Dec 00. £3,100.*

507

Set of 4 north Italian walnut framed hall chairs. *Cheffins, Cambridge. Oct 00. £3,100.*

495

William IV mahogany two-tier cabinet, 58in wide. *Canterbury Auc. Galleries, Kent. Oct 00. £3,100.*

500

George III oak dresser, later feet, 60in. *Clarke Gammon, Guildford. Dec 02. £3,100.*

Prices quoted are hammer and exclude the buyer's premium. Adding 15% will give approx. buying price.

508

Art Deco walnut dining suite, extending table, 85.5 x 40in, 6 chairs with cream leather overstuffed seat, sideboard, and serving table. *Andrew Hartley, Ilkley. Feb 04. £3,000.*

496

Mahog. centre table, 18thC design, with Irish 18thC cabriole legs. 48in wide. *Canterbury Auc. Galleries, Kent. Feb 00. £3,100.*

504

Victorian mahog. extending dining table, 2 leaves, 1.37m wide x 1.46m open to 2.66m. *Sworders, Stansted Mount-fitchet. Dec 03. £3,100.*

509

Geo. IV Pollard Oak break-fast table, veneered in figured panels, 50in dia. *Canterbury Auc. Galleries, Kent. Feb 04. £3,000.*

497

Victorian figured walnut tilt top dining table, 60in dia. *Dockree's, Manchester. Dec 00. £3,100.*

505

Late 17thC oak cabinet on stand, 104.5cm high. *Rupert Toovey, Washington, Sussex. Jan 04. £3,100.*

501

19thC Dutch walnut double bombe chest with serpentine top, 2ft 11in. *Gorringes, Lewes. Feb 01. £3,100.*

510

Regency ebony strung mahogany bowfront sideboard, 2 central drawers, ring turned tapered legs, 5ft. *Gorringes, Lewes. June 00. £3,000.*

498

Set 6 + 2 Edwardian mahog. Hepplewhite style dining chairs. *Wintertons Ltd, Lichfield. Nov 00. £3,100.*

502

Early 18thC oak press cupboard, 49in wide, 71in high. *Tring Market Auctions, Herts. Sep 02. £3,100.*

506

19thC rosewood cheval mirror, tunnel stretcher. *Sworders, Stansted Mount-fitchet. Mar 04. £3,100.*

511

Set of 4 + 2 Geo. III mahog. dining chairs in the Sheraton style. *Andrew Hartley, Ilkley. Aug 00. £3,000.*

Hammer Price £3,000

George I figured walnut chest of drawers. Lots Road Auctions, Chelsea. Nov 00. £3,000.

George IV mahogany serpentine chest, 47in width. Wintertons Ltd, Lichfield. Sep 00. £3,000.

Secretaire, Napoleon III rosewood, white marble top, 52in wide. (stamped 'Durand, Paris'). Lots Road Auctions, Chelsea. Mar 01. £3,000.

Mid 19thC French marquetry centre table, coloured wood veneers, 51.5in wide, 30in high. Tring Market Auctions, Herts. Sep 02. £3,000.

Late Regency faded mahogany sofa table, 3ft 1.5in. Woolley & Wallis, Salisbury. Aug 00. £3,000.

Edwardian painted satinwood elbow chair in the manner of George Seddon. A. Hartley, Ilkley. Feb 01. £3,000.

Early 18thC walnut chest on chest, 3ft 5in. Gorringes, Lewes. June 00. £3,000.

Pair of late 19thC ebonised boulle, pietra dura tortoiseshell cabinets, 35in wide. Amersham Auction Rooms, Bucks. Nov 01. £3,000.

Edwardian satinwood bijouterie table, 16.5in wide, 29.5in high. Andrew Hartley, Ilkley. Dec 00. £3,000.

George III mahogany, brass bound wine cooler, 17in wide. Canterbury Auc. Galleries, Kent. Apr 01. £3,000.

Adzed oak refectory table by Robert 'Mouseman' Thompson, 94.25in long, 34.25in wide. A. Hartley, Ilkley. Feb 01. £3,000.

Aesthetic rosewood, harewood sideboard, c1880, in manner of Collinson and Lock, 161cm high x 198cm wide. Sotheby's, Billingshurst. June 01. £3,000.

Mahog. library table, crossbanded top, gilt embossed green leather inset, 19thC, 50.5in wide. Andrew Hartley, Ilkley. June 01. £3,000.

Set of 8 William IV mahogany dining chairs, foliate carved curved cresting rails, drop in seats. Gorringes, Lewes. Apr 01. £3,000.

William IV rosewood library table, with chess board inlaid in green and black marble, 40in wide by 29.5in high. Canterbury Auc. Galleries, Kent. June 01. £3,000.

Regency mahogany Gillows style metamorphic library stool, horsehair seat hinged to create 4 rectangular treads with turned brass supports, 3ft 4in. Gorringes, Lewes. Mar 01. £3,000.

Edwardian mahog. display cabinet, Edwards and Roberts, 4ft 6in. Gorringes, Lewes. Oct 01. £3,000.

Mid 18thC walnut library armchair, upholstered in needlework, (probably German). Woolley & Wallis, Salisbury. Aug 00. £3,000.

530

Edwardian inlaid mahogany side cabinet, 4ft wide, 5ft 5in high. *Sworders, Stansted Mountfitchet. Apr 01. £3,000.*

531

19thC burr walnut serpentine credenza, ormolu mounts, marquetry, 5ft 5in. *Gorringes, Lewes. Apr 01. £3,000.*

532

Regency mahogany drinking table of semi circular form, 69in wide. *Andrew Hartley, Ilkley. June 01. £3,000.*

533

Early 18thC Queen Anne figured walnut chest, quarter veneered and line inlaid top. *Lots Road Auctions, Chelsea. Sep 02. £3,000.*

534

Victorian walnut inlaid gilt bronze mounted credenza, 190cm. *Sworders, Stansted Mountfitchet. Mar 04. £3,000.*

535

George III oak dresser with 3-shelf rack, 3 drawers over chamfered legs and potboard, on stile feet, 5ft. *Gorringes, Lewes. July 02. £3,000.*

536

French Louis XV style rosewood display cabinet, large inset lacquer panel painted with a Watteauesque pastoral scene, 71in high x 54in wide. *Wintertons Ltd, Lichfield. Mar 01. £3,000.*

> The numbering system acts as a reader reference as well as linking to the Analysis of each Section

537

George III oak farmhouse table. *Mellors & Kirk, Nottingham. Feb 03. £3,000.*

538

Pair of mid 19thC lacquered side cabinets, gilt metal mounts, black marble tops, applied pietra dura, 32.5in wide. *Amersham Auc. Rooms, Bucks. Mar 04. £3,000.*

Hammer Price £3,000

539

Adzed oak Robert Mouseman Thompson dining table, 84in long, 33.75in wide with a set of 6 + 2 lattice back chairs to match. *Andrew Hartley, Ilkley. Apr 04. £3,000.*

540

Victorian satin walnut and parcel gilt writing table in the manner of Seddon, 4ft 4in wide. *Gorringes, Bexhill. Mar 03. £3,000.*

541

Set of 6 + 2 19thC George III design mahogany wheelback dining chairs. *Gorringes, Lewes. Jan 03. £3,000.*

542

Victorian inlaid walnut credenza, associated mirrored back, 213cm wide. *Sworders, Stansted Mountfitchet. Sep 03. £3,000.*

543

Regency rosewood concave open bookcase, 2 adjustable shelves, 3ft 8in. *Gorringes, Lewes. Jan 04. £3,000.*

544

Traditional double oak tester bed, 2nd half 20thC, 200cm high, 162cm wide, 220cm long. *R. Wintertons, Burton on Trent. Aug 03. £3,000.*

545

William and Mary oak side table, single frieze drawer, 91cm. *Sworders, Stansted Mountfitchet. Oct 02. £3,000.*

546

Victorian burr walnut piano top davenport with jack-in-a-box stationary compartment, pull out writing slope, 1ft 11in. *Gorringes, Lewes. Dec 00. £3,000.*

547

Oak dresser, Caernarfonshire, c1780-1800, 204cm high. *Byrne's, Chester. Oct 03. £3,000.*

Here is not 'shabby chic....', rather pieces which would typically add grace and charm to older properties, blending in with the faded and 'gently ravaged' interiors created by centuries of 'romantic' neglect.

The emerging story is of three woods dominating the English antique furniture scene during the last 400 years. Firstly, it was oak, hard, longlasting, home-grown and European, which is found from the Tudor and Stuart periods, the 'Age of Oak' right through to the nineteenth and twentieth century reproductions. Popularised by the Arts and Crafts Movement, oak dominated again, particularly in the first half of the twentieth century. But there had in this period, always been walnut, again from England and Europe. This was in continuous use for high quality furniture from the sixteenth century and was hugely popular at the end of the seventeenth and into the early eighteenth century in solid furniture and veneers, including burr wood. But then, as the Americas opened up and perhaps because walnut became unobtainable from France, a warm, hard, exciting wood called mahogany arrived. Known as early 'Spanish' or 'San Domingo' it was extremely dark and heavy and excellent for carving. Cuban mahogany was imported from about 1750 and was much used in veneers because of its fine ripple and curl grain. Honduras followed and was used from the later eighteenth century onwards for cheaper work as it lacked the quality of Cuban.

These three woods dominate these pages. And in this Section even though there are fifty or more each examples of walnut and oak, mahogany dominates with over 140 examples. Rosewood musters a credible twenty five and now the reader has an opportunity to study more than a dozen satinwood lots at **669**, **670**, **762**, **829**, **844**, **846**, and **868**. Our native ash, elm and yew account for only half a dozen lots. Again there is only one example of pine, **630**, and again this is Continental, being a painted pine marriage chest, dated 1736, which fetched £2,600 at Sworders, Stansted Mountfitchet, Essex in 2003. Incidentally, this is a piece which would typically add grace and charm to older properties, blending in with the faded and 'gently ravaged' interiors created by centuries of 'romantic' neglect! For a survey of the old fashioned comfort of the lived-in interior which I must add, is not 'shabby chic', see *The Well-Worn Interior*, by Robin Forster and Tim Whittaker, published by Thames & Hudson at £24.95. ISBN 0 500 511 39 X.

On page 41, I am struck immediately by the Art Deco walnut dining suite at **550**. Think of it, a dining table more than eight feet long and forty inches wide, eight chairs including two carvers, plus a matching sideboard

for only £2,900 in October 2000 at Andrew Hartley in Ilkley in North Yorkshire. It is also worth checking out a similar suite at **785** which has an additional cupboard but unfortunately only five chairs. This fetched £2,200 at Gorringes, Bexhill in November 2003. Interested readers can also check out the similar prices of £2,800 and £2,700 for Art Deco burr walnut cocktail cabinets at **594** and **602**. Or check out the *Index*. My eye was also attracted to the Queen Anne walnut gateleg table at **588**. This wonderful example, with its attractive turned out or splayed legs fetched £2,800 at Mellors and Kirk in Nottingham in April 2003. Note also the Charles II oak food hutch, dated 1667 at **636** for £2,600.

Windsor chairs are worth tracking through the *Index*. Here there is a very credible near set of six nineteenth century elbow chairs, **577**, which reached £2,800 at Henry Adams, Chichester in September 2002. And at **612** a set of eight nineteenth century ash and elm Windsor armchairs found £2,700 a year earlier in Yorkshire. See also a set of five at **637**. Earlier single chairs can fetch considerable sums such as the Buckinghamshire Windsor at **801**, selling in its own county at Amersham Auction Rooms for £2,100 and the elm stick back Windsor at **849**, bearing traces of old green paint (never remove old surfaces) which found £2,000. Art Nouveau furniture can be traced through the *Index* but see the display cabinet which sold at Morphets in Harrogate in 2001 for £2,900 **553**, and the Liberty style oak sideboard at **871** which reached £2,000 at Clarke Gammon in April 2004. Gothic Revival furniture can be checked out through the *Index* but as we have mentioned repro oak already, it is worth drawing the readers' attention to the pair of library chairs at **564** which sold at Cheffins, Cambridge in October 2000 for £2,800. Have these chairs risen in value since?

More about out-of-favour bureaux and in-favour early walnut. Turn to page 50 to find three examples which all sold for £2,400 in different counties in different years. Don't treat early walnut bureaux like early oak or mahogany. Similar prices for similar pieces selling in different parts of the country at different times or even at the same time, indicate the wisdom and the knowledge of the market nationwide. The critics of this book must acknowledge the usefulness of having many examples to choose from which have been placed in numerical price order accompanied by a comprehensive *Index*.

Hammer Prices £2,950-£2,800

548

Early 19thC English George I figured walnut chest, 38in wide. *Lots Road Auctions, Chelsea. Mar 01. £2,950.*

549

Georgian mahogany and line inlay sideboard, with concave drawer and cupboard ends. *Biddle & Webb, Birmingham. Sep 00. £2,900.*

550

Art Deco walnut dining suite, canted table, 97 x 40in, 6 + 2 chairs, stepped pedestal sideboard 66in wide. *Andrew Hartley, Ilkley. Oct 00. £2,900.*

551

Large George III mahogany lodge chair, arched toprail, adjustable headrest with Masonic emblems. *Cheffins, Cambridge. Oct 00. £2,900.*

552

Geo. II red walnut (?) bureau, with drawers, pigeon holes, 32in wide. *Sworders, Stansted Mountfitchet. July 01. £2,900.*

553

Art Nouveau mahog. display cabinet, satin and harewood inlaid of stylised flowers and panels, 44in. *Morphets, Harrogate. Mar 01. £2,900.*

554

George III mahogany bureau/ bookcase, 43.25in wide, 91.5in high. *Dockree's, Manchester. Feb 01. £2,900.*

555

Mahogany specimen chest, 37in wide, 49.75in high, early to mid 19thC. *A. Hartley, Ilkley. Dec 00. £2,900.*

556

Pr. walnut/tulipwood cross-banded side cabinets, 19thC & later, Louis XV style, 21in wide. *Halls Fine Art Auctions, Shrewsbury. Oct 03. £2,900.*

557

George III mahogany chest on chest, 103cm wide. *Cheffins, Cambridge. Oct 00. £2,900.*

558

George III mahogany Gainsborough chair. *Peter Wilson, Nantwich. Nov 01. £2,900.*

> The illustrations are in descending price order. The price range is indicated at the top of each page.

559

18thC walnut faced chest on chest, original brass furniture, pine sides, bracket feet, 41in wide. *Sworders, Stansted Mountfitchet. Apr 01. £2,900.*

560

Late Regency rosewood cylinder bureau, with a three quarter brass gallery edge of Greek key design, 102cm wide, 104cm high. *Hamptons, Godalming. May 02. £2,900.*

561

Early 19thC mahogany sideboard, 63 x 26 x 36in. *Hamptons, Godalming. Mar 02. £2,900.*

562

Victorian mahogany military chest, drawer fronts veneered in figured walnut, 39in wide. *Tring Market Auctions, Herts. May 02. £2,900.*

563

Set of six Regency rosewood single dining chairs, caned seats, brass strung sabre legs. *Sworders, Stansted Mount-fitchet. Sep 03. £2,900.*

564

Pair of Victorian oak Gothic revival library chairs. *Cheffins, Cambridge. Oct 00. £2,800.*

565

Regency flame mahog. linen press. *Lots Road Auctions, Chelsea. Nov 00. £2,800.*

Hammer Price £2,800

566

Regency design breakfast table. *Lots Road Auctions, Chelsea. Oct 00. £2,800.*

567

Edwardian satinwood/ebony line inlaid bonheur du jour. *Rupert Toovey, Washington, Sussex. Dec 02. £2,800.*

568

Modern pietra dura marble table top. *Rosebery's, London. Dec 00. £2,800.*

569

Early 19thC rosewood sofa table, 2 frieze drawers and opposing dummies, 142cm x 64cm. *Thos Mawer & Son, Lincoln. Nov 02. £2,800.*

570

19thC walnut Davenport, 38in high, 23in wide. *Amersham Auction Rooms, Bucks. May 01. £2,800.*

571

George III mahogany linen press, 4ft 2in. *Gorringes, Lewes. Sep 00. £2,800.*

572

19thC walnut davenport, 3/4 galleried back with rising till, 3 small drawers and 4 pigeon holes, 22in wide. *Hamptons, Godalming. Sep 01. £2,800.*

573

Set of 6 + 2 dining chairs in the Chippendale style. *Canterbury Auction Galleries, Kent. Dec 01. £2,800.*

574

Regency mahogany and ebony strung secretaire bookcase. *Lots Road Auctions, Chelsea. May 01. £2,800.*

575

Set of 8 William IV mahogany dining chairs. *Lots Road Auctions, Chelsea. Apr 02. £2,800.*

576

Oak dresser base. *Kivell & Sons, Bude. Mar 03. £2,800.*

577

Very near set of six 19thC yew wood stick-back Windsor elbow chairs. *Henry Adams, Chichester. Sep 02. £2,800.*

578

Oak court cupboard. *Kivell & Sons, Bude. Mar 03. £2,800.*

579

Queen Anne style walnut kneehole dressing table/desk, small proportions, 27in wide. *Clarke Gammon, Guildford. Dec 02. £2,800.*

580

Late 19thC ormolu mounted ebonised amboyna credenza, ebony banding, glazed cupboards, 72in long. *Maxwells, Wilmslow. Sep 02. £2,800.*

581

Set 6 +2 George III mahog. dining chairs, drop in seats in pink striped brocade. *Canterbury Auc. Galleries, Kent. Aug 02. £2,800.*

582

George II walnut kneehole desk, 31.25in wide, 32.5in high. *Tring Market Auctions, Herts. Nov 02. £2,800.*

583

Regency mahogany cellaret, sarcophagus form with lead lined interior, lions paw feet, 1ft 8in. *Gorringes, Lewes. Apr 01. £2,800.*

584

Louis XVI design kingwood and marquetry serpentine commode, rouge marble top, ormolu foliate scroll mounts, 4ft 4in. *Gorringes, Lewes. Dec 00. £2,800.*

585

George III oak low panelled dresser, 84.5in wide. Andrew Hartley, Ilkley. Feb 03. £2,800.

586

Regency wall mirror, oval plate within carved giltwood rope twist surround, 116cm wide. Sworders, Stansted Mountfitchet. Mar 04. £2,800.

587

Geo. III mahogany standing corner cupboard, 32.5in wide, 83in high. Andrew Hartley, Ilkley. June 03. £2,800.

588

Queen Anne walnut gateleg table, 138 x 135cm. Mellors & Kirk, Nottingham. Apr 03. £2,800.

589

19thC chest, chinoiserie decor, 93cm. Lots Road Auctions, Chelsea. Nov 03. £2,800.

590

Set 10 + 2 early 20thC mahog. dining chairs, drop in seats. Lots Road Auctions, Chelsea. Nov 03. £2,800.

591

Robert Thompson, adzed oak wardrobe, iron latch/hinges, incised mouse trademark, 1960s, 66in high. A. Hartley, Ilkley. Dec 03. £2,800.

Prices quoted are hammer and exclude the buyer's premium. Adding 15% will give approx. buying price.

592

Victorian mahog. extending dining table, plus 3 leaves, 122in x 54in. A. Hartley, Ilkley. Dec 03. £2,800.

593

Victorian burr walnut davenport, metamorphic stationery compartment, piano front, leather lined writing slide, 3ft 4in high. Gorringes, Bexhill. Nov 03. £2,800.

Hammer Prices £2,800-£2,700

594

Art Deco burr walnut cocktail cabinet of demi lune form, fluted doors, mirrored interior, 36in wide. Andrew Hartley, Ilkley. Feb 04. £2,800.

595

18thC Irish pierced brass footman, top with unicorn & crowned lion either side of a central wheel with a harp and lute on each side, 68cm. Sworders, Stansted Mountfitchet. Feb 04. £2,800.

596

6 + 2 dining chairs, late 19thC oak in Carolean style, floral needlework covers. Lots Road Auctions, Chelsea. Mar 04. £2,800.

597

George III mahogany and brass bound wine cooler, hinged lid, lead lined, 62cm. Sworders, Stansted Mountfitchet. Mar 04. £2,800.

598

18thC walnut chest. Lots Road Auctions, Chelsea. Oct 00. £2,800.

599

William and Mary and later walnut chest, inlaid crossbanding, 40.5in wide. Clarke Gammon, Guildford. Apr 04. £2,800.

600

Set 6 + 2 William IV mahog. dining chairs. D. Duggleby, Scarborough. June 01. £2,750.

601

Late 19thC mahogany dower chest, cock beading and cast brass bail handles, 68in wide. Amersham Auction Rooms, Bucks. June 01. £2,700.

602

Art Deco burr walnut/bird's eye maple semi-circular cocktail cabinet, 72in high, 49in wide. Clarke Gammon, Guildford. Apr 01. £2,700.

Hammer Prices £2,700-£2,600

603

Early Victorian figured mahogany cellaret, 102cm wide. *Bristol Auction Rooms, Bristol. Mar 02. £2,700.*

604

Regency rosewood sofa table. *Lambert & Foster, Tenterden. Sep 02. £2,700.*

605

Oak Welsh dresser, rack back, cupboard base, 177cm. *Stride & Son, Chichester. June 02. £2,700.*

606

19thC burr walnut desk, stamped T Wilson, 68 Great Queen Street, London, c1860, 145cm wide. *Wintertons Ltd, Lichfield. Nov 02. £2,700.*

607

Walnut chest crossbanded, quarter veneered top, late 17th/early 18thC, 39in wide. *Andrew Hartley, Ilkley. Apr 04. £2,700.*

608

Geo. III oak press cupboard, cornice initialled 'R.A.P.', dated 1743, 4ft 9in. *Gorringes, Bexhill. Dec 02. £2,700.*

609

19thC oak breakfront bookcase, 218cm wide. *Bristol Auc. Rooms, Bristol. Jan 03. £2,700.*

610

19thC rosewood breakfast table, birds/floral marquetry centre and bird's eye maple scroll and floral border, 4ft. (Mr Simpson cabinet maker, Oetzman's Tottenham Court Rd. *Gorringes, Lewes. Dec 00. £2,700.*

611

George III mahogany linen press, moulded lambrequin cornice, 56in wide. *Andrew Hartley, Ilkley. Oct 00. £2,700.*

612

Set of 8 ash and elm windsor armchairs, 19thC. *Andrew Hartley, Ilkley. Oct 01. £2,700.*

613

Regency pollard oak drum table, 4 drawers, 44in dia. *Amersham Auction Rooms, Bucks. Feb 04. £2,700.*

614

George IV mahogany sarcophagus shaped cellaret, 63cm wide. *Wintertons Ltd, Lichfield. Nov 02. £2,700.*

615

Georgian mahogany tilt top table with bird-cage movement. *W & H Peacock, Bedford. Mar 03. £2,700.*

616

Charles & Ray Eames Model No 670 chair and Model No 671 footstool for Herman Miller Furniture Co., rosewood faced plywood seat shells, leather cushions, cast aluminium base. *Cheffins, Cambridge. Apr 04. £2,700.*

617

Regency faded rosewood library table, 2 drawers, 4ft 8in x 2ft 4in. *Gorringes, Lewes. Sep 00. £2,700.*

618

Neo Rococo mahogany serpentine desk, c1890, stamped Jetley, 74cm high, 135cm wide. *Wintertons Ltd, Lichfield. May 03. £2,700.*

619

19thC Continental centre table, giltwood/marble top, 55in wide. *Lots Road Auctions, Chelsea. Apr 01. £2,600.*

620

19thC Continental marquetry table top cabinet, 17in wide. af. *Lots Road Auctions, Chelsea. May 01. £2,600.*

621

Victorian mahogany window seat, carved flowerhead end, 57.5in long. *Andrew Hartley, Ilkley. Apr 01. £2,600.*

622

Victorian burr walnut credenza. *Lots Road Auctions, Chelsea. July 01. £2,600.*

623

Wake table, late 18thC Irish mahogany. Lots Road Auctions, Chelsea. May 02. £2,600.

624

Regency mahog. bow fronted linen press, 4ft 6in. Gorringes, Bexhill. May 02. £2,600.

625

18thC German red walnut bombe serpentine fronted commode, 3ft 5in. Gorringes, Lewes. Apr 01. £2,600.

626

Victorian burr walnut writing table, green skiver, frieze drawer, ovulo banding, Copes patent bronze caps, castors, 3ft 3in x 1ft 10in. Gorringes, Lewes. Apr 01. £2,600.

627

Late George III mahogany chest on chest, 67in high. Amersham Auction Rooms, Bucks. Aug 02. £2,600.

628

George III mahogany chest, brushing slide, 2ft 10in. Gorringes, Lewes. Apr 01. £2,600.

629

Late 17thC Italian walnut cabinet, 8 drawers, 3 small cupboards, central cupboard concealing secret compartments, 2ft 2in wide. Gorringes, Lewes. Apr 01. £2,600.

> The numbering system acts as a reader reference as well as linking to the Analysis of each Section

630

18thC Continental painted pine marriage chest, inscribed 'Anna, Brollin 1736', landscape panels, 135cm high. Sworders, Stansted Mountfitchet. Feb 03. £2,600.

631

George III oak pot board dresser, 5ft 2in wide, 6ft 10in high. Sworders, Stansted Mountfitchet. July 01. £2,600.

Hammer Price £2,600

632

19thC mahogany partners desk, reeded top, tooled leather skiver, 4ft 1in. Gorringes, Lewes. Sep 02. £2,600.

633

Regency cross banded mahogany breakfast table, 5ft x 3ft 2in. Gorringes, Lewes. Sep 02. £2,600.

634

George III oak dresser, c1780, 85cm high, 198cm wide. Wintertons Ltd, Lichfield. Jan 03. £2,600.

635

Victorian Heals Arts and Crafts golden oak wardrobe in the manner of Charles Bevan, 6ft 4in. Gorringes, Lewes. July 03. £2,600.

636

Charles II oak food hutch, triple plank top (poss. later), frieze drawer, dated 1667, stile feet (one restored), 3ft 7.5in wide. Gorringes, Lewes. Jan 04. £2,600.

637

Set 5 19thC yew and elm Yorkshire high back Windsor chairs. (faults/repairs), Gorringes, Bexhill. Mar 03. £2,600.

638

George III oak press cupboard. Mellors & Kirk, Nottingham. Feb 03. £2,600.

639

Edwardian mahog./satinwood crossbanded writing desk by Jas. Shoolbred & Co. Rupert Toovey, Washington, Sussex. Dec 02. £2,600.

640

Italian carved walnut cassone. (late 17thC blanket chest). Stride & Son, Chichester. Dec 03. £2,600.

641

Louis Vuitton, brown and cream, canvas clad trunk, leather edges, lined, tray fitted interior, 28 x 44 x 24in. Amersham Auction Rooms, Bucks. June 03. £2,600.

45

Hammer Prices £2,600-£2,500

642

Edwardian Carlton House desk, mahogany/line inlaid, 122cm wide. Lots Road, Chelsea. Nov 03. £2,600.

643

19thC Italian Pietra Dura occasional table, tilt top, 55cm dia. Locke & England, Leamington Spa. Jan 03. £2,600.

644

George III oak enclosed dresser, 60.5in wide, 77.5in high. Andrew Hartley, Ilkley. Apr 04. £2,600.

645

19thC French kingwood and walnut jardiniere, 43.75in high. Andrew Hartley, Ilkley. Dec 00. £2,600.

646

Victorian mahogany secretaire military chest. Rosebery's, London. Sep 01. £2,600.

647

19thC walnut three piece bedroom suite, wardrobe, 92in wide, dressing table & washstand with white marble top. Andrew Hartley, Ilkley. Feb 03. £2,600.

648

Regency mahog. crossbanded, boxwood strung breakfast table, hinged top, stamped 'W & C Wilkinson, 14 Ludgate Hill, 19395', 160.5cm dia. Sworders, Stansted Mountfitchet. Mar 04. £2,600.

649

Set 6 + 2 Edwardian Chippendale design mahogany dining chairs. Gorringes, Lewes. Mar 04. £2,600.

650

Late 19thC French mahogany credenza, elaborate ormolu mounts, frieze drawer, central door flanked by bowed doors, toupie feet, 4ft 6in. Gorringes, Lewes. Mar 01. £2,600.

651

George III D end dining table. Lots Road Auctions, Chelsea. Oct 00. £2,600.

652

Geo. IV rosewood occasional table, 22.25in wide. Andrew Hartley, Ilkley. Feb 01. £2,600.

653

Set of 12 Georgian style mahogany dining chairs. Sworders, Stansted Mountfitchet. Oct 01. £2,600.

654

Victorian rosewood pedestal dining table. John Taylors, Louth. Nov 03. £2,550.

655

19thC continental mahogany settee with show wood frame, 68in long. Sworders, Stansted Mountfitchet. Mar 01. £2,500.

656

Geo. III mahogany breakfast sideboard, satinwood bands, brass gallery, uprights & urn finials, 68in. wide. Dee Atkinson & Harrison, Driffield. Mar 04. £2,500.

657

William IV mahogany window seat. Rosebery's, London. Sep 01. £2,500.

658

18thC oak dresser base. Rosebery's, London. Sep 01. £2,500.

659

Late Victorian rosewood cylinder bureau, marquetry inlay, fitted interior, 31in. Sworders, Stansted Mountfitchet. Mar 01. £2,500.

660

George III mahogany chest on chest, 112cm wide. Cheffins, Cambridge. Oct 00. £2,500.

661

Joined oak/marquetry court cupboard, 17thC and later, 158cm wide. Bristol Auction Rooms. Jan 02. £2,500.

662

Late 18thC Irish pollard oak cellarette, 27in wide. Amersham Auction Rooms, Bucks. Feb 02. £2,500.

663

Geo. III mahogany secretaire chest on chest. Lots Road, Chelsea. Apr 02. £2,500.

664

Set of 6 + 1 Chippendale Revival mahogany dining chairs, fluted scroll top rails, pierced interlaced splats on acanthus carved cabriole legs. Gorringes, Lewes. Apr 01. £2,500.

665

Geo. III mahogany serpentine sideboard crossbanded with stringing, parquetry banding, 71.75in wide. A. Hartley, Ilkley. Feb 04. £2,500.

666

Late George III satinwood and kingwood crossbanded side table, c1810, 31 x 52 x 19.25in. Wintertons Ltd, Lichfield. Feb 02. £2,500.

667

Maltese walnut chest, drawers inlaid with a pair of birds, top inlaid star, sides inlaid Maltese cross, 71cm. Stride & Son, Chichester. Apr 02. £2,500.

> The illustrations are in descending price order. The price range is indicated at the top of each page.

668

Regency mahog. library table, 2 real and 2 dummy drawers, 63.75in x 34in. Gorringes, Lewes. July 03. £2,500.

669

Edwardian satinwood breakfront side cabinet inlaid with fanned paterae swags and ribbonfolds, architectural pediment over glazed door, flanked by mirrors, base with panelled door concave glazed cupboards, 4ft 6in. Gorringes, Lewes. Mar 01. £2,500.

Hammer Price £2,500

670

Pair of Sheraton style satinwood pedestal cupboards with strung, inlaid and pen work decoration, panelled door enclosing 3 drawers, 21in wide. Sworders, Stansted Mountfitchet. Apr 01. £2,500.

671

Charles II small joined oak gateleg table, 69cm high, 71cm wide. Wintertons Ltd, Lichfield. Mar 02. £2,500.

672

Victorian walnut and floral marquetry credenza of serpentine form, 60in wide. Andrew Hartley, Ilkley. June 02. £2,500.

673

Pair of oak backed stools, 17thC, 124cm high. Richard Wintertons, Burton on Trent. Aug 03. £2,500.

674

Late 19thC walnut Wellington chest, 6 graduated drawers, one with secretaire, fall front concealing facsimile drawers, 22in wide. Amersham Auction Rooms, Bucks. June 02. £2,500.

675

Regency mahogany bowfront sideboard, ebony line inlaid top, 153cm. Henry Adams, Chichester. Sep 02. £2,500.

676

George III mahogany chest on chest, 3ft 11in. Gorringes, Lewes. Mar 04. £2,500.

677

Regency rosewood side cabinet, doors enclosing shelves, 3ft. Gorringes, Lewes. Sep 03. £2,500.

Hammer Prices £2,500-£2,400

678

Mid Victorian walnut writing table, 44in wide. Hamptons, Godalming. Sep 01. £2,500.

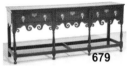

679

18thC Oak open dresser with moulded edged top, scrolled apron, 75.5in wide. Andrew Hartley, Ilkley. Apr 04. £2,500.

680

George III mahogany demi-lune card table, fold over top, 94cm wide. Sworders, Stansted Mountfitchet. Feb 04. £2,500.

681

Victorian burr walnut break front credenza, gilt metal mounts, 92in wide. Andrew Hartley, Ilkley. Aug 01. £2,500.

682

Late Victorian rosewood cylinder bureau, marquetry inlay, fitted interior, 31in wide. Sworders, Stansted Mountfitchet. Mar 01. £2,500.

683

Victorian walnut framed three piece salon suite, chaise longue 68in wide. A. Hartley, Ilkley. Aug 01. £2,500.

684

George II feather banded walnut bureau, fall enclosing 10 small drawers, central cupboard over 2 short and 3 long drawers. 3ft. Gorringes, Bexhill. Oct 01. £2,500.

685

Regency carved wood/gilded overmantel mirror, 53in wide, 35.75in high. A. Hartley, Ilkley. Dec 00. £2,500.

686

18thC mahogany architects table in Chippendale style, 107cm wide. Marilyn Swain, Grantham. Dec 03. £2,500.

687

Late 18th/early 19thC Dutch walnut/marquetry bombe chest, 92cm. Sworders, Stansted Mountfitchet. Mar 04. £2,500.

688

Early Victorian mahogany breakfront wardrobe, centre fitted 5 sliding trays, 100in wide. Canterbury Auction Galleries. Feb 04. £2,500.

689

Victorian giltwood/rococo style overmantel mirror. Lots Road Auctions, Chelsea. Sep 03. £2,450.

690

Geo. IV mahogany Canterbury, 20in. Morphets, Harrogate. Mar 01. £2,450.

691

Early Victorian mahogany extending dining table having two D ends, 48.5in wide, 103in long. Andrew Hartley, Ilkley. Dec 00. £2,400.

692

George II feather banded walnut side table, one long drawer, 2ft 9in. af. Gorringes, Bexhill. Oct 01. £2,400.

693

George III mahogany chest, 46in wide. Lots Road Auctions, Chelsea. Mar 02. £2,400.

694

Regency flame mahogany linen press, 47in. Lots Road, Chelsea. Jan 02. £2,400.

695

George I walnut chest on stand, 3ft 6in. Gorringes, Lewes. Mar 01. £2,400.

696

Bureau plat, 19thC rosewood, kingwood and gilt metal mounted. Lots Road Auctions, Chelsea. May 02. £2,400.

697

19thC Dutch walnut and marquetry serpentine bombe commode, 2ft 4in. Gorringes, Lewes. Apr 01. £2,400.

48

698

Mid 19thC ebonised/boulle serpentine credenza, with bell flower and bead cast gilt brass mounts, 167cm. *David Duggleby, Scarborough. June 02. £2,400.*

699

Geo. III oak bureau bookcase. *Locke & England, Leamington Spa. Sep 02. £2,400.*

700

19thC oak dresser, moulded cornice, 72in high, 60in wide. *Amersham Auction Rooms, Bucks. Sep 02. £2,400.*

701

Early 18thC walnut/herring-bone crossbanded chest on stand. *W & H Peacock, Bedford. Jan 03. £2,400.*

702

Regency mahogany sideboard table. *Mellors & Kirk, Nottingham. Feb 03. £2,400.*

703

Fruitwood, pine/oak settle, curved outline, 18th/early 19thC, 64.5in. *A. Hartley, Ilkley. Oct 02. £2,400.*

> Prices quoted are hammer and exclude the buyer's premium. Adding 15% will give approx. buying price.

704

17thC oak dresser, 233cm wide. *Henry Adams, Chichester. Jan 03. £2,400.*

705

George III mahogany chest, 3ft 1in. *Gorringes, Lewes. Jan 03. £2,400.*

706

Regency rosewood and brass inlaid sofa table, 162cm extended. (needs restoration). *Lots Road Auctions, Chelsea. Nov 03. £2,400.*

Hammer Price £2,400

707

Lady's late 19thC walnut and kingwood writing table, stamp Wilkinson & Son, 8 Old Bond Street and No. 10964, 30.5in wide. *Amersham Auc. Rooms, Bucks. Mar 03. £2,400.*

708

Geo. III secretaire bookcase, mahogany, strung inlaid, 122cm. *Lots Road Auctions, Chelsea. Mar 04. £2,400.*

709

Period oak joint stool with bold turned baluster legs and box stretchers, 18in wide. *Tring Market Auctions, Herts. Nov 03. £2,400.*

710

Early Victorian burr maple occasional table with carved frieze, 29in high. *Gorringes, Bexhill. Sep 03. £2,400.*

711

Adzed oak dressing table by Robert Mouseman Thompson, 54in wide. *Andrew Hartley, Ilkley. Oct 03. £2,400.*

712

Set 6 + 2 Geo. III mahogany dining chairs. (2 single chairs modern replacement copies). *Canterbury Auction Galleries, Kent. Dec 03. £2,400.*

713

Regency mahogany tea table, folding top, 3ft. *Gorringes, Lewes. Jan 04. £2,400.*

714

Set 7 + 2 Geo. III mahogany dining chairs in blue dralon, Hepplewhite style. *Gorringes, Bexhill. Nov 03. £2,400.*

715

Victorian walnut side cabinet by Holland & Sons, 153cm wide, door stamped 5496, stencil mark. *Mellors & Kirk, Nottingham. Apr 03. £2,400.*

Hammer Prices £2,400-£2,300

716

Early 18thC walnut bureau, feather banded, satinwood string, inlaid decor, 39in wide. Amersham Auc. Rooms, Bucks. Apr 02. £2,400.

717

Victorian mahog. extending dining table opening to 214 x 120cm. Henry Adams, Chichester. July 02. £2,400.

718

George II walnut bureau, pin sides, top/slope with twin figured panels, herringbone inlay bandings, crossbanded. Canterbury Auc. Galleries, Kent. Dec 00. £2,400.

719

Continental walnut display cabinet on stand, 34in wide. Andrew Hartley, Ilkley. Oct 00. £2,400.

720

19thC mahogany kneehole writing table. Lambert & Foster, Tenterden. Apr 01. £2,400.

721

Early Victorian burr elm tilt top occasional table, 70cm dia. Sworders, Stansted Mountfitchet. Feb 04. £2,400.

722

Late 18thC French farmhouse table. Lots Road Auctions, Chelsea. Oct 00. £2,400.

723

Set of 6 + 2 reproduction Chippendale design dining chairs. Sworders, Stansted Mountfitchet. Apr 01. £2,400.

724

Late Georgian oak dresser, open plate rack, six drawers and two panelled doors, 200 x 165cm. Rosebery's, London. Mar 04. £2,400.

725

George I burr walnut bureau, feather/crossbanding, stepped interior, 2ft 11in. Gorringes, Lewes. June 03. £2,400.

726

Victorian rosewood glazed medal cabinet, drawers 1-53, plaque 'Presented to the Society of Arts by Sir Edward Thomason 1879', 76.5cm. damage, 3 drawers missing. Locke & England, Leamington Spa. Sep 03. £2,400.

727

19thC mahog. partners desk, leathered writing surface, 152 x 99cm. Sworders, Stansted Mountfitchet. Feb 04. £2,400.

728

Mahogany bonheur-du-jour, crossbanded in satinwood, impressed maker's crown mark No 289, 42.5in high. D. Duggleby, Scarborough. July 01. £2,400.

729

Oak dresser, west country, c1720, later brasses, 130cm wide. R. Wintertons, Burton on Trent. Oct 03. £2,400.

730

Regency mahog. sideboard, 122cm. Lots Road Auctions, London. Apr 04. £2,400.

731

Victorian figured walnut kneehole desk by Heal & Son, London, brown tooled leather, 54 x 24 x 30in high. Canterbury Auction Galleries, Kent. Feb 04. £2,400.

732

George III mahog. butterfly Pembroke table. Gorringes, Bexhill. July 01. £2,300.

733

Set of six George III Hepplewhite design mahog. dining chairs. Gorringes, Lewes. June 01. £2,300.

734

Late 19th/early 20thC French mahogany cylinder bureau, Vernis Martin painted panels, marble top, 81cm wide. *Lots Road Auctions, Chelsea. Feb 03. £2,300.*

735

George III figured mahogany chest of drawers. *Rupert Toovey & Co, Washington, Sussex. Feb 03. £2,300.*

736

William IV mahog. extending dining table, manner of Waring & Gillows, 3 extra leaves, telescopic action, 281 x 121cm extended. *D M Nesbit & Company, Southsea. June 03. £2,300.*

737

George III mahogany cabinet on chest, Gothic inspired astragal glazed doors, secretaire drawer with fitted interior, 87in high, 46in wide. *Amersham Auction Rooms, Bucks. Feb 04. £2,300.*

738

George III mahog. secretaire bookcase. *Mellors & Kirk, Nottingham. Feb 03. £2,300.*

739

Geo. III mahog. dining table, 3 sections, drop leaf centre section, 104 x 49in extended. *Canterbury Auc. Galleries, Kent. Aug 03. £2,300.*

> The numbering system acts as a reader reference as well as linking to the Analysis of each Section

740

Regency mahogany cellaret, 19.5in wide. *Clarke Gammon, Guildford. Dec 02. £2,300.*

741

Regency linen press. *Lots Road Auctions, Chelsea. Sep 00. £2,300.*

742

Pair of Victorian giltwood armchairs, c1870, Louis XVI style. *Wintertons Ltd, Lichfield. Sep 03. £2,300.*

743

Yorkshire oak rocking armchair, winged back, arched top rail, rope seat, 18thC. *Andrew Hartley, Ilkley. Apr 03. £2,300.*

744

Regency amboyna/rosewood games table, marquetry inlaid in ebony, 30in high. *Gorringes, Bexhill. Sep 03. £2,300.*

745

Maple & Co pollarded oak leather topped pedestal desk, 4ft 6in x 2ft 1in. *Gorringes, Lewes. Dec 03. £2,300.*

746

Early Victorian mahogany buffet. *Lots Road Auctions, Chelsea. Oct 00. £2,300.*

Hammer Price £2,300

747

George III mahog. octagonal wine cooler, cross banded in tulipwood, line inlaid in boxwood, brass bound, 20in dia. *Gorringes, Bexhill. Feb 04. £2,300.*

748

George III figured mahogany demi-lune table, crossbanded folding top, 99.5cm width. *Bristol Auction Rooms, Bristol. Jan 04. £2,300.*

749

19thC mahogany and Dutch marquetry inlaid settee. *Crows, Dorking. Feb 01. £2,300.*

750

George III oak and mahogany crossbanded dresser, c1780, 198cm wide. *Wintertons Ltd, Lichfield. Jan 03. £2,300.*

751

Late George III mahog. sofa table, c1820, extended length 142cm. *Wintertons Ltd, Lichfield. May 03. £2,300.*

Hammer Prices £2,300-£2,200

752

Walnut writing desk, Louis XV style, stringing, Kingwood banding, gilt metal mounts, 19thC, 45in wide. A. Hartley, Ilkley. Feb 02. £2,300.

753

Victorian mahog. extending dining table, moulded edge top, 3 leaves, 301 x 122cm extended. Bristol Auction Rooms. Apr 02. £2,300.

754

Victorian brass bound teak military chest, 39in. Gorringes, Bexhill. Sep 02. £2,300.

755

Geo. III mahog. bureau bookcase, adjustable shelving, fitted bureau, later handles, 47in wide. Andrew Hartley, Ilkley. Apr 04. £2,300.

756

Set of 6 + 2 20thC Georgian revival mahog. dining chairs. Lots Road Auctions, Chelsea. Feb 03. £2,300.

757

19thC Irish mahog. writing table with moulded rectangular top, 4ft. Gorringes, Lewes. Oct 02. £2,300.

758

Geo. III mahog. chest, fitted brushing slide, 4 graduated drawers, 2ft 6in. Gorringes, Lewes. Mar 01. £2,300.

759

Regency figured mahogany cellaret. (faults). Rupert Toovey & Co, Washington, Sussex. Aug 03. £2,300.

760

Regency ebony strung mahog. breakfront sideboard, 5ft 5in. Gorringes, Lewes. July 01. £2,300.

761

Victorian brass bound mahogany secretaire military chest in 2 sections, 39in wide. Canterbury Auc. Galleries, Kent. June 02. £2,300.

762

Set of Edwardian painted satinwood quartetto tables of oblong form. Andrew Hartley, Ilkley. Feb 01. £2,300.

763

George II mahog. tea table, c1735, hinged rectangular and rounded top, 74cm high, 84cm wide. Wintertons Ltd, Lichfield. Jan 04. £2,300.

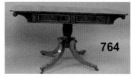

764

Regency rosewood sofa table, crossbanded and inlaid, 55in wide. Tring Market Auctions, Herts. Mar 02. £2,250.

765

George III style mahogany dining table, extra leaf, 79in extended. Sworders, Stansted Mountfitchet. Oct 01. £2,200.

766

Set of 10 + 2 Chippendale design mahog. dining chairs, drop in seats. Gorringes, Lewes. Apr 02. £2,200.

767

Edwardian satinwood wardrobe, 78in high. A. Hartley, Ilkley. Aug 01. £2,200.

768

Geo. IV mahog. crossbanded tilt top breakfast table, 50.5in dia. Wintertons Ltd, Lichfield. Feb 02. £2,200.

769

Coffee table with pietra dura marble and painted top. Rosebery's, London. Dec 00. £2,200.

770

19thC figured walnut and inlaid 'piano top' Davenport. Rosebery's, London. Sep 00. £2,200.

Hammer Price £2,200

771

George IV rosewood nest of quartetto tables, 21in wide. *Andrew Hartley, Ilkley. Apr 01. £2,200.*

772

William IV mahogany secretaire wellington chest, 92cm wide. *Cheffins, Cambridge. Oct 00. £2,200.*

773

Edwardian Sheraton style mahogany bookcase, 72.75in wide. *Clarke Gammon, Guildford. Apr 03. £2,200.*

774

Arts and Crafts Movement oak settle, possibly by Liberty & Co, box seat, 185cm high, 76cm wide. *Mellors & Kirk, Nottingham. Sep 03. £2,200.*

775

George III linen press inlaid in satinwood, sycamore and rosewood, 130cm. *Locke & England, Leamington Spa. Jan 03. £2,200.*

776

19thC rosewood, inverted breakfront bookcase, 74in wide. *Amersham Auc. Rooms, Bucks. Nov 02. £2,200.*

The illustrations are in descending price order. The price range is indicated at the top of each page.

777

William IV mahog. extending dining table, 8 lotus headed tapering turned legs, two leaves, concertina action, 72cm high. *Mellors & Kirk, Nottingham. June 03. £2,200.*

778

Georgian mahog. secretaire bookcase, 160cm wide. *Thos Mawer & Son, Lincoln. Feb 03. £2,200.*

779

Geo. III mahog. bow fronted standing corner cupboard, central slide, 220cm high, 94cm wide. *Mellors & Kirk, Nottingham. Sep 03. £2,200.*

780

Edward VII mahogany and marquetry breakfront china cabinet, crossbanded in satinwood and line inlaid, 181cm high. *Mellors & Kirk, Nottingham. Sep 03. £2,200.*

781

Easy chair & stool designed by Charles Eames, made by Herman Miller in rosewood, black finished metal & black leather. *Canterbury Auction Galleries. June 02. £2,200.*

782

Victorian mahog. 3 pedestal dining table, sections with drop flaps, 324cm long extended, 121cm wide. *Sworders, Stansted Mountfitchet. Mar 04. £2,200.*

783

Regency mahogany secretaire bookcase, astragal glazed, base with secretaire drawer, leather writing surface. *Hamptons. Godalming. July 02. £2,200.*

784

Early Victorian rosewood whatnot canterbury, pierced gallery top with turned finials raised on 'C' scrolls, 43 x 56 x 104cm. *Hamptons, Godalming. July 02. £2,200.*

785

Art Deco burr walnut and birdseye maple dining suite prob. Epstein, with dining table, 2 extra leaves, 6ft max, 2ft 6in wide, 5 chairs, sideboard & cupboard. *Gorringes, Bexhill. Nov 03. £2,200.*

Hammer Prices £2,200-£2,100

786

George II mahog. kneehole desk, top, walnut banding over slide and frieze drawer, 32.5in wide. *Andrew Hartley, Ilkley. Apr 04. £2,200.*

787

William IV mahog. bow front chest, brass lion mask handles, 36in. *Denhams, Warnham. Feb 04. £2,200.*

788

Dutch walnut marquetry secretaire abattant, 19thC, 40.25in wide. *Clarke Gammon, Guildford. Oct 02. £2,200.*

789

19thC Killarney work arbutus, marquetry tripod table, 28.5in dia. (one support cracked, one cracked with old repairs - c1870). *Canterbury Auction Galleries. Feb 04. £2,200.*

790

Regency mahogany pedestal sideboard, manner of Gillows, 4ft 2in wide. *Gorringes, Bexhill. Feb 04. £2,200.*

791

Sheraton Revival satinwood sideboard of demi lune form, kingwood banding, stringing, 54in wide. *Andrew Hartley, Ilkley. Dec 01. £2,200.*

792

Set 5 + 1 Regency mahogany chairs. *Andrew Hartley, Ilkley. Feb 01. £2,200.*

793

Charles Eames, Hermann Miller rosewood and black leather lounge chair (650) & ottoman (651). *Gorringes, Lewes. Dec 00. £2,200.*

794

Walnut library table, inlaid satinwood crossbanding, 48in wide. (Stamped 'Holland & Sons). *Clarke Gammon, Guildford. June 02. £2,200.*

795

Early 18thC gilt overmantel mirror, 18.5 x 51in overall. *Canterbury Auc. Galleries, Kent. Aug 03. £2,100.*

796

Late 17thC oak cupboard, 50in wide, 45in high, rearranged. *Dockree's, Manchester. Feb 01. £2,100.*

797

Vic. oak breakfront bookcase of Reformed Gothic interest, 314cm wide. *Bristol Auction Rooms. Sep 02. £2,100.*

798

Geo. III rosewood canterbury, 18.5in. *Sworders, Stansted Mountfitchet. Apr 01. £2,100.*

799

Set of 6 + 2 Geo. III mahog. dining chairs. *Sworders, Stansted Mountfitchet. July 01. £2,100.*

800

Waring & Gillow, Geo. style mahog. sideboard, drawer stamped 'Waring & Gillow L'pool', 214cm. *Cheffins, Cambridge. Dec 00. £2,100.*

801

18th/19thC Buckinghamshire regional, yew and elm framed Windsor chair. *Amersham Auction Rooms, Bucks. Mar 02. £2,100.*

802

Set of 6 + 2 Sheraton period mahogany dining chairs. (some restoration). *Sworders, Stansted Mountfitchet. Mar 01. £2,100.*

803

George III mahogany chest, 31in wide. *Andrew Hartley, Ilkley. June 01. £2,100.*

804

George III 3 section mahog. dining table. *Bristol Auction Rooms. Nov 02. £2,100.*

805

Regency rosewood table with cross banded top, 126cm. *Henry Adams, Chichester. Sep 02. £2,100.*

806

Georgian secretaire chest, walnut cross, feather banded. *Lots Road Auctions, Chelsea. Nov 02. £2,100.*

807

Mid Victorian walnut Davenport, 35in high, 21in wide. *Amersham Auction Rooms, Bucks. Nov 02. £2,100.*

808

Joined oak dresser, South Wales c1820, 136.5cm wide. *Bristol Auction Rooms, Bristol. June 03. £2,100.*

809

Late Victorian figured walnut piano top davenport, 1ft 11in. *Gorringes, Lewes. July 03. £2,100.*

810

George IV mahogany, cross-banded satinwood strung sofa table, 70cm wide extended 142cm. *Wintertons Ltd, Lichfield. Jan 03. £2,100.*

811

Robert Mouseman Thompson, oak chest of drawers, 77cm. *Richard Wintertons, Burton on Trent. July 03. £2,100.*

Prices quoted are hammer and exclude the buyer's premium. Adding 15% will give approx. buying price.

812

George III oak dresser, 5ft 2in wide. *Gorringes, Bexhill. Feb 04. £2,100.*

813

Regency mahogany 3-tier buffet, leaf carved pediment back, 3ft 2in. (2 side spindles missing). *Gorringes, Lewes. Dec 03. £2,100.*

Hammer Prices £2,100-£2,000

814

Set 6 early Victorian mahog. dining chairs, rosette carved cresting rails. *Gorringes, Bexhill. Oct 01. £2,100.*

815

Large Regency mahogany canterbury, 19in. *Gorringes, Lewes. Sep 00. £2,100.*

816

George III mahog. serpentine chest, crossbanded, baise lined slide over 2 long drawers, deep drawer as two dummies, 42.5in. *A. Hartley, Ilkley. Oct 01. £2,100.*

817

19thC mahogany 'D' dwarf bookcase, 51in wide, 37in high. *Dockree's, Manchester. Feb 01. £2,050.*

818

Two panelled oak wardrobes, mid 20thC, handcrafted in the Old English style. *Richard Wintertons, Burton on Trent. Aug 03. £2,050.*

819

George III mahogany dumb waiter. *Lots Road Auctions, Chelsea. May 01. £2,050.*

820

George III oak dresser with mahogany crossbanding, 73.5in wide. *Andrew Hartley, Ilkley. Oct 00. £2,000.*

821

Victorian giltwood convex mirror, pierced acanthus border, concave ball rim, eagle pediment, 130cm high x 78cm wide. *Wintertons Ltd, Lichfield. July 02. £2,000.*

822

George III mahogany bureau bookcase, 48in wide, 89in high. *Dockree's, Manchester. Sep 00. £2,000.*

Hammer Price £2,000

Mid 18thC mahogany tripod table, 30in dia. *Hamptons, Godalming. Sep 01. £2,000.*

Victorian mahogany pedestal desk, gilt-tooled green leather writing surface, stamped 'Edw. Winter', 54 x 33in. *Lots Road Auctions, Chelsea. Mar 01. £2,000.*

Regency mahog. secretaire bookcase, c1820, glazed doors, fall front, fitted interior, 205 x 104cm. *Rosebery's, London. Mar 04. £2,000.*

George III mahog. chest, 30in wide. *Lots Road Auctions, Chelsea. May 01. £2,000.*

Geo. III style livery cupboard on chest, early 20thC, 63in wide x 70.5in high. *Morphets, Harrogate. Mar 01. £2,000.*

George II oak dresser, 76in wide. *Clarke Gammon, Guildford. Apr 01. £2,000.*

Edwardian satinwood and marquetry display cabinet, swans neck pediment and Z glazed doors, serpentine panels, 4ft 9in. *Gorringes, Lewes. Feb 01. £2,000.*

c1790 bow front mahog. side-board with inlay, convenience cupboard and metal gallery back. *R. Wintertons, Burton on Trent. Apr 02. £2,000.*

Regency mahogany and rosewood crossbanded side cabinet. *Lots Road Auctions, Chelsea. May 01. £2,000.*

Regency rosewood side cabinet, black marble top brass inlaid frieze, glazed doors, 97 x 97cm. *Rosebery's, London. Mar 04. £2,000.*

Late 17th/early 18thC Italian giltwood wall mirror, 110cm high. (as found, part later). *Lots Road Auctions, Chelsea. Feb 03. £2,000.*

18thC George II walnut chest. *Lots Road Auctions, Chelsea. June 01. £2,000.*

George III oak dresser, 190cm wide. *Cheffins, Cambridge. Oct 00. £2,000.*

19thC commode, French burr walnut with marble top, 51in wide. *Lots Road Auctions, Chelsea. May 01. £2,000.*

Walnut chest mainly George I, later drop handles and key escutcheons, 100cm wide. *Hamptons, Godalming. May 02. £2,000.*

Late Georgian bonheur du jour. *Tring Market Auctions, Herts. Jan 02. £2,000.*

Early 19thC mahogany bow fronted small chest of drawers, 34in wide. *Dockree's, Manchester. Feb 01. £2,000.*

19thC Japanese hardwood and shibayama decorated cabinet, sliding doors, panels inlaid with mother o'pearl, tortoiseshell, gilt burnished lacquer, birds amongst foliage and flowers. *Gorringes, Lewes. Sep 00. £2,000.*

George III mahogany and inlaid teapoy, 2 removable caddies and 2 cylindrical compartments, 13.5in wide. Clarke Gammon, Guildford. June 02. £2,000.

Set of six salon chairs, late 19th/early 20thC, Louis XVI style. Lots Road Auctions, Chelsea. May 02. £2,000.

Art Deco mahogany dressing mirror, with layer of shagreen. Lots Road Auctions, Chelsea. Nov 03. £2,000.

Edwardian painted satinwood Pembroke table with panels of lovers and cherubs, pearl strands and floral garlands, 2 drawers, 2ft 6in. Gorringes, Lewes. Apr 01. £2,000.

Set 6 George III Chippendale design, mahogany framed dining chairs, upholstered drop in seats. £2,000. Amersham Auction Rooms, Bucks. May 02. £2,000.

Pair Geo. III style satinwood semi circular side cabinets, 45in wide. Clarke Gammon, Guildford. Apr 02. £2,000.

The numbering system acts as a reader reference as well as linking to the Analysis of each Section

Regency pollard oak card table with 'D' shape folding top, 3ft. Gorringes, Bexhill. Sep 02. £2,000.

Late George III mahogany secretaire bookcase. Lambert & Foster, Tenterden. May 02. £2,000.

Hammer Price £2,000

Elm stick back Windsor armchair bearing traces of old green paint. Stride & Son, Chichester. June 02. £2,000.

Victorian walnut side cabinet, floral marquetry, ormolu mounts, glazed doors, 49 x 42in. Hamptons, Godalming. Mar 02. £2,000.

19thC fiddleback mahogany wellington chest, 23 x 18 x 51in. Hamptons, Godalming. Mar 02. £2,000.

George III mahogany tilt top pedestal table, birdcage action, on three 'Isle of Man' style carved legs, 26.5in wide. Tring Market Auctions, Herts. Sep 02. £2,000.

Mahogany wardrobe, c1840 and later, 122cm wide. Peter Wilson, Nantwich. July 02. £2,000.

Set of 6 + 2 Hepplewhite design mahogany dining chairs. Gorringes, Lewes. Oct 02. £2,000.

19thC Indo Portuguese carved mahogany centre table. Lots Road Auctions, Chelsea. Nov 00. £2,000.

Sheraton mahog. satinwood and tulip wood banded side table, 3ft. Gorringes, Lewes. Jan 04. £2,000.

19thC mahogany expanding dining table, drop leaf D-end top, concertina action. (no leaves). Rosebery's, London. Sep 03. £2,000.

Hammer Price £2,000

858

Regency rosewood and brass inlaid foldover top card table. *W & H Peacock, Bedford. Jan 03. £2,000.*

859

18thC/early 19thC oak dresser. *Biddle & Webb, Birmingham. Jan 04. £2,000.*

860

Full tester four poster bed, 1890s, French, in Henry II style. *Lots Road Auctions, Chelsea. Mar 03. £2,000.*

861

Geo. III oak standing corner cupboard, cavetto cornice, crossbanded in mahogany, 107cm wide. *Mellors & Kirk, Nottingham. June 03. £2,000.*

58

862

Victorian oak partners desk, tooled leather inset, 1.66 x 1.05m. *Sworders, Stansted Mountfitchet. Mar 03. £2,000.*

863

18thC oak low dresser with later raised back, 167cm wide. *D M Nesbit & Co, Southsea. May 03. £2,000.*

864

Victorian mahogany breakfront wardrobe, by Edwards & Roberts, 7ft high, 8ft 4in wide. *Gorringes, Bexhill. June 03. £2,000.*

865

Regency rosewood work table, 18.25in wide. *Andrew Hartley, Ilkley. Apr 2004. £2,000.*

866

Set of four Russian Karelian birch bergeres, upholstered seats and scoop backs, early 19thC. *Clarke Gammon, Guildford. Dec 03. £2,000.*

867

Regency mahogany work table, brass-line inlaid, crossbanded top, 56cm. *H. Adams, Chichester. Sep 02. £2,000.*

868

Edwardian satinwood and marquetry oval etagere, 2ft 9in wide. *Gorringes, Bexhill. Mar 03. £2,000.*

869

Set of 6 + 2 Regency mahog. brass inlaid dining chairs. *Thos Mawer & Son, Lincoln. Nov 02. £2,000.*

870

George III mahogany wine table, c1780. *Wintertons Ltd, Lichfield. Nov 03. £2,000.*

871

Art Nouveau Liberty style oak sideboard, pierced sides and inlaid floral decoration, 60in wide, reverse stamped '7605 Design, 4787 and 1. *Clarke Gammon, Guildford. Apr 04. £2,000.*

872

Pair of Empire urn stands, limewood, c1810, 42cm high. *Lots Road Auctions, London. May 04. £2,000.*

873

17th/18thC black japanned cabinet on later giltwood stand, with 4 sections from a Japanese lacquer screen, 30in wide, stand 36in wide. *Canterbury Auc. Galleries, Kent. Feb 04. £2,000.*

874

George III mahogany chest on chest. *Lambert & Foster, Tenterden. May 02. £2,000.*

875

19th/early 20thC Louis XVI style kingwood and gilt metal mounted cabinet, 172cm high. *Rupert Toovey, Washington, Sussex. Dec 03. £2,000.*

Section VI <£2,000 to £1,500

The Editor has never felt comfortable with Art Nouveau furniture, whilst admiring the art of the movement. One might suggest the style sits uncomfortably and self consciously beyond the ideal of the classic marriage of form and function.

Without involving ourselves in tedious arithmetic, mahogany continues to dominate oak and walnut. Rosewood follows closely behind. Then there is a good sprinkling of satinwood, two of the most interesting of these being a fine Regency mahogany banded dwarf chiffonier, **913**, which sold at Rupert Toovey in Washington for £1,900 in August 2003, and a late eighteenth century demi-lune card table, **914**, which sold at Gorringes, Bexhill in September 2002 for the same price. The nineteenth century is now showing well and including the late Georgian period, accounts for more lots than the eighteenth century. The seventeenth century is poorly represented. Yew, elm and ash are still in short supply with less than a dozen examples altogether. See **936**, **1019**, **1174**, **1204** etc. **1019** is actually an interesting combination of elm and oak in a George III settle.

One of the more interesting lots is a Georgian fruitwood dresser at **877** which sold at Dockree's, Manchester in March 2000. Regardless of the intervening years being a period of readjustment and reappraisal, I should like to bet that this wonderful fruitwood example has been a sound investment. There are again only a few pine examples, see **1098** and **1110** on page 72. To our knowledge eight feet long, nineteenth century pine tables do not appear very often. This example fetched £1,600 in February 2004. More of pine later.

882 is one of the most interesting and expensive oak spoon racks ever, but certainly a most desirable and rare object measuring about 17 inches x 25 inches and including a base drawer. This fine piece of probably eighteenth or early nineteenth century oak is highly decorative but frivolous at a hammer price of £1,950! Remember in the *Introduction* to be a little fussy where davenports are concerned? Well this probably doesn't apply to the specimen walnut and marquetry lot at **898** which set the buyer back £1,900 plus commission. On to page 62 and two further Art Nouveau lots at **915** and **924**, the first having a huge pedigree, if one can attach the name of Heal's or Liberty's. Also see the Arts and Crafts Liberty and Co. sideboard at **920**. Now this is only a personal opinion but I have never felt comfortable with such furniture. It sits uncomfortably and self-consciously beyond my ideals of the classic English form married perfectly to function, as in the chest-on-chest at **925**, or the furniture of Robert 'Mouseman' Thompson for whom fussiness and show were so alien.

On page 63 check out the Mart Stam for Thonet stainless steel club chairs which fetched a crazy £1,800 at Phillips, Scotland in 2000. Compare them with the eight seventeenth century style Derbyshire pattern dining chairs on the same page at **949** which fetched the same sum. Which would you rather have? Moving on to page 65 is a seventeenth century oak wainscot chair with a carved panel back which sold at D. M. Nesbit & Co, Southsea in July 2003 for the same £1,800. From medieval times, wainscot meant oak, quarter-cut and adze-trimmed boards, eight to ten inches wide. They were much imported from Europe and the Low Countries and used for furniture and panelling. Hence the more recognisable meaning which attaches to wainscot, panelling or boarding on a room wall which reaches from the floor to a limited height.

Note the pair of replica parquetry inlaid demi-lune side tables, **977**, in the Sheraton style but dating from the late twentieth century! These almost-new reproductions fetched £1,800 at Byrnes in Chester in March 2004. This is probably around half the value or less than for Georgian or Revival examples. There are several Eames chairs in this work. See **978** but also check out the *Index* so that you can become familiar with their values. Now see the superb rosewood collector's cabinet at **999** with its bird's-eye maple faced drawers. Imagine the impact of furnishing a home using these two contrasting woods.

1025 is an oak bacon cupboard with arched, panelled doors. No date is supplied but it fetched £1,700 in July 2003. I would dearly love to know more about this piece or to have been a fly on the wall in the Rooms at the time. Perhaps a reader can enlighten us? In the same sale were a pair of antique walnut open armchairs, **1040**, with later painted decoration for the same price. Now for joint stools. There is a late seventeenth century example, **1050** which fetched £1,650 in August 2002 at Canterbury Auction Galleries. Check out stools through the *Index*. Notice the Art Deco suite at **1096** and the pair of Deco style leather armchairs at **1179**. Compare two Queen Anne pieces, the panelled oak lambing chair at **1185** and the walnut wing armchair at **1187**. Finally, view the pair of Italian walnut side cabinets at **1164** which reached £1,500 at Lots Road Auctions in Chelsea. The description suggests that in part they possibly date from the seventeenth century. I wonder what has happened to them over the last 300 years and where are they now?

Hammer Prices £1,950-£1,900

876

Display cabinet in figured burr walnut veneer, early 20thC, 54.5in wide. David Duggleby, Scarborough. Apr 00. £1,950.

877

George III early 19thC fruitwood dresser, 67.5in wide, 83in high. Dockree's, Manchester. Sep 00. £1,950.

878

18thC and later oak dresser, 188cm x 196cm. Wintertons Ltd, Lichfield. Mar 00. £1,950.

879

Late George II oak chest on stand, 3ft wide. Hamptons, Godalming. Nov 01. £1,950.

880

George III lacquered/painted hanging corner cabinet, 36in high. Sworders, Stansted Mountfitchet. Apr 01. £1,950.

881

George III cellarette, fluted concave sides, cross banding and yew-wood spandrels, unfitted interior. (replacement base board). Peter Wilson, Nantwich. July 02. £1,950.

882

Oak spoon rack, shaped back with two rows of holders and scrolled surmount, 16.75in wide. Andrew Hartley, Ilkley. June 02. £1,950.

883

George III oak open dresser, 80in wide. Andrew Hartley, Ilkley. Feb 04. £1,950.

884

Early 18thC walnut lowboy, 79cm wide. (replaced rear leg). Sworders, Stansted Mountfitchet. Dec 02. £1,950.

885

Lady's Edwardian satinwood writing desk, 36in wide, 38in high. Andrew Hartley, Ilkley. Dec 02. £1,950.

886

Oak dresser base, George III, last quarter 18thC, faults, 184cm wide. Sotheby's, Billingshurst. May 00. £1,900.

887

Early Victorian mahogany partners desk. Rosebery's, London. Sep 00. £1,900.

888

Victorian rosewood chiffonier, 3-shelf fretwork back over two Berlin needlework panelled doors, 3ft 1in. Gorringes, Lewes. Apr 00. £1,900.

889

George III mahogany secretaire/bookcase. Dockree's, Manchester. May 00. £1,900.

890

William IV mahogany tilt top dining table, 53in dia. Dee, Atkinson & Harrison, Driffield. Dec 00. £1,900.

891

Late Victorian walnut dining table by Shoolbred, 2 spare leaves, windout action to 8ft. Lots Road Auctions, Chelsea. June 01. £1,900.

892

William IV mahogany music canterbury, 19.75in wide. Woolley & Wallis, Salisbury. Aug 00. £1,900.

893

Victorian James Shoolbred & Co. mahogany and marquetry desk, 3ft 6in. Gorringes, Lewes. Oct 00. £1,900.

894

Geo. IV rosewood davenport, 50cm wide. Cheffins, Cambridge. Oct 00. £1,900.

895

Victorian chair back settee with a carved walnut frame. Sworders, Stansted Mountfitchet. Oct 01. £1,900.

896

Regency rosewood sofa table, frieze drawer, lions paw feet, 3ft 3in x 2ft 3in. Gorringes, Lewes. Dec 00. £1,900.

897

Six Regency sabre leg chairs, drop in seats in gold brocade. Hamptons, Godalming. Jan 02. £1,900.

898

19thC burr walnut/marquetry davenport, raised stationery cupboard back, drawer with writing slope, base cupboard, 1ft 9in. Gorringes, Lewes. Mar 01. £1,900.

899

Regency mahog. wine cooler, 22 x 17 x 19in. Hamptons, Godalming. Nov 01. £1,900.

900

Edwardian inlaid mahogany kneehole desk, raised single shelf back, 4ft. Gorringes, Lewes. Mar 01. £1,900.

> The illustrations are in descending price order. The price range is indicated at the top of each page.

901

Victorian flame mahogany bookcase, 88in high. Fellows & Sons, Hockley, Birmingham. Dec 02. £1,900.

902

Victorian triple wardrobe, flame mahogany, 192cm. Lots Road Auctions, Chelsea. Mar 03. £1,900.

903

William IV davenport, brass gallery, 43cm wide. (in need of restoration). Hamptons, Godalming. May 02. £1,900.

904

Edwardian mahog. wind out dining table, 3 leaves, square tapering and fluted legs, 9ft max. x 4ft. Sworders, Stansted Mountfitchet. July 01. £1,900.

905

6 + 2 reproduction carved mahogany dining chairs, drop in seats. Sworders, Stansted Mountfitchet. July 01. £1,900.

906

Regency mahogany pedestal sideboard, 6ft wide. Sworders, Stansted Mountfitchet. Apr 01. £1,900.

907

Set of six Regency mahogany framed dining chairs. Amersham Auction Rooms, Bucks. Mar 03. £1,900.

908

Early 18thC walnut chest of drawers of small proportions. Richard Winterton, Burton on Trent. Feb 03. £1,900.

909

Late 19thC figured mahogany secretaire à abattant by Edwards & Roberts, 43in wide, 55in high. Maxwells, Wilmslow. Sep 02. £1,900.

910

19thC inlaid walnut cylinder bureau, pull-out slide operating the fall and base drawer, 2ft 7in. Gorringes, Lewes. Apr 00. £1,900.

911

Regency giltwood convex girandole mirror, eagle and anthemion crest, ebonised slip, two branches, twin serpents, 30in wide. Gorringes, Lewes. Apr 01. £1,900.

Hammer Prices £1,900-£1,850

912

Edwardian Sheraton revival bow front vitrine. *Richard Wintertons, Burton on Trent. Apr 02. £1,900.*

913

Regency satinwood/mahog. banded dwarf chiffonier, 42in high. *R. Toovey, Washington, Sussex. Aug 03. £1,900.*

914

Geo. III satinwood demi lune card table, folding top inlaid shell motif, 38in. *Gorringes, Bexhill. Sep 02. £1,900.*

915

Art Nouveau oak mirror back sideboard, c1900, possibly Heals or Liberty's, back stamped '42', 54in wide. *Halls Fine Art Auctions, Shrewsbury. Mar 04. £1,900.*

916

Victorian walnut and upholstered dressing stool, c1860, 120 x 71cm. *Wintertons Ltd, Lichfield. Jan 04. £1,900.*

917

Regency mahogany collectors chest, 59cm wide. *Bristol Auc. Rooms. May 02. £1,900.*

918

Portuguese red painted mule chest having ornate brass studded front, on later walnut stand, 110cm. *Stride & Son, Chichester. July 03. £1,900.*

919

Sheraton revival rosewood and marquetry cylinder desk. *Lambert & Foster, Tenterden. Oct 00. £1,900.*

920

Arts and Crafts 'Liberty & Co' oak sideboard, c1900, 74in wide. *Halls Fine Art, Shrewsbury. Sep 03. £1,900.*

921

Regency mahogany sideboard, drop down doors, 181cm. *Sworders, Stansted Mountfitchet. Feb 04. £1,900.*

922

Geo. III mahogany urn stand, 65cm high. *Mellors & Kirk, Nottingham. June 03. £1,900.*

923

Rosewood breakfast table, 19thC, 48in wide. *A. Hartley, Ilkley. Oct 01. £1,850.*

924

Art Nouveau display cabinet. *Louis Taylor, Stoke on Trent. Mar 01. £1,850.*

925

George III mahogany chest on chest, 47.5in wide. *Andrew Hartley, Ilkley. Feb 01. £1,850.*

926

Pier mirror, 18thC giltwood, gesso. *Lots Road Auctions, Chelsea. Oct 02. £1,850.*

927

George III mahog. serpentine chest, crossbanded stringing and parquetry, 47in. *Andrew Hartley, Ilkley. Dec 01. £1,850.*

928

Black leather sofa, Hoffman design, square back and arms raised on square supports. *Lots Road Auctions, Chelsea. Oct 00. £1,850.*

929

Victorian mahogany crank wind extending dining table, 44.5 x 97.5in extended. *Dockree's, Manchester. May 00. £1,850.*

930

19thC carved walnut bookcase, 5ft 5in wide, 8ft high. *Sworders, Stansted Mountfitchet. Apr 01. £1,850.*

Sheraton period mahogany tallboy, 112 x 54 x 183cm. (restorations). Hamptons, Godalming. July 02. £1,850.

Regency gilt framed convex wall mirror, eagle cresting, pair of later scrolled candle sconces, 100cm. Sworders, Stansted Mountfitchet. Feb 04. £1,850.

Victorian walnut chaise longue, upholstery as seen. Ambrose, Loughton. Sep 00. £1,800.

Regency flame mahog. side cabinet. Lots Road Auctions, Chelsea. Nov 00. £1,800.

Victorian amboyna banded coromandel loo table, 4ft 8in. Gorringes, Lewes. July 00. £1,800.

Pair of mid 19thC Yorkshire region yew and elm Windsor elbow chairs. Gorringes, Lewes. July 01. £1,800.

Mart Stam for Thonet. A pair of club chairs, 1929. Phillips, Scotland. May 00. £1,800.

Edwardian inlaid mahogany display cabinet. Clevedon Salerooms, Bristol. Mar 01. £1,800.

Kidney shaped desk, mid 19thC Continental walnut, 53in wide. Lots Road Auctions, Chelsea. Mar 01. £1,800.

William IV sofa table, rosewood veneered, brass inlay and stringing. (restored) 37in wide. Woolley & Wallis, Salisbury. Aug 00. £1,800.

Hammer Prices £1,850-£1,800

George III mahogany bureau bookcase, astragal glazed doors. (associated parts). Lots Road Auctions, Chelsea. Apr 01. £1,800.

George III mahog. Pembroke table, 31in x 20in. Gorringes, Lewes. Feb 01. £1,800.

Prices quoted are hammer and exclude the buyer's premium. Adding 15% will give approx. buying price.

19thC Anglo Indian padouk dining table, 54in. Gorringes, Lewes. June 00. £1,800.

19thC flame mahogany linen press. Lots Road Auctions, Chelsea. Apr 01. £1,800.

19thC mahogany sideboard. Andrew Hartley, Ilkley. Dec 00. £1,800.

Victorian rosewood centre table, 32.5in wide, maker's label. Andrew Hartley, Ilkley. Dec 00. £1,800.

19thC English teak and brass bound campaign chest. Lots Road Auctions, Chelsea. Apr 01. £1,800.

Early 18thC figured walnut chest. Lots Road Auctions, Chelsea. May 01. £1,800.

Set 6 + 2 17thC style Derbyshire pattern dining chairs. Dockree's, Manchester. June 01. £1,800.

Hammer Price £1,800

950

Oak gateleg table, 17th/ early 18thC, 64.25 x 56in. *Andrew Hartley, Ilkley. Apr 01. £1,800.*

951

Late 19thC French kingwood veneered & floral serpentine marquetry side cabinet, cast bronze lion mask and other ornamental motifs, 43in wide. *Amersham Auction Rooms, Bucks. Nov 01. £1,800.*

952

Regency rosewood open book-case, later marble top, 47.5in x 35.5in high. *A. Hartley, Ilkley. Oct 01. £1,800.*

953

Victorian burr walnut writing table in Louis XVI taste, 59 x 34 x 30in. *Hamptons, Godalming. Jan 02. £1,800.*

954

Early Victorian mahogany serving table, 150cm. *Sworders, Stansted Mount-fitchet. Feb 03. £1,800.*

955

Mid 19thC ormolu mounted satinwood/mahogany planter, decoration in the manner of Donald Ross, 28in. *Gorringes, Lewes. Sep 00. £1,800.*

956

Sheraton Revival demi lune card table, inlaid satinwood batwing motif and mahogany ovals, 3ft. *Gorringes, Bexhill. Sep 02. £1,800.*

957

Victorian rosewood mirror backed side cabinet, 64in wide. *Andrew Hartley, Ilkley. Feb 01. £1,800.*

958

Regency rosewood worktable, drawer and green silk bag on lions paw castors, 15.5in wide. *Sworders, Stansted Mountfitchet. Apr 01. £1,800.*

959

Oak Gothic revival trefoil table. *Dreweatt Neate, Newbury. May 02. £1,800.*

960

George III style solid oak Shropshire dresser, 72in long. *Peter Wilson, Nantwich. Feb 02. £1,800.*

961

Regency chinoiserie table top work cabinet, 6 ivory handled doors, black lacquered, 36cm wide. *Peter Wilson, Nantwich. July 02. £1,800.*

962

Edwardian inlaid mahogany bedroom suite, triple break-front wardrobe, 7ft x 7ft 1in high, dressing chest, chest of drawers, bedside cabinet. *Sworders, Stansted Mount-fitchet. July 01. £1,800.*

963

Oak mule chest, late 17thC, profusely carved with trailing thistle heads and roses, 52 x 23 x 30in. *Hamptons, Godalming. Nov 01. £1,800.*

964

c1890 mahogany tripod supper table with bath edge and cabriole legs. *Richard Wintertons, Burton on Trent. Oct 02. £1,800.*

965

18thC walnut chest on stand, 97cm. *Henry Adams, Chichester. Sep 02. £1,800.*

966

19thC maplewood X-frame stool, patera, roundel terminals. *Tring Market Auctions, Herts. Jan 03. £1,800.*

967

19thC mahogany library bookcase, 101cm wide. *Thos. Mawer & Son, Lincoln. Nov 02, £1,800.*

968

Victorian rosewood canterbury, 3 divisions, bombe base with single drawer. *Rosebery's, London. June 03. £1,800.*

969

18thC walnut chest, crossbanded top, string inlaid drawers, 3ft wide. *Gorringes, Lewes. Jan 04. £1,800.*

970

17thC oak wainscot chair, carved panel back, scrolled arms. *D M Nesbit & Co., Southsea. July 03. £1,800.*

971

William IV mahogany wind-out extending dining table. *W & H Peacock, Bedford. July 03. £1,800.*

972

Regency mahogany side cabinet, inverted breakfront, grey marble top, 95cm wide. *Lots Road Auctions, Chelsea. Nov 03. £1,800.*

973

George III mahogany linen press, 132cm. *Sworders, Stansted Mountfitchet. July 03. £1,800.*

974

Edwardian mahog. drawing room suite, Art Nouveau floral panels inlaid with bone, settee, 37.75in wide, 2 armchairs, 4 single chairs. *Andrew Hartley, Ilkley. June 01. £1,800.*

> The numbering system acts as a reader reference as well as linking to the Analysis of each Section

975

Mid Victorian inlaid walnut breakfront credenza, ormolu mounts, grill doors, 5ft 6in. *Gorringes, Lewes. Mar 04. £1,800.*

976

Geo. III rosewood veneered and inlaid linen press secretaire, 114cm wide. *Ambrose, Loughton. Feb 02. £1,800.*

Hammer Price £1,800

977

Pair replica parquetry inlaid demi-lune side tables, Sheraton style, late 20thC, 48in wide. *Byrne's, Chester. Mar 04. £1,800.*

978

Charles & Ray Eames model 670 & 671 chair & footstool, c1958, rosewood veneered frame, black leather cushions, 'Herman Miller', produced for 'Hille' London. complete with spare base. *Rosebery's, London. Mar 04. £1,800.*

979

Victorian walnut pier cabinet, burr walnut panels inlaid with stringing and marquetry, pagoda top, glazed doors, 120 x 106cm. *Sworders, Stansted Mountfitchet. Feb 04. £1,800.*

980

Edwardian mahog. Sheraton Revival display cabinet, 76cm. *Locke & England, Leamington Spa. May 03. £1,800.*

981

Set of 3 Regency mahogany hall chairs, c1800, cockerel crest of Cox family. *Rosebery's, London. Mar 04. £1,800.*

982

Regency rosewood top breakfast table, 122cm dia. *Sworders, Stansted Mountfitchet. Feb 04. £1,800.*

983

Set of 8 Victorian oak single dining chairs, carved arched backs, leather overstuffed seats. *Sworders, Stansted Mountfitchet. June 03. £1,800.*

984

17thC oak gateleg table, plank top, old repairs/replacement parts, 64in extended length. *Halls Fine Art Auctions, Shrewsbury. Oct 03. £1,800.*

985

Small George III mahogany chest, brushing slide, 27.5in. *Gorringes, Lewes. Jan 04. £1,800.*

Hammer Prices £1,780-£1,700

986

Mahogany secretaire bookcase, 127cm wide. Bristol Auc. Rooms. Jan 03. £1,780.

987

Georgian mahogany boxwood strung library bookcase, 102cm wide. Thos Mawer & Son, Lincoln. Apr 02. £1,775.

988

Set of six William IV mahog. dining chairs, scroll crests, bar backs, drop in seats. Clevedon Salerooms, Bristol. Feb 02. £1,750.

989

19thC mahogany inlaid sideboard. John Taylors, Louth. May 00. £1,750.

990

Antique oak dresser, with an associated plate rack, 6ft wide. Sworders, Stansted Mountfitchet. Apr 01. £1,750.

991

19thC satinwood dwarf bookcase, giltwood mounts (af), 6ft long. Sworders, Stansted Mountfitchet. July 01. £1,750.

992

George III mahogany chest of small proportion, 34in wide. Tring Market Auctions, Herts. Sep 02. £1,750.

993

19thC mahog. partner's desk, later green leather, 168cm wide. Lots Road Auctions, Chelsea. Aug 03. £1,750.

994

Victorian oak sideboard by Christopher Pratt, Bradford, 84in wide, 64in high. Andrew Hartley, Ilkley. Dec 03. £1,750.

995

Edwardian inlaid mahogany nine-piece drawing room suite. W & H Peacock, Bedford. Feb 03. £1,750.

996

Early 18thC oak lowboy, 32in wide. Tring Market Auctions, Herts. Nov 03. £1,750.

997

Early 19thC mahogany table top cabinet in the form of a miniature chest, 14.75in wide. Tring Market Auctions, Herts. May 02. £1,750.

998

Unusual Geo. III mahogany desk, secretaire drawer and 4 short drawers on a pair of pedestal bases, 61in wide. Sworders, Stansted Mountfitchet. July 01. £1,750.

999

19thC rosewood collector's cabinet, birds eye maple faced drawers, 2ft 8in. Gorringes, Bexhill. Oct 01. £1,750.

1000

George IV beech library armchair, simulated rosewood, outscrolled crest, caned seat and back. Dreweatt Neate, Newbury. Apr 00. £1,750.

1001

Late 18thC giltwood three glass overmantel mirror, 134 x 115cm. Sworders, Stansted Mountfitchet. Feb 04. £1,700.

1002

Mid 19thC commode, Louis Philippe, feather figured flame mahogany, 50in wide. Lots Road Auctions, Chelsea. Mar 01. £1,700.

1003

Set 6 + 1 Sheraton period mahogany dining chairs. Woolley & Wallis, Salisbury. Aug 00. £1,700.

1004

Napoleon III, burr walnut, secretaire commode, grey marble top, 52in wide. Lots Road Auctions, Chelsea. Mar 01. £1,700.

1005

Late Victorian rosewood and marquetry kneehole writing table, 3ft 6in. *Gorringes, Lewes. June 00. £1,700.*

1006

Victorian birds eye maple and marquetry breakfast table, 5ft, severe split to top. *Gorringes, Lewes. June 00. £1,700.*

1007

Near pr. early 19thC Dutch mahogany/floral marquetry inlaid demi lune side tables, 30.25in x 29.75in. *Gorringes, Lewes. June 00. £1,700.*

1008

19thC oriental painted chest on stand, 38in wide. (old iron brace repairs). *Woolley & Wallis, Salisbury. Aug 00. £1,700.*

1009

Georgian corner cupboard (distressed). *John Taylors, Louth. May 00. £1,700.*

1010

19thC French occasional table, floral marquetry, panels of trellis florettes in parquetry, 32.75in. *Woolley & Wallis, Salisbury. Aug 00. £1,700.*

1011

George I miniature walnut bureau, 23cm wide. *Cheffins, Cambridge. Oct 00. £1,700.*

> The illustrations are in descending price order. The price range is indicated at the top of each page.

1012

William IV chiffonier, veneered in rosewood, 3ft. *Woolley & Wallis, Salisbury. Aug 00. £1,700.*

1013

Late George III mahogany cabinet bookcase, 42in wide. *Amersham Auction Rooms, Bucks. May 01. £1,700.*

Hammer Price £1,700

1014

Regency period simulated rosewood Bergere chair. *Sworders, Stansted Mount-fitchet. July 01. £1,700.*

1015

Regency mahogany card table. *Rosebery's, London. Apr 00. £1,700.*

1016

Early George III oak lowboy, 83cm wide. *Cheffins, Cambridge. Oct 00. £1,700.*

1017

Victorian mahog. extending dining table (2 extra leaves), 47 x 56in extending to 93in. *Lambert & Foster, Tenterden. May 00. £1,700.*

1018

Victorian wellington chest, 30in wide. *Peter Wilson, Nantwich. Feb 02. £1,700.*

1019

George III oak and elm box settle, 44.5in wide. *Andrew Hartley, Ilkley. Oct 01. £1,700.*

1020

Regency rosewood canterbury, four division top and base drawer. *Gorringes, Lewes. Jan 02. £1,700.*

1021

Victorian mahog. extending dining table, top with two leaves, 242 x 120cm extended. *Bristol Auction Rooms. Mar 02. £1,700.*

1022

19thC Continental walnut stool, buttoned drop-in seat, elaborately carved. *Gorringes, Lewes. Mar 01. £1,700.*

1023

Pair Geo. III mahog. dining chairs. *Lots Road Auctions, Chelsea. July 02. £1,700.*

Hammer Price £1,700

1024

George III mahogany chest on chest, c1785, 114cm wide. Wintertons Ltd, Lichfield. May 02. £1,700.

1025

Oak bacon cupboard, arch panel doors above 2 drawers, 135cm. Stride & Son, Chichester. July 03. £1,700.

1026

William IV mahog. breakfast table, top with wide rosewood crossbanding, 52in dia. Canterbury Auc. Galleries, Kent. Oct 02. £1,700.

1027

Regency mahogany library bergere armchair with scroll arms and leather squab seat. Gorringes, Lewes. Sep 00. £1,700.

1028

Late 19thC burr walnut and marquetry inlaid card table, of Louis XVI style, 90cm. Henry Adams, Chichester. Sep 02. £1,700.

1029

Geo. III mahog. bureau bookcase. Lots Road Auctions, Chelsea. Oct 02. £1,700.

1030

17thC oak coffer. W & H Peacock, Bedford. Jan 03. £1,700.

1031

George IV mahogany library table. Mellors & Kirk, Nottingham. Feb 03. £1,700.

1032

Regency mahogany/inlaid brass library table, 29in high, 48in dia. Amersham Auction Rooms, Bucks. Sep 03. £1,700.

1033

Early 19thC mahog. writing table, 61 x 54cm. (in need of restoration). Crows, Dorking. Jan 03. £1,700.

1034

Victorian walnut/gilt metal mounted credenza, 'Sevres' porcelain plaque, 61in wide, damage. Canterbury Auction Galleries. Dec 03. £1,700.

1035

19thC French rosewood chiffonier, 51.5in. Gorringes, Lewes. Jan 03. £1,700.

1036

18thC oak dresser, moulded top over 3 short drawers, 2ft 9in, 6ft 1in wide. Gorringes, Bexhill. Feb 04. £1,700.

1037

Victorian mahogany mirror backed sideboard, 79in wide, 72.5in high. Andrew Hartley, Ilkley. Feb 04. £1,700.

1038

19thC rosewood 2 tier table. Rupert Toovey, Washington, Sussex. Feb 03. £1,700.

1039

Victorian mahog. extending dining table, screw action to take 2 leaves, 237 x 122cm extended. Bristol Auction Rooms. Jan 04. £1,700.

1040

Pair of antique walnut open armchairs, later painted cream decoration, floral tapestry seats. Stride & Son, Chichester. July 03. £1,700.

1041

George IV mahogany bow fronted side table, 92cm. Locke & England, Leamington Spa. Sep 02. £1,700.

1042

Edwardian mahogany and line inlaid bijouterie table by Edwards & Roberts. Rupert Toovey, Washington, Sussex. Dec 02. £1,700.

1043

19thC iron, brass and black leather campaign bed, 87cm wide. *Lots Road Auctions, Chelsea. May 04. £1,700.*

1044

Regency brass inlaid mahogany cheval mirror. *W & H Peacock, Bedford. Mar 03. £1,700.*

1045

George III mahogany wine cooler on stand, lacking lead liner, 18in dia. *Hamptons, Godalming. Mar 02. £1,700.*

1046

Geo. IV mahogany/rosewood linen press probably Channel Islands, 137 x 239 x 55cm. *Hamptons, Godalming. July 02. £1,700.*

1047

George III oak chest on chest, 121cm wide. *Ambrose, Loughton. May 00. £1,700.*

1048

Late 18thC Dutch oak and floral marquetry bow front commode, 47in wide. *Amersham Auction Rooms, Bucks. Mar 02. £1,650.*

Prices quoted are hammer and exclude the buyer's premium. Adding 15% will give approx. buying price.

1049

Regency mahogany breakfast table, radiating flame veneers, cross banded edge, 132cm dia. *Rosebery's, London. Sep 02. £1,650.*

1050

Late 17thC oak joint stool, 17 x 10.5 x 22in high, underside stamped I.M. *Canterbury Auc. Galleries, Kent. Aug 02. £1,650.*

1051

Mid 19thC library table, green tooled leather, 6 drawers, 72in wide. *Tring Market Auctions, Herts. May 02. £1,650.*

1052

William IV rosewood centre table, heavy gadrooned rim, carved feet, 36in wide. *Peter Wilson, Nantwich. Nov 01. £1,650.*

1053

William IV mahog. linen press, 52in wide. *Tring Market Auctions, Herts. Sep 02. £1,650.*

1054

Victorian walnut breakfront cabinet, panels of parquetry, central door flanked by two glazed doors, 107cm high x 179cm. *Dreweatt Neate, Newbury. Apr 00. £1650.*

1055

Late Georgian mahog. twin pedestal D-end dining table, two extra leaves, not original condition, extending to 227 x 120cm. *Henry Adams, Chichester. Sep 02. £1,650.*

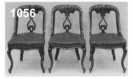

1056

Set of eight early Victorian mahogany dining chairs, serpentine deeply buttoned red leather, French cabriole legs. *David Duggleby, Scarborough. Apr 00. £1,650.*

1057

Victorian mahogany pedestal desk. *R. Toovey, Washington, Sussex. Oct 03. £1,650.*

1058

Regency rosewood and brass inlaid card table, swivel top, 36in wide. *Andrew Hartley, Ilkley. Apr 04. £1,650.*

1059

William IV rosewood centre table, 52in wide. *A. Hartley, Ilkley. Oct 03. £1,650.*

1060

George IV mahogany framed bergere, rollover collared back, caned panels and seat. *Amersham Auction Rooms, Bucks. Nov 01. £1,650.*

69

Hammer Prices £1,650-£1,600

George III linen press, 50in wide. *Wintertons Ltd, Lichfield. Sep 01. £1,650.*

19thC style mahogany breakfront open bookcase, 2.4m wide. *Sworders, Stansted Mountfitchet. Sep 03. £1,650.*

Italian rosewood sofa table, inlaid bone/boxwood floral motifs, 32in x 28in, and pair of matching side chairs, 19th/early 20thC. *D. Duggleby, Scarborough. Apr 00. £1,600.*

18thC figured mahog. chest, c1780. *Lots Road Auctions, Chelsea. May 01. £1,600.*

William and Mary oak mule chest, 137cm wide. *Cheffins, Cambridge. Oct 00. £1,600.*

Miniature black japanned chinoiserie decorated bureau. *Rosebery's, London. Sep 00. £1,600.*

Edwardian mahogany and satinwood banded escritoire, 62cm wide. *Wintertons Ltd, Lichfield. May 00. £1,600.*

5-seater car seat sofa upholstered in brown/burnt orange with white piping, 10ft 10in. *Lots Road Auctions, Chelsea. July 01. £1,600.*

Egg chair by Arne Jacobsen, manufactured by Fritz Hansen. *Woolley & Wallis, Salisbury. Aug 00. £1,600.*

William IV mahogany linen press, 141cm wide. *Cheffins, Cambridge. Oct 00. £1,600.*

George III oak drop flap dining table, 172cm when open. *Cheffins, Cambridge. Oct 00. £1,600.*

Small Regency bow front chest. *Lots Road Auctions, Chelsea. Sep 00. £1,600.*

Geo. I walnut chest of drawers, 95cm wide. *Cheffins, Cambridge. Oct 00. £1,600.*

Chinoiserie decorated black lacquer bedroom suite. *Rosebery's, London. May 00. £1,600.*

Victorian mahogany pedestal desk. *Lots Road Auctions, Chelsea. May 01. £1,600.*

Geo. III mahogany campaign hanging press, 57.5in wide. *Andrew Hartley, Ilkley. Feb 01. £1,600.*

Small pr. of Venetian giltwood wall mirrors, c1900. *Rosebery's, London. June 01. £1,600.*

Mahogany tester double bedstead, 5ft 1in wide x 8ft high. *Woolley & Wallis, Salisbury. Aug 00. £1,600.*

Mid Victorian gentleman's and lady's armchair, walnut, upholstery as seen. *Ambrose, Loughton. Sep 00. £1,600.*

1080

Pair of late Victorian mahog. bergere chairs. Cheffins, Cambridge. Oct 00. £1,600.

1081

Early 19thC Dutch mahog. and floral marquetry Lit en Bateau, 4ft 2in x 6ft 10in long. Lots Road Auctions, Chelsea. Nov 00. £1,600.

1082

Victorian walnut kneehole writing desk, 51in wide. Dee, Atkinson & Harrison, Driffield. Dec 00. £1,600.

1083

Commode, Napoleon III flame mahogany, maroon marble top, plinth base, 53in wide. Lots Road Auctions, Chelsea. Mar 01. £1,600.

1084

Late 18thC mahog. campaign cabinet, two doors enclosing shelves and drawers, 2ft 6in, on contemporary chamfered leg stand. Gorringes, Lewes. Mar 01. £1,600.

1085

Early 19thC mahogany secretaire chest of drawers, a stationery drawer marked in pencil by cabinet maker suggesting date of 1821 and origin Shropshire, 47in wide. Peter Wilson, Nantwich. Nov 00. £1,600.

1086

19thC French pollard oak serpentine collectors cabinet, 3ft 6in. Gorringes, Lewes. June 00. £1,600.

The numbering system acts as a reader reference as well as linking to the Analysis of each Section

1087

Victorian mahogany pedestal desk. Lots Road Auctions, Chelsea. May 02. £1,600.

1088

Late 19th/20thC reproduction of a George II oak/mahogany veneered bureau bookcase, 39in wide, 88in high. Amersham Auction Rooms, Bucks. Sep 02. £1,600.

Hammer Price £1,600

1089

19thC Dutch apprentices linen press in walnut and floral marquetry. Gorringes, Lewes. Mar 02. £1,600.

1090

19thC faded mahogany linen press. G W Finn & Sons, Canterbury. Sep 00. £1,600.

1091

George III mahogany chest of 3 drawers below a brushing slide, raised on bracket feet, 37in wide. Sworders, Stansted Mountfitchet. Apr 01. £1,600.

1092

Victorian burr walnut Sutherland table, serpentine oval top, 2ft 11in. Gorringes, Lewes. July 00. £1,600.

1093

Early 18thC oak low dresser, 73in wide. Tring Market Auctions, Herts. Sep 02. £1,600.

1094

Early 20thC walnut sofa in George I style, 197cm wide. Lots Road Auctions, Chelsea. Feb 03. £1,600.

1095

18th/early 19thC European marriage chest in the form of a miniature bureau with ivory panels, 8.5in x 12in high. Tring Market Auctions, Herts. May 02. £1,600.

1096

Sofa suite incl. two matching armchairs, cream and green leather. Lots Road Auctions, Chelsea. July 01. £1,600.

1097

Edwardian satinwood/painted Bonheur du Jour, 108cm wide. Lots Road Auctions, Chelsea. July 02. £1,600.

Hammer Price £1,600

1098

Early 19thC cream painted pine dressing chest with faux bamboo mouldings, 47in wide. *Amersham Auction Rooms, Bucks. Apr 02. £1,600.*

1099

Late 18thC Dutch mahogany chest, top inlaid with satinwood patera, tied ribbon and swags over ovals of vases of flowers, 3ft 3in. *Gorringes, Lewes. Feb 01. £1,600.*

1100

Set of 6 + 1 late 18th/early 19thC oak dining chairs, of 'Country Hepplewhite' design. *Canterbury Auction Galleries, Kent. Oct 01. £1,600.*

1101

Art Nouveau satinwood and mother of pearl inlaid, mahog. desk, fall front, fitted interior, 56in high. *Amersham Auction Rooms, Bucks. Sep 03. £1,600.*

1102

Early 19thC mahog. metamorphic vanity unit. *Gorringes, Bexhill. July 01. £1,600.*

1103

George III mahog. Pembroke table, crossbanded, inlaid panelled frieze, 30.5in wide. *Andrew Hartley, Ilkley. Apr 01. £1,600.*

1104

Late 18thC elm coffer, plank construction, shallow drawer, 17in high, 22.5in wide. *Amersham Auction Rooms, Bucks. Feb 04. £1,600.*

1105

Early 19thC oak cupboard, moulded cornice, carved guilloche frieze, twin panel cupboard doors, 40in wide. *Amersham Auction Rooms, Bucks. Sep 01. £1,600.*

1106

George III elm curved settle, 7 moulded panels, box base, 76in wide. *Andrew Hartley, Ilkley. Dec 03. £1,600.*

1107

Georgian rosewood card table, crossbanded top, frieze drawer, 38in. *Denhams, Warnham. Feb 04. £1,600.*

1108

Pair of 19thC painted side tables. *Rosebery's, London. Sep 01. £1,600.*

1109

1920s Art Nouveau inspired, light oak dining suite with carved, stylised fruit and whiplash motifs: wind-out dining table, 100in long, with 2 extra leaves, a set of 4 + 2 stud upholstered chairs. *Amersham Auction Rooms, Bucks. May 02. £1,600.*

1111

French Empire mahogany dressing table, c1810, 80cm wide. *Lots Road Auctions, Chelsea. Sep 03. £1,600.*

1112

Regency painted waterfall bookcase, scroll pediment, door with simulated brass grill, 1ft 8in. *Gorringes, Lewes. Sep 03. £1,600.*

1113

Art Nouveau mahog. glazed display cabinet, coloured wood floral motifs, 45in wide. *Tring Market Auctions, Herts. May 02. £1,600.*

1110

Large 19thC pine kitchen table, two end drawers, H stretcher; 97 x 274cm. *Sworders, Stansted Mountfitchet. Feb 04. £1,600.*

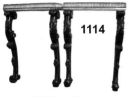

1114

Pair of William IV mahog. and parcel gilt console tables, each 58cm wide. *Lots Road Auctions, Chelsea. Apr 04. £1,600.*

1118

Set 6 + 2 Hepplewhite style mahogany dining chairs. *Gorringes, Bexhill. Dec 02. £1,600.*

Hammer Price £1,600

1122

19thC French mahogany/brass mounted commode, grey marble top, 130cm wide. *Lots Road Auctions, Chelsea. Mar 03. £1,600.*

1127

Early Victorian mahog. roll top desk, well fitted interior, 106 x 120cm. *Rosebery's, London. June 03. £1,600.*

1115

20thC Black Forest style carved wood hat stand, 82in high, another similar, 80in, both distressed. *Gorringes, Lewes. Mar 04. £1,600.*

1119

Yew Windsor armchair of north country type, 19thC. *Andrew Hartley, Ilkley. Feb 03. £1,600.*

> The illustrations are in descending price order. The price range is indicated at the top of each page.

1123

George III mahog./rosewood crossbanded writing/work table, 2 drawers, one with leathered slope, 2ft. *Gorringes, Lewes. Jan 04. £1,600.*

1128

George II period mahogany card table, 2ft 6.5in wide. *Mervyn Carey, Tenterden. June 03. £1,600.*

1116

George II walnut chest on associated stand, 3ft 6in. *Gorringes, Bexhill. Dec 02. £1,600.*

1120

Victorian mahogany breakfront linen press, 2.4m wide. *Sworders, Stansted Mountfitchet. Dec 03. £1,600.*

1124

Victorian ebonised/amboyna banded credenza, c1885, 169cm wide. *Wintertons Ltd, Lichfield. May 03. £1,600.*

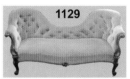

1129

Victorian rosewood humped back sofa. *Lots Road Auctions, Chelsea. Sep 03. £1,600.*

1130

Victorian inlaid and ebonised credenza, gilt metal mounts, porcelain panel in Sevres manner, 165cm. *D M Nesbit, Southsea. June 03. £1,600.*

1117

Geo. III mahogany standing corner cabinet, 94cm wide. *Sworders, Stansted Mountfitchet. Feb 04. £1,600.*

1121

19thC German Black Forest carved softwood stick stand. *Rupert Toovey, Washington, Sussex. Dec 03. £1,600.*

1125

Set of 6 single Regency mahog. dining chairs. *Gorringes, Lewes. Jan 04. £1,600.*

1126

George III mahogany chest on chest. *D M Nesbit & Co., Southsea. Apr 03. £1,600.*

1131

George III mahogany tray top commode, tambour front and base drawer, chamfered legs, 1ft 8in. *Gorringes, Lewes. Feb 01. £1,600.*

Hammer Prices £1,600-£1,550

1132

19thC Louis XV style kingwood marquetry jardiniere stand, lift off cover, 31.5in wide, 30.5in high. *Tring Market Auctions, Herts. Mar 03. £1,600.*

1133

Set 6 Victorian walnut dining chairs, carved balloon backs, *David Duggleby, Scarborough. Apr 00. £1,550.*

1134

George III mahog. sideboard. *Eastbourne Auction Rooms, Sussex. Mar 02. £1,550.*

1135

Set 6 + 2 Regency mahogany dining chairs, 2 of later date. *Bristol Auction Rooms, Bristol. May 02. £1,550.*

1136

Late 17thC oak chest of drawers. *John Taylors, Louth. June 00. £1,550.*

1137

17thC north European pine and iron bound chest, initials and dated 1697. *Cheffins, Cambridge. Oct 00. £1,550.*

1138

Set of six Regency mahogany framed dining chairs. *Amersham Auction Rooms, Bucks. June 01. £1,550.*

1139

Early Victorian mahogany wardrobe, 100.25in wide, 89.5in high. *Andrew Hartley, Ilkley. June 02. £1,550.*

1140

Georgian joined elm dresser base, swan neck handles, 172cm wide. *Bristol Auction Rooms. July 02. £1,550.*

1141

19thC mahog. secretaire book-case, 100cm. *Henry Adams, Chichester. Sep 02. £1,550.*

1142

George III satinwood card table crossbanded in harewood, 91cm wide. *Hamptons, Godalming. May 02. £1,550.*

1143

Oak enclosed dresser and rack, 74.5in x 67in. *Dee, Atkinson & Harrison, Driffield. Mar 04. £1,550.*

1144

Georgian walnut bureau, 32.25in wide. *A. Hartley, Ilkley. Oct 02. £1,550.*

1145

Long Victorian mahogany window seat, 152cm long. *Sworders, Stansted Mount-fitchet. Feb 04. £1,550.*

1146

19thC mahog. military chest. *Locke & England, Leamington Spa. Nov 02. £1,550.*

1147

Antique mahogany octagonal tripod table, cross banded tip up top, 61cm. *Stride & Son, Chichester. July 03. £1,550.*

1148

Edwardian inlaid satinwood jardiniere. *Sworders, Stansted Mountfitchet. May 00. £1,550.*

1149

Sheraton Revival painted satin wood display cabinet, 3ft 9in wide. *Mervyn Carey, Tenterden. Mar 03. £1,550.*

1150

Victorian burr walnut Canter-bury of unusual form, 24in wide. *Tring Market Auctions, Herts. Jan 03. £1,550.*

1151

French rosewood table a ouvrage, c1880, top with a marquetry basket of flowers, 56cm wide. Peter Wilson, Nantwich. July 02. £1,550.

1152

19thC faded mahog. satin-wood banded, marquetry inlaid vitrine, 67cm wide. Thos Mawer & Son, Lincoln. Nov 02. £1,550.

Prices quoted are hammer and exclude the buyer's premium. Adding 15% will give approx. buying price.

1153

George III mahogany chest on chest with inlaid canted corners, 48.5in wide. Dockree's, Manchester. Feb 01. £1,520.

1154

Geo. III mahog. chest, minor restoration required, 34.5in wide. Tring Market Auctions, Herts. Sep 02. £1,520.

1155

Victorian carved walnut salon suite, in Rococo Revival style, 54in wide. Andrew Hartley, Ilkley. Aug 00. £1,500.

1156

Louis XV style kingwood and ormolu commode, Vernis Martin panels. Rosebery's, London. Sep 00. £1,500.

1157

19thC mahogany marquetry inlaid tea table. Crows, Dorking. Feb 01. £1,500.

1158

George III mahogany chest of drawers, 47in wide. Wintertons Ltd, Lichfield. Sep 01. £1,500.

1159

Edwardian mahogany and inlaid bureau. Phillips, Leeds. Apr 00. £1,500.

1160

Edwardian mahogany 7 piece salon suite: settee, two open armchairs and four standard chairs. Clarke Gammon, Guildford. Apr 01. £1,500.

1161

19thC Sheraton revival mahog. sideboard, 149cm. Cheffins, Cambridge. Dec 00. £1,500.

1162

Victorian walnut canterbury, 24.75in wide. Andrew Hartley, Ilkley. Dec 00. £1,500.

1163

Set 4 William IV mahog. hall chairs, cartouche shaped backs, C scrolls on, wrythen fluted supports. Gorringes, Lewes. Dec 00. £1,500.

1164

Pair of Italian walnut side cabinets, parts possibly dating from 17thC Lots Road Auctions, Chelsea. Nov 00. £1,500.

Hammer Prices £1,550-£1,500

1165

George III mahog. canterbury, 1ft 6in. Gorringes, Lewes. June 00. £1,500.

1166

19thC mahogany folding card table, 33in wide. A. Hartley, Ilkley. Dec 00. £1,500.

1167

George I figured walnut chest, quarter veneered and feather strung, 102cm wide. Cheffins, Cambridge. Dec 00. £1,500.

1168

George III mahogany chest of drawers, original gilt swan neck handles, 45in x 21in x 37in. (Possibly Gillows of Lancaster) Hamptons, Godalming. Sep 01. £1,500.

Hammer Price £1,500

1169

Mid 19thC French commode, Louis Phillippe feather figured flame mahogany, 50in. Lots Road Auctions, Chelsea. May 01. £1,500.

1170

George III flame mahog. bow-front chest, small proportions, 36in. Lots Road Auctions, Chelsea. May 01. £1,500.

1171

Victorian walnut pedestal desk, 50.25in wide. Andrew Hartley, Ilkley. Apr 01. £1,500.

1172

Regency mahogany serving table, 168cm wide. Cheffins, Cambridge. Oct 00. £1,500.

1173

Regency mahogany night cupboard, 22in wide, 35.5in high. Andrew Hartley, Ilkley. Feb 01. £1,500.

1174

Set of 4 + 2 ash ladder back chairs, 19thC. A. Hartley, Ilkley. Aug 01. £1,500.

1175

Pair of Venetian mirrors in rococo style c1900. Rosebery's, London. Sep 00. £1,500.

1176

Queen Anne design desk in burr walnut, top with triple leather panels, 138cm wide. Lots Road Auctions, Chelsea. Sep 02. £1,500.

1177

Geo. III banded walnut chest, later superstructure and writing flap, 3ft. Gorringes, Lewes. Sep 00. £1,500.

1178

Late Geo. III mahog. bookcase, 52in wide. Lots Road Auctions, Chelsea. Mar 00. £1,500.

1179

Pair of Art Deco style leather armchairs. Lots Road Auctions, Chelsea. Aug 01. £1,500.

1180

George III walnut bow front chest, crossbanding/stringing, quarter veneered top, 35.5in wide. Andrew Hartley, Ilkley. Apr 01. £1,500.

1181

Victorian mirror, paper label of Howard & Sons of London, Cabinet Makers, 74in wide. Amersham Auction Rooms, Bucks. June 03. £1,500.

1182

George III mahogany breakfast table, unusual dropflap action, over gun barrel turned upright 134.5 x 122cm. Bristol Auc. Rooms. June 02. £1,500.

1183

William IV mahog. cellarette. Marilyn Swain Auctions, Grantham. Aug 01. £1,500.

1184

George III satinwood fold over demi-lune card table, 36in wide. Dee, Atkinson & Harrison, Driffield. Aug 01. £1,500.

1185

Queen Anne, panelled oak lambing chair. Amersham Auction Rooms, Bucks. Nov 02. £1,500.

1186

Mid 19thC Dutch veneered tallboy, 26in high, 38in wide. Amersham Auction Rooms, Bucks. Apr 01. £1,500.

1187

Queen Anne walnut wing armchair. Cheffins, Cambridge. Mar 00. £1,500.

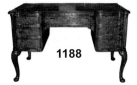

1188

Early 20thC burr walnut desk, George II style, 122cm wide. *Lots Road Auctions, Chelsea. Feb 03. £1,500.*

1189

Victorian burr walnut low breakfront bookcase, plinth base restored, 6ft 3in wide. *Gorringes, Bexhill. Mar 03. £1,500.*

1190

Mid Georgian mahog. fold-over card table, counter wells and replacement baize, 34.5in wide. *Tring Market Auctions, Herts. Mar 03. £1,500.*

1191

Regency mahog. linen press, with 4 sliding trays above 2 short and 2 long drawers, 4ft 3in wide. *Sworders, Stansted Mountfitchet. Apr 01. £1,500.*

1192

19thC French giltwood and gesso pier cabinet, white marble top, 3ft 5in. *Gorringes, Lewes. Oct 02. £1,500.*

1193

Mahogany tambour fronted commode, c1900, poss. continental. *R. Wintertons, Burton on Trent. Feb 02. £1,500.*

1194

Regency rosewood chaise longue, scroll/foliage carved frame, lotus carved legs, stamped Kirby. *Gorringes, Lewes. Apr 01. £1,500.*

The numbering system acts as a reader reference as well as linking to the Analysis of each Section

1195

Geo. III mahog. gentleman's press, 71 x 52in. *Sworders, Stansted Mountfitchet. Apr 01. £1,500.*

1196

19thC Irish giltwood and gesso wall mirror, blue/clear glass facetted jewelled border within a beaded and fluted frame, 2ft 9in x 1ft 9in. *Gorringes, Lewes. Mar 04. £1,500.*

1197

Victorian walnut Bureau De Dame, stationery compartment, inlaid lid, carved legs, 44in wide. *Sworders, Stansted Mountfitchet. Apr 01. £1,500.*

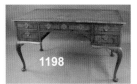

1198

Queen Anne design walnut kneehole writing table, c1920, 54in wide. *Sworders, Stansted Mountfitchet. Apr 01. £1,500.*

1199

Victorian mahogany three tier buffet, 4ft 6in. *Gorringes, Bexhill. May 02. £1,500.*

1200

Set of 6 + 2 Victorian mahog. balloon back dining chairs. (repairs). *Sworders, Stansted Mountfitchet. Apr 01. £1,500.*

1201

Edwardian painted satinwood work table, with tray and silk lined interior, painted with cherubs, garlands and a portrait of a lady. *Gorringes, Lewes. Apr 01. £1,500.*

Hammer Price £1,500

1202

George III mahogany dwarf estate cabinet, drawers inlaid with ivory letters of most of the alphabet, 70 x 36 x 81cm. *Hamptons, Godalming. July 02. £1,500.*

1203

Geo. III demi-lune satinwood card table of Sheraton style, 95cm. *Henry Adams, Chichester. July 02. £1,500.*

1204

Four 19thC elm wavy ladder back arm chairs, and spindle back chair. *Sworders, Stansted Mountfitchet. July 01. £1,500.*

1205

Late 19thC walnut/marquetry centre table, top with foliate decoration and crossbanded border, cast metal guilloche edge, 30in high, 48in wide. *Amersham Auction Rooms, Bucks. July 02. £1,500.*

1206

Regency rosewood writing table, green leather over 2 drawers, 3ft 6in. *Gorringes, Lewes. Mar 04. £1,500.*

Hammer Price £1,500

1207

Set of 6 Regency rosewood dining chairs, carved crests, caned seats. *Amersham Auc. Rooms, Bucks. Mar 04. £1,500.*

1208

Geo. IV standing mahogany corner cupboard, c1830, stained harewood and satinwood centre shell inlay, 94cm wide. *Wintertons Ltd, Lichfield. Jan 04. £1,500.*

1209

Late Victorian giltwood and upholstered three piece salon suite, c1900, in Louis XV style. *Wintertons Ltd, Lichfield. Mar 04. £1,500.*

1210

Regency gilt brass inlaid rosewood card table, rotating fold-over D-shaped top, 35in wide. *Amersham Auction Rooms, Bucks. Feb 04. £1,500.*

1211

Set of 6 William IV mahogany dining chairs, c1835, scroll crest rails, leather upholstered bowed seats. *Wintertons Ltd, Lichfield. Jan 04. £1,500.*

1212

Regency rosewood occasional table. *R. Toovey, Washington, Sussex. Jan 04. £1,500.*

1213

19thC Dutch walnut and marquetry miniature cabinet, 1ft 8in wide. *Gorringes, Lewes. Jan 04. £1,500.*

1214

Biedermeier mahogany secretaire a abattant, gilt metal mounts, 19thC, 39in wide, 54in high. *Andrew Hartley, Ilkley. June 03. £1,500.*

1215

George III mahogany and crossbanded chest, stamped 'Willson, 68 Great Queens Street, London', 43.5in wide. *Dee, Atkinson & Harrison, Driffield. Mar 04. £1,500.*

1216

Welsh oak dresser, 17thC and later, 56in wide. *Clarke Gammon, Guildford. June 03. £1,500.*

1217

Geo. III mahog. bureau, fall front enclosing fitted interior, 60cm wide. *Mellors & Kirk, Nottingham. Sep 03. £1,500.*

1218

Set of 6 Georgian style mahog. ribbon back chairs, c1900, drop in seats, 109cm. *Bristol Auction Rooms. Nov 03. £1,500.*

1219

Victorian giltwood sofa, upholstered in cream brocade, 215cm wide. *Mellors & Kirk, Nottingham. Sep 03. £1,500.*

1220

Set of six Geo. IV mahogany dining chairs, c1820, prob. Scottish, incised tableau top rail, drop in leather seats. *Wintertons Ltd, Lichfield. Mar 04. £1,500.*

1221

Regency rosewood breakfront chiffonier, 73in wide. *Amersham Auction Rooms, Bucks. May 03. £1,500.*

1222

19thC mahogany serpentine fronted sideboard, 153cm wide. *Lambert & Foster, Tenterden. Aug 03. £1,500.*

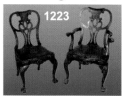

1223

Set of 4 + 1 early 20thC George I style walnut dining chairs. *Lots Road Auctions, Chelsea. June 01. £1,500.*

Section VII <£1,500 to £1,000

It is sometimes impossible even for expert auctioneers to be absolutely certain in their attributions. As a consequence, buyers often see themselves as pitting their wits against the auction and their competitors - a world of excitement and risk.

The earliest piece in this extensive Section appears to be the large sixteenth century linenfold oak coffer at **1432**, which with inevitable repairs and restoration fetched £1,200 at Hamptons, Godalming in 2001. I have deliberately used the verbal notion of 'appears', at the beginning of this analysis, not to question the credentials of **1432**, but to raise the important issue of 'appearance and reality'. In fact this lot is almost certainly no illusion and in almost all cases throughout this work, auctions descriptions qualify the nature of the lots. It must be so otherwise they would be discredited. In fact, the auctions industry is a very credible institution. However, it can be a problem for the amateur or the collector or even the novice buyer to understand cataloguing terms.

Many catalogues offer an explanation of terms relating to say, art or books, but similar explanations relating to furniture are difficult to find. Take Sheraton. The *Index* shows entries for *Sheraton, Sheraton design, Sheraton manner, Sheraton period, Sheraton Revival, Sheraton style, Sheraton taste* and *Sheraton type*! It is similarly confusing when confronted with Chippendale, Hepplewhite, Gillow etc. In defense of the auctions and this book, one should add that in most cases the combined illustrations, descriptions, estimates, and prices which now add into the equations, in many cases clarify any doubt. In certain cases it is impossible even for experts to be certain in their attributions and as a consequence, buyers often see themselves as pitting their wits against the auction and other bidders. This is a world of excitement and some risk! There remains in some descriptions, ambiguity which may predispose prospective clients to buy new. This is a pity. Buying antiques and secondhand furniture is altogether practical and sensible, even astute, resourceful and certainly prudent.

Three items of pine appear, the first a Georgian armoire, **1262**, dated 1778 which fetched £1,400 at Lots Road Auctions, Chelsea in 2001. Then there is an Orkney chair at **1321**, and thirdly the lot which prompted my pine attribution, a nineteenth century East European painted pine armoire at **1532**, which fetched £1,100. There is a serious market for painted antique pine. Whilst it would be almost impossible to trace such a theme through the *Index*, readers should consider this genre as a clear European phenomenon over the last 300 or so years. One of the more interesting pieces is the nineteenth century French provincial buffet or sideboard at **1360**, which fetched £1,300 in 2003. Cherrywood and walnut are an unusual combination. French provincial furniture is an interesting theme and set to go up in value in years to come. Check the *Index* for sideboards.

Returning to our earlier theme, check out the nineteenth century Chippendale design mahogany silver table at **1397**. Here there is no ambiguity being clearly a nineteenth century reproduction. Now check **1582**. Here is a tea table actually of the Hepplewhite period, not by Hepplewhite, who ran a small London cabinet-making business. He died in 1786, but is famous for *The Cabinet-Maker's and Upholsterer's Guide,* published in 1788, two years after his death, and a revised edition in 1794 containing new designs which reflected the current taste for restrained, light, new-classicism. Now check out **1615**, a twentieth century bureau bookcase, which stylistically echoes no one style, rather an uncomfortable looking reproduction. See **1620**, the 1920s Hepplewhite style chairs, which in contrast perfectly sympathise with the late eighteenth century. Or check out the Sheraton style chairs at **1738**, quality reproductions, which could be nineteenth but are more likely to be twentieth century.

1429, a George I oak library alcove bookcase suggests the concept of creating an alcove to reinstate this rare piece in a period setting. The eighteenth century oak press cupboard at **1456**, sold for £1,200 in 2003. What potential has this piece as an investment in the years to come? Check out also eight carved dining chairs in seventeenth century style at **1475**. Could you find a matching reproduction table? The answer is probably, yes. Certainly they would make a statement in the dining room probably at less than the price of buying new! Also note another Art Deco walnut dining suite at **1496** and at **1509**, a seventeenth century oak chest for the same money. **1568** shows a very rare ash kitchen cupboard, undated, which surely has gone up in value since 2000. Check out the Sheraton Revival inlaid mahogany dumb waiter or buffet at **1644**, which fetched £1,000 at Mellors & Kirk in Nottingham in 2003. Also note the twentieth century oak gateleg table by Cumper of Salisbury at **1652**, which at £1,000 exceeds the price you would pay for many a seventeenth or eighteenth century example. Don't overlook the set of nineteenth century, painted mahogany dining chairs at **1655** which fetched £1,000 in 2004 in Cambridge. What an incredible statement they will make for conservatory dining.

79

Hammer Prices £1,480-£1,450

1224

Geo. III mahog. fold over tea table, 36in wide. Peter Wilson, Nantwich. Nov 00. £1,480.

1225

Early 19thC large giltwood console table, marble top, 36in wide. Tring Market Auctions, Herts. Jan 03. £1,480.

1226

George III mahogany framed Gainsborough open armchair, velvet upholstery, lacking castors. Sworders, Stansted Mountfitchet. Mar 04. £1,480.

1227

18thC Flemish oak commode, later planked top, 34.5in wide. Amersham Auction Rooms, Bucks. Dec 01. £1,470.

1228

Charles II oak chest initialled W L and dated 1676, 123cm wide. Wintertons Ltd, Lichfield. July 02. £1,450.

1229

19thC mahogany folding tea table, 36in wide. A. Hartley, Ilkley. Dec 00. £1,450.

1230

Regency mahog. 'D' shaped fold over and swivel top tea table, 36in wide. Dockree's, Manchester. Feb 01. £1,450.

1231

Victorian walnut table, twist turned stretcher, restoration, 45in wide. Sworders, Stansted Mountfitchet. July 01. £1,450.

1232

George III mahogany chest, 37in wide. Andrew Hartley, Ilkley. Apr 01. £1,450.

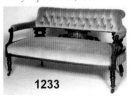

1233

Victorian satinwood inlaid, rosewood framed parlour suite: three person settee and 2 matching tub style chairs. Amersham Auction Rooms, Bucks. July 02. £1,450.

1234

19thC marble and ormolu occasional table, breche violet marble top, on green toleware legs, stamped 'L Kahn', 21.5 x 12 x 29in. Hamptons, Godalming. Sep 01. £1,450.

1235

George III mahog./satinwood inlaid secretaire chest on chest. Amersham Auc. Rooms, Bucks. Oct 01. £1,450.

1236

George II mahogany small kneehole desk, 87cm wide. Bristol Auction Rooms, Bristol. Mar 02. £1,450.

1237

Late 18thC demi-lune side table, Sheraton taste, satinwood crossbanded, large fan inlay, frieze inlaid with central Prince of Wales motif, 46 x 19.5 x 32.5in. Alterations/restorations. Hamptons, Godalming. Mar 02. £1,450.

1238

William IV chiffonier in rosewood, 39in wide. Hamptons, Godalming. Nov 01. £1,450.

1239

George I oak crossbanded chest on stand, 66in high, 40in wide. Sworders, Stansted Mountfitchet. Apr 01. £1,450.

1240

George III mahog. tripod tea table, single piece top, adapted birdcage and turned column, 28.5in dia. Sworders, Stansted Mountfitchet. Apr 01. £1,450.

1241

Ebonised credenza, c1880, burr walnut, 219cm base. Peter Wilson, Nantwich. Feb 02. £1,450.

1242

Geo. III mahog. bureau, fall front, fitted interior, 42.75in wide. A. Hartley, Ilkley. Dec 01. £1,450.

1243

George III mahog. linen press, 126 x 204 x 58cm. Hamptons, Godalming. July 02. £1,450.

1244

17thC low oak chest, moulded, painted and inlaid doors, enclosing three drawers, 44in wide. Sworders, Stansted Mountfitchet. July 01. £1,450.

The illustrations are in descending price order. The price range is indicated at the top of each page.

1245

Edwardian mahog. bijouterie table of heart form, hinged lid, 21in wide. A. Hartley, Ilkley. Apr 03. £1,450.

1246

Malachite inlaid belge noir marble pedestal table, prob. Derbyshire, c1850, 46cm dia. Bristol Auction Rooms, Bristol. Dec 03. £1,450.

1247

Regency mahogany demi-lune foldover card table, 37in wide. Tring Market Auctions, Herts. Nov 03. £1,450.

1248

Mid 19thC figured walnut bonheur du jour, 41in wide. Tring Market Auctions, Herts. Sep 02. £1,450.

1249

19thC Scandinavian salon suite, painted floral sprays: 3 seater canape, pair of side chairs. Lots Road Auctions, Chelsea. Mar 04. £1,450.

1250

Victorian mahogany partners desk, crossbanded, inset leather, 60in wide. A. Hartley, Ilkley. Aug 03. £1,450.

1251

18thC oak cupboard on chest, inlaid frieze over 2 doors, 51.75in wide. A. Hartley, Ilkley. Apr 04. £1,450.

Hammer Prices £1,450-£1,400

1252

Edwardian mahog. bergere armchair, oval vignette, rest painted with classical decoration. Sworders, Stansted Mountfitchet. Feb 04. £1,450.

1253

Early 18thC oak cupboard, top rail carved with initials 'I.R.A 1725', 132cm wide. Sworders, Stansted Mountfitchet. Feb 04. £1,450.

1254

Victorian mahog. extending dining table, 3 extra leaves, 268cm approx extended. Sworders, Stansted Mountfitchet. Feb 04. £1,450.

1255

Victorian lady's figured walnut cylinder bureau, gilt metal gallery, French manner, 31in. Canterbury Auction Galleries, Kent. Aug 03. £1,450.

1256

Edwardian inlaid mahogany serpentine display cabinet, 42in. Tring Market Auctions, Herts. Mar 02. £1,420.

1257

William IV mahogany hall bench. Lots Road Auctions, Chelsea. Apr 01. £1,400.

1258

Victorian figured mahogany sideboard, 87in long. Dee, Atkinson & Harrison. Driffield. Feb 01. £1,400.

1259

Regency bow front chest. Lots Road Auctions, Chelsea. Oct 00. £1,400.

1260

George IV mahog. work table, Gillows manner, pleated semi-circular pull-out workbox. Canterbury Auction Galleries, Kent. Feb 01. £1,400.

Hammer Price £1,400

1261

1265

Early George III mahogany bureau, 95cm wide. Cheffins, Cambridge. Oct 00. £1,400.

Regency mahogany cheval mirror. Rosebery's, London. Jan 00. £1,400.

1262

Late 18th/early 19thC painted armoire, initials A. K. & date 1778, 73in wide. Lots Road, Chelsea. May 01. £1,400.

1266

19thC French provincial fruit-wood bureau plat, extending side leaves, two drawers, 74in wide. Lots Road Auctions, Chelsea. July 01. £1,400.

1263

1267

17thC oak coffer. Lots Road Auctions, Chelsea. Apr 02. £1,400.

George III mahog. wardrobe, 99cm wide. Cheffins, Cambridge. Oct 00. £1,400.

1264

Geo. III mahog. linen press, 209cm high. Hamptons, Godalming. July 01. £1,400.

1268

George I walnut bureau. Clarke Gammon, Guildford. Sep 01. £1,400.

1270

Regency convex wall mirror, carved solid mahogany frame, 26in dia. Sworders, Stansted Mountfitchet. Apr 01. £1,400.

1271

Pair 18thC style walnut open armchairs, floral marquetry decoration. Hamptons, Godalming. May 02. £1,400.

1272

Oak wardrobe, carved frieze, animal masks over 4 arched panelled doors, 9ft long x 8ft high. Sworders, Stansted Mountfitchet. July 01. £1,400.

1273

Set 8 mahogany dining chairs, 20thC. Lots Road Auctions, Chelsea. Mar 02. £1,400.

1274

George III mahog. demi lune card table, satinwood cross-banded, ebony stringing, folding top, 30in. A. Hartley, Ilkley. Aug 01. £1,400.

1275

Regency banded mahogany bowfront chest, fitted slide, 4 drawers, 3ft. Gorringes, Lewes. Dec 00. £1,400.

1276

Card table, Regency rosewood, with baize lined foldover top. Lots Road Auctions, Chelsea. Nov 01. £1,400.

1277

Six early Victorian mahogany balloon back single dining chairs. Sworders, Stansted Mountfitchet. Apr 01. £1,400.

1278

William IV mahog. sideboard, beaded edged front. Lots Road Auctions, Chelsea. May 02. £1,400.

1279

Regency inlaid mahogany cabinet, astragal glazed doors, fitted secretaire, 106cm wide. Bristol Auction Rooms, Bristol. Dec 01. £1,400.

Late George III mahogany bowfront chest on chest, 76in high. Hamptons, Godalming. Sep 01. £1,400.

1280

Geo. II oak clothes press in 2 sections, 146cm wide, 193cm high. *Hamptons, Godalming. May 02. £1,400.*

1281

Set of 6 Edwardian mahogany/inlaid dining chairs, stuffover needlework seats. *Rosebery's, London. Mar 02. £1,400.*

1282

George III mahogany chest, moulded edged crossbanded top, 34.5in wide. *A. Hartley, Ilkley. Dec 01. £1,400.*

1283

Set of four adzed oak chairs by Robert 'Mouseman' Thompson. *Andrew Hartley, Ilkley. June 03. £1,400.*

1284

Victorian walnut work table, quarter veneered lid, fitted interior centred by a pierced fret well cover, 22.5in wide. *Andrew Hartley, Ilkley. Feb 02. £1,400.*

1285

Edwardian rosewood and marquetry inlaid lady's writing desk, stamped Jas Shoolbred and Co., 106cm. *Henry Adams, Chichester. July 02. £1,400.*

1286

Geo. III Hepplewhite mahog. card table with serpentine folding top, 3ft 2in. *Gorringes, Lewes. Apr 01. £1,400.*

> Prices quoted are hammer and exclude the buyer's premium. Adding 15% will give approx. buying price.

1287

Small 18thC country oak dresser, 59in wide. *Maxwells, Wilmslow. Sep 02. £1,400.*

1288

Regency mahogany whatnot, 50cm wide. *Lots Road, Chelsea. Jan 03. £1,400.*

Hammer Price £1,400

1289

Regency rosewood breakfront side cabinet, green marble top, 71.5in. *Tring Market Auctions, Herts. Sep 02. £1,400.*

1290

Mid Victorian pedestal table, specimen marble mosaic top, 32in dia. *Tring Mkt Auctions, Herts. Nov 02. £1,400.*

1291

Late George II walnut and feather banded chest, 107cm wide. *Wintertons Ltd, Lichfield. Nov 02. £1,400.*

1292

Set of eight Victorian carved mahogany balloon-backed chairs. *W & H Peacock, Bedford. July 03. £1,400.*

1293

Regency rosewood bergere armchair, stamped W Huxley. *Sworders, Stansted Mount-fitchet. Dec 02. £1,400.*

1294

Set of eight Georgian style dining chairs in mahogany. *Lots Road Auctions, Chelsea. May 03. £1,400.*

1295

Edwardian satinwood inlaid mahogany display cabinet, 45in wide. *Amersham Auction Rooms, Bucks. July 02. £1,400.*

1296

Edwardian satinwood/foliate inlaid corner display cabinet. *Rupert Toovey, Washington, Sussex. Feb 03. £1,400.*

1297

Geo. III oak country dresser, N Wales, c1800, associated open plate rack constructed partly from earlier elements, 197 x 166cm. *Rosebery's, London. Mar 02. £1,400.*

Hammer Price £1,400

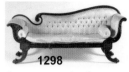

1298

Regency carved mahogany settee, 214cm. *Bristol Auction Rooms. July 03. £1,400.*

1299

Late Geo. III mahog. chest of small proportions, 33in wide. *Canterbury Auction Galleries, Kent. Dec 03. £1,400.*

1300

George III oak breakfront dresser base, 6ft. *Gorringes, Lewes. Dec 03. £1,400.*

1301

Late 19thC oak/crossbanded mahogany chest, 59in wide. *Amersham Auction Rooms, Bucks. Feb 04. £1,400.*

1302

Geo. III mahogany secretaire bookcase, 230 x 125cm. (top poss. associated). *Rosebery's, London. Sep 03. £1,400.*

1303

Oak enclosed dresser, 18thC and later, 74in wide. *Andrew Hartley, Ilkley. Apr 03. £1,400.*

1304

Victorian Sheraton revival satinwood side cabinet painted, decorated with classical medallions, swags and ribbons, 3ft 8in wide. *Gorringes, Bexhill. Nov 03. £1,400.*

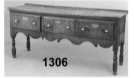

1305

Late 19thC Chinese daybed, black lacquered, figurative decoration, 201cm long. *Lots Road Auctions, Chelsea. Jan 04. £1,400.*

1306

Mid 18thC oak dresser base, replaced brass handles, 68in. *Gorringes, Lewes. Mar 04. £1,400.*

1307

Early Geo. III mahog. linen press, 50in wide. *A. Hartley, Ilkley. Feb 04. £1,400.*

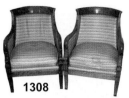

1308

Pair of 20thC Restoration style bergeres in mahogany. *Lots Road Auctions, Chelsea. Mar 04. £1,400.*

1309

George III mahogany bureau bookcase, astragal glazed doors, fitted interior, 41in wide. *Andrew Hartley, Ilkley. Feb 04. £1,400.*

1310

George III mahog. sofa table, 47in x 24in x 28in high. *Canterbury Auction Galleries, Kent. Feb 04. £1,400.*

1311

Late 18thC oak dresser base, moulded edge to two plank top, 78in wide, later 3 tier open front rack to back. *Canterbury Auc. Galleries, Kent. Feb 04. £1,400.*

1312

Regency rosewood breakfast table, 122cm dia. *Lots Road Auctions, Chelsea. Apr 04. £1,400.*

1313

17thC panelled oak chest in 2 sections, 38in wide. (later brass swan neck handles). *Canterbury Auc. Galleries, Kent. Feb 04. £1,400.*

1314

Side cabinet, Edwardian rosewood/marquetry, 258cm high. *Lots Road Auctions, Chelsea. Mar 03. £1,400.*

1315

Regency rosewood work table, boxwood line inlaid, 1ft 7in wide, 1ft 2in deep. *Gorringes, Bexhill. Mar 04. £1,400.*

1316

Victorian walnut 'Knitting' table, top veneered in burr walnut with candle branch to side, 15in dia. *Canterbury Auction Galleries, Kent. Feb 04. £1,400.*

Late 18thC oak dresser base with plain top, 65in wide. *Canterbury Auction Galleries, Kent. Feb 04. £1,400.*

Georgian mahog. bureau bookcase, 42in wide, 89in high. *Maxwells, Wilmslow. Sep 02. £1,400.*

Set 6 + 2 early 19thC mahog. chairs. *Lots Road Auctions, Chelsea. Nov 00. £1,380.*

Victorian figured mahogany linen press, 49in wide. *Dee, Atkinson & Harrison, Driffield. Apr 01. £1,350.*

19thC stained pine Orkney child's chair. *Diamond Mills, Felixstowe. Oct 01. £1,350.*

19thC giltwood, gesso over-mantel. *Lots Road Auctions, Chelsea. Sep 03 £1,350.*

The numbering system acts as a reader reference as well as linking to the Analysis of each Section

George III mahog. pembroke table, tulipwood crossbanding, 45 x 32 x 28in. *Hamptons, Godalming. Mar 02. £1,350.*

Vernis Martin display cabinet, veneered in rosewood, shaped marble top, gilt mounts, 27.5in wide. *Sworders, Stansted Mountfitchet. Apr 01. £1,350.*

Small walnut bow fronted chest, with a slide, 24in wide. *Sworders, Stansted Mountfitchet. Apr 01. £1,350.*

Regency rosewood games/work table, inlaid chequer board, fitted frieze drawer, turned wood handles, 22in wide. *Andrew Hartley, Ilkley. Dec 01. £1,350.*

Late George III mahogany sideboard, 140cm wide, 56cm deep. *Wintertons Ltd, Lichfield. Dec 01. £1,350.*

Set of 6 + 2 Georgian mahog. dining chairs, Sheraton type, drop in seats. *A. Hartley, Ilkley. Dec 03. £1,350.*

French 19thC kingwood bombé shaped side cupboard, 90cm. *Henry Adams, Chichester. July 02. £1,350.*

Hammer Prices £1,400-£1,350

Set 4 + 2 mid 19thC mahog. dining chairs, scrolled arms, upholstered in wine dralon. *Canterbury Auc. Galleries, Kent. Oct 02. £1,350.*

19thC figured walnut whatnot, inset mirror, 47in. *Canterbury Auction Galleries, Kent. Dec 03. £1,350.*

Edwardian mahogany display cabinet, label for Christopher Pratt, Bradford, 42in wide. *Andrew Hartley, Ilkley. June 03. £1,350.*

Mahog. bookcase of Georgian design, 39.25in wide. *Andrew Hartley, Ilkley. Dec 03. £1,350.*

Hammer Prices £1,350-£1,300

1334

Adzed oak serving table, 1932, 81in wide. A. Hartley, Ilkley. Dec 03. £1,350.

1335

William IV rosewood break-fast table, figured veneered top, triangular base, 50in dia. Canterbury Auc. Galleries, Kent. Feb 04. £1,350.

1336

Regency mahog. sideboard, central drawers over tambour slide door, 166.5cm wide. Sworders, Stansted Mount-fitchet. Feb 04. £1,350.

1337

Regency rosewood pier table, mirrored back, 89 x 95cm. Rosebery's, London. Mar 04. £1,350.

1338

George III figured mahogany & ebony strung small centre table. Bristol Auction Rooms, Bristol. Nov 01. £1,350.

1339

19thC rising side table, brown oak, poss. by W Smee & Sons, 47 x 21 x 45in. Hamptons, Godalming. Mar 02. £1,350.

1340

Regency beech framed and simulated rosewood chaise longue, 197cm. Cheffins, Cambridge. Oct 00. £1,300.

1341

Regency mahogany drop leaf table, 51 x 69in x 27in high. Dee, Atkinson & Harrison, Driffield. Dec 00. £1,300.

1342

Mid 19thC mahogany side cabinet of Adam design, 55in wide. Peter Wilson, Nantwich. Nov 00. £1,300.

1343

19thC mahogany linen press. G W Finn & Sons, Canterbury. Sep 00. £1,300.

1344

18thC oak settle, geometric carved back, down-swept arms terminating in lions heads, 53in wide. Gorringes, Lewes. Feb 01. £1,300.

1345

George III mahog. dressing chest of smaller proportions, 34in wide. Dockree's, Manchester. Feb 01. £1,300.

1346

George III mahog. bowfront chest of drawers, 92cm wide. Cheffins, Cambridge. Oct 00. £1,300.

1347

Late 19thC Dutch mahogany/satinwood marquetry dressing chest, 58in high, 38.5in wide. Amersham Auction Rooms, Bucks. Nov 02. £1,300.

1348

Early victorian set of seven mahogany chairs. Mervyn Carey, Tenterden. Dec 00. £1,300.

1349

George III mahog. cellarette, interior in four compartments, 19.25in wide. Andrew Hartley, Ilkley. Dec 00. £1,300.

1350

Late 18th/early 19thC carved giltwood wall mirror. Rupert Toovey, Washington, Sussex. Dec 03. £1,300.

1351

19thC French kingwood parquetry bombe commode, 34in wide. Wintertons Ltd, Lichfield. Sep 00. £1,300.

1352

Early Victorian mahogany wardrobe, stamped Gillows, Lancaster. (virtually unused condition). Hamptons, Godalming. Sep 02. £1,300.

1353

Pair of late 19thC specimen inlaid occasional tables. *Lots Road Auctions, Chelsea. Sep 01. £1,300.*

1354

Art Nouveau mahog./satinwood inlaid cabinet, c1910, 92cm wide. *Wintertons Ltd, Lichfield. Dec 01. £1,300.*

> The illustrations are in descending price order. The price range is indicated at the top of each page.

1355

19thC Chinese black lacquer work table. *Canterbury Auction Galleries, Kent. June 02. £1,300.*

1356

19thC French gilt framed four fold screen. *Canterbury Auction Galleries, Kent. June 02. £1,300.*

1357

Late 18thC oak dower chest with crossbanded decoration. *Amersham Auction Rooms, Bucks. Dec 01. £1,300.*

1358

Large three seater George Smith sofa in Howard style, tan leather and matching stool. *Lots Road Auctions, Chelsea. Mar 03. £1,300.*

1359

Regency rosewood chiffonier, 42in wide. *Amersham Auction Rms, Bucks. Aug 01. £1,300.*

1360

19thC French provincial buffet, cherrywood, walnut, 146cm wide. af. *Lots Road Auctions, Chelsea. Jan 03. £1,300.*

1361

19thC mahog. sofa table, wide satinwood banded, kingwood line top, one drawer stamped 3487, 94cm, restored. *Henry Adams, Chichester. Sep 02. £1,300.*

Hammer Price £1,300

1362

George III inlaid mahogany bowfront sideboard, 171cm. *Henry Adams, Chichester. Sep 02. £1,300.*

1363

George III mahogany butlers tray on a faux bamboo stand. *R. Wintertons, Burton on Trent, Staffs. Apr 02. £1,300.*

1364

Regency satinwood card table, inlaid crossbanding and decoration, 35 x 36in overall. *Clarke Gammon, Guildford. Oct 02. £1,300.*

1365

Regency hall bench, shaped back, painted with elephant coat of arms, 107cm wide. *Lots Road Auctions, Chelsea. Dec 02. £1,300.*

1366

18thC walnut commode, North Italy, 78cm wide. *Cheffins, Cambridge. Oct 00. £1,300.*

1367

George III mahog. kneehole desk , 2ft 9in. *Gorringes, Lewes. Oct 02. £1,300.*

1368

Antique oak box settle. *W & H Peacock, Bedford. Jan 03. £1,300.*

1369

Pair day beds, Empire style, gilt decorated, headboards carved eagle heads flanking rosette and anthemion decor above a drop-in mattress, 3ft wide. *Lots Road Auctions, Chelsea. Oct 00. £1,300.*

1370

Ladies Edwardian mahogany desk. *Louis Taylor, Stoke on Trent. June 02. £1,300.*

1371

Victorian Irish mahogany campaign secretaire chest, maker's label Ross & Co. Dublin, 39in wide. *Lots Road Auctions, Chelsea. Aug 01. £1,300.*

Hammer Prices £1,300-£1,250

1372

Victorian mahogany extending dining table, telescopic action to take 3 leaves, 270 x 120cm extended. Bristol Auction Rooms, Bristol. Sep 03. £1,300.

1373

French mirror. Lots Road Auctions, Chelsea. Oct 00. £1,300.

1374

Late Victorian aesthetic ebonized mahogany side cabinet on 8 feet, door inset with a painted panel on a gilt ground by R. J. Mackay, 69in wide. (Poss. Edwards and Roberts). Clarke Gammon, Guildford. Apr 04. £1,300.

1375

William IV mahogany framed caned bergere library chair, needlework cushion. Cheffins, Cambridge. Apr 04. £1,300.

1376

Victorian rosewood serving table with a white marble top, 168cm. Lots Road Auctions, Chelsea. Oct 03. £1,300.

1377

Late 19thC canape, painted and gilt heightened, upholstered in patterned covers, 145cm. Lots Road Auctions, Chelsea. Mar 04. £1,300.

1378

Victorian figured walnut serpentine top card table, 37in. Gorringes, Lewes. Jan 04. £1,300.

1379

Late 19thC Louis XV style, walnut card table, rotating foldover top, 36in wide. Amersham Auction Rooms, Bucks. June 03. £1,300.

1380

Victorian walnut pedestal desk, stamped W. Walker & Sons, Bunhill Row, London E.C. Lots Road Auctions, Chelsea. Mar 04. £1,300.

1381

Victorian walnut/ebonised credenza, inset Sevres style plaques, mirrored back, 5ft high. Gorringes, Bexhill. Sep 03. £1,300.

1382

Oak lambing chair, winged panelled back with waved top rail, 18thC. Andrew Hartley, Ilkley. Apr 03. £1,300.

1383

George III adjustable reading table, double ratcheted top, 2 candle slides, 2ft 3in. (by repute belonged to William Pitt the Younger). Gorringes, Lewes. Dec 03. £1,300.

1384

Set of 6 fine quality 18thC Dutch Queen Anne style splat back dining chairs. Denhams, Warnham. Aug 03. £1,300.

1385

Victorian gilt gesso overmantel mirror, (repainted) 1.7m wide x 1.85m high. Sworders, Stansted Mountfitchet. Feb 03. £1,300.

1386

17thC oak dresser, raised back, 61in. Denhams, Warnham. Oct 03. £1,300.

1387

Demi lune mahogany inlaid fold over card table. Kivell & Sons, Bude. Dec 02. £1,280.

1388

Pair early 19thC yew wood Windsor chairs. Hamptons, Godalming. Sep 01. £1,250.

1389

Victorian walnut davenport, 22in wide. Amersham Auction Rooms, Bucks. Nov 01. £1,250.

1390

French kingwood/marquetry commode, 19thC, 36in wide. Andrew Hartley, Ilkley. June 01. £1,250.

1391

19thC rosewood Sutherland table, 44in wide. A. Hartley, Ilkley. Dec 01. £1,250.

Prices quoted are hammer and exclude the buyer's premium. Adding 15% will give approx. buying price.

1392

Geo. III inlaid mahog. gentlemans wardrobe, a base drawer and 3 dummy drawers, 49in wide. Sworders, Stansted Mountfitchet. Apr 01. £1,250.

1393

George III mahogany chest on chest, lacking a cornice, secretaire drawer, with Victorian ebonised knobs, 98cm wide. Peter Wilson, Nantwich. Nov 01. £1,250.

1394

George III mahogany mule chest, 63in wide x 30in high. Sworders, Stansted Mountfitchet. Apr 01. £1,250.

1395

William & Mary inlaid walnut chest of drawers, later handles and bracket feet, 36.5in wide. Sworders, Stansted Mountfitchet. Apr 01. £1,250.

1396

Georgian III mahogany bow front chest of drawers, 41in wide. Sworders, Stansted Mountfitchet. Apr 01. £1,250.

1397

Chippendale design mahog. silver table, 19thC, 28 x 20in. af. Sworders, Stansted Mountfitchet. Apr 01. £1,250.

1398

Geo. III oak corner cupboard banded in mahogany, 79cm wide. Peter Wilson, Nantwich. July 02. £1,250.

Hammer Price £1,250

1399

19thC mahog. salon suite: sofa, 2 armchairs, 4 side chairs. Locke & England, Leamington Spa. July 03. £1,250.

1400

Late Regency period mahog. stool, 38 x 18in approx. Diamond Mills & Co, Felixstowe. Oct 01. £1,250.

1401

Set 4 + 2 George I design walnut dining chairs. Gorringes, Lewes. Sep 02. £1,250.

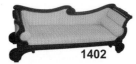

1402

William IV mahogany sofa, 242cm. Lots Road Auctions, Chelsea. Sep 02. £1,250.

1403

Oak monk's bench, hinged plank top on shaped arms raised on turned columnar supports, moulded edged hinged seat, 17thC and later, 27.25in wide. A. Hartley, Ilkley. June 02. £1,250.

1404

Geo. III mahog. tilt top table, 30in dia. Sworders, Stansted Mountfitchet. July 01. £1,250.

1405

18thC figured walnut desk, 76cm. (later top). Henry Adams, Chichester. July 02. £1,250.

1406

George III mahog. dressing chest, 40in wide. Amersham Auction Rooms, Bucks. May 02. £1,250.

1407

Victorian carved mahogany standing corner cupboard, 31.5in wide. Andrew Hartley, Ilkley. Aug 03. £1,250.

Hammer Prices £1,250-£1,200

1408

19thC mahog. bookcase, 51in wide. *Fellows & Sons, Hockley, B'ham. July 03. £1,250.*

1409

French mirror. *Lots Road, Chelsea. Oct 00. £1,250.*

1410

17thC oak chest of drawers. (alterations). *Rupert Toovey, Washington, Sussex. Oct 03. £1,250.*

1411

19thC mahog. secretaire book-case, associated top, 105cm wide. af. *Lambert & Foster, Tenterden. Aug 03. £1,250.*

1412

George IV mahogany library armchair, c1830, cane back and seat with scroll leafy armrests. *Wintertons Ltd, Lichfield. Jan 04. £1,250.*

1413

William IV mahog. breakfast table, 3ft 2in. *Gorringes, Lewes. Jan 04. £1,250.*

1414

Early Victorian figured mahogany linen press, 148cm wide. *Bristol Auction Rooms, Bristol. Jan 04. £1,250.*

1415

19thC Italian giltwood wall mirror, 48 x 26in overall. *Canterbury Auc. Galleries, Kent. Oct 01. £1,250.*

1416

Regency rosewood canterbury, 50 x 41cm. (one finial missing). *Sworders, Stansted Mount-fitchet. Feb 04. £1,250.*

1417

19thC rosewood chiffonier, mirrored back, plinth base, 130cm. *Sworders, Stansted-Mountfitchet. Feb 04. £1,250.*

1418

Victorian mahogany library table. *W & H Peacock, Bedford. Mar 03. £1,250.*

1419

William IV mahogany break-front bookcase, adjustable shelves, 183cm. *Sworders, Stansted Mountfitchet. Mar 04. £1,250.*

1420

George II mahogany chest of small proportions, brushing slide, 31in wide. (splits to top and later brass handles). *Canterbury Auc. Galleries, Kent. Feb 04. £1,250.*

1421

Set of six mahogany George IV period sabre legged dining chairs. *Dockree's, Manchester. Sep 00. £1,200.*

1422

Maple & Co. oak surprise table. *Ambrose, Loughton. Jan 01. £1,200.*

1423

Edwardian satinwood elbow chair, shield back, centred by Prince of Wales feathers. *Andrew Hartley, Ilkley. Feb 01. £1,200.*

1424

Geo. III mahogany demi-lune card table, 38in wide. *Andrew Hartley, Ilkley. Oct 00. £1,200.*

1425

French quartetto tables, brass edging. *Lots Road Auctions, Chelsea. Sep 00. £1,200.*

1426

Geo. III mahogany bureau, enclosing pigeon holes, drawers and replacement green tooled leather writing surface. *Wintertons Ltd, Lichfield. Feb 01. £1,200.*

1427

Victorian walnut games table, rotating foldover top, 36in. *Amersham Auction Rooms, Bucks. June 01. £1,200.*

The numbering system acts as a reader reference as well as linking to the Analysis of each Section

1428

Georgian and later dresser. *Lots Road Auctions, Chelsea. Oct 00. £1,200.*

1429

George I oak library alcove bookcase, 130cm wide, 278cm high. *Cheffins, Cambridge. Oct 00. £1,200.*

1430

Early 19thC burr satinwood top Sutherland tea table, 39in wide. *Clevedon Salerooms, Bristol. June 01. £1,200.*

1431

Victorian rosewood veneered bookcase, 53in wide x 92in high. *Wintertons Ltd, Lichfield. May 01. £1,200.*

1432

Large 16thC oak linen fold panel coffer, 29cm high. (repairs and restoration). *Hamptons, Godalming. July 01. £1,200.*

1433

Georgian mahogany corner serving cabinet, 64in wide x 36.5in deep. *Hamptons, Godalming. Sep 01. £1,200.*

1434

Early 18thC North European fruitwood and walnut side table, 89.5cm wide. *Cheffins, Cambridge. Oct 00. £1,200.*

Hammer Price £1,200

1435

George III mahog. Pembroke table, satinwood crossbanding and stringing, 33in. *Andrew Hartley, Ilkley. Apr 01. £1,200.*

1436

19thC mahogany work table, kidney shaped with stringing and gilt metal mounts, 22.5in wide. *Andrew Hartley, Ilkley. Feb 01. £1,200.*

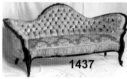

1437

Late Victorian walnut sofa, 76in wide overall. *Dockree's, Manchester. Feb 01. £1,200.*

1438

Victorian walnut card table. *Eastbourne Auction Rooms, Sussex. Mar 02. £1,200.*

1439

Venetian looking glass (mirror), engraved plates and mounted flower detail, 88in high. *Lots Road Auctions, Chelsea. Apr 01. £1,200.*

1440

Pr. 19thC mahog. stools, floral needlework drop in seats, 16in high. *Amersham Auction Rooms, Bucks. Apr 02. £1,200.*

1441

William IV rosewood centre table, two end drawers, octagonal stem with saltire platform and rounded feet, 4ft 3in x 2ft 3in. *Gorringes, Lewes. Feb 01. £1,200.*

1442

Mid Victorian mahogany military chest in two parts, 115 x 107cm. *Rosebery's, London. Mar 02. £1,200.*

1443

Edwardian strung and inlaid mahogany side cabinet, 34in wide. *Sworders, Stansted Mountfitchet. Apr 01. £1,200.*

1444

Pair of late George III cream & green painted elbow chairs, overstuffed seats. *Hamptons, Godalming. Mar 02. £1,200.*

Hammer Price £1,200

1445

Oak livery cupboard, moulded edged plank top over lunette carved frieze, panelled fascia with central door, 17thC, 38.5in wide. *Andrew Hartley, Ilkley. June 02. £1,200.*

1446

Set 4 + 2 Chippendale style mahogany dining chairs. *Gorringes, Bexhill. Oct 02. £1,200.*

1447

Late Georgian mahogany chest, 88cm wide. *Locke & England, Leamington Spa. Jan 03. £1,200.*

1448

Set 8 Louis XVI style dining chairs. *Lots Road Auctions, Chelsea. Oct 02. £1,200.*

1449

Early Victorian rosewood five tier shelf unit, 72in wide. *Canterbury Auc. Galleries, Kent. Aug 03. £1,200.*

1450

19th/early 20thC mahogany partner's desk, 183 x 120cm. *Henry Adams, Chichester. Jan 03. £1,200.*

1451

William III oak chest, c1700, 94cm wide. *Wintertons Ltd, Lichfield. Jan 03. £1,200.*

1452

19thC Italian bureau, blue painted with landscape, 83cm wide. *Lots Road Auctions, Chelsea. Feb 03. £1,200.*

1453

Victorian mahogany hall bench, stamped Gillow, 87cm wide. *Lots Road Auctions, Chelsea. May 03. £1,200.*

1454

Late Victorian mahogany revolving bookcase. *Lots Road Auctions, Chelsea. Jan 03. £1,200.*

1455

Aesthetic oak and ebonised bookcase, 126cm wide. *Sworders, Stansted Mountfitchet. July 03. £1,200.*

1456

Panelled oak press cupboard, 18thC, 60.5in wide. *A. Hartley, Ilkley. Feb 03. £1,200.*

1457

Regency mahogany secretaire bookcase, 105cm wide. *Bristol Auction Rooms, Bristol. Apr 03. £1,200.*

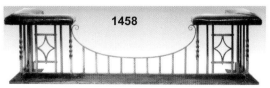

1458

Late Victorian copper and leather upholstered club fender, c1900, 61cm high, 225cm wide. *Wintertons Ltd, Lichfield. Mar 03. £1,200.*

1459

Regency rosewood card table, foldover top, 36in wide. *Amersham Auction Rooms, Bucks. Mar 03. £1,200.*

1460

Regency mahogany sideboard of D shaped form, 3ft 6in wide. *Gorringes, Bexhill. July 03. £1,200.*

1461

Geo. III mahog. tripod table, figured top above bird-cage block, 21 x 28.5in. *Hamptons, Godalming. Nov 01. £1,200.*

1462

Small Georgian mahogany bow fronted sideboard, 39cm. *Fellows & Sons, Hockley, Birmingham. July 03. £1,200.*

1463

19thC French looking glass (mirror) in giltwood and gesso, with a laurel wreath cresting, 41 x 68in. Lots Road Auctions, Chelsea. July 01. £1,200.

1464

Set of 6 George I style walnut leather upholstered armchairs. Rosebery's, London. Sep 03. £1,200.

The illustrations are in descending price order. The price range is indicated at the top of each page.

1465

William IV rosewood breakfast table, top banded in burr maple, 4ft dia. Gorringes, Bexhill. Sep 03. £1,200.

1466

Edwardian mahog. and inlaid bowfront display cabinet, length 46.5in. Fellows & Sons, Hockley, Birmingham. Oct 03. £1,200.

1467

Sheraton mahog./crossbanded drum top table, 4 real and 4 dummy drawers, 3ft. Gorringes, Lewes. Dec 03. £1,200.

1468

Pair Louis XVI style giltwood open armchairs, 19thC. Bristol Auction Rooms, Bristol. Dec 03. £1,200.

1469

William IV mahog. drop leaf dining table, 2 leaves, 1.14 x 1.28m extended. Sworders, Stansted Mountfitchet. Feb 04. £1,200.

1470

Victorian walnut credenza, glazed doors, 136 x 106cm. Sworders, Stansted Mountfitchet. Feb 04. £1,200.

1471

Late 18thC rosewood cross banded mahogany two flap writing and work table. Mervyn Carey, Tenterden. Nov 03. £1,200.

1472

Victorian burr walnut piano davenport, metamorphic stationery compartment, fitted interior, 3ft high. Gorringes, Bexhill. Feb 04. £1,200.

1473

Set of three 19thC Dutch marquetry dining chairs and a similar chair. Gorringes, Lewes. Jan 04. £1,200.

1474

Set 7 + 1 mahogany dining chairs, 19th/early 20thC Chippendale revival design. Richard Wintertons, Burton on Trent. Feb 04. £1,200.

1475

Set 6 + 2 early 20thC oak framed chairs, overstuffed green leather seats. Amersham Auction Rooms, Bucks. Nov 03. £1,200.

1476

Late 19thC rosewood/floral marquetry writing table, brass bound serpentine top, 2ft 3in. Gorringes, Lewes. Mar 04. £1,200.

1477

Regency mahogany dumb waiter. Sworders, Stansted Mountfitchet. Feb 04. £1,200.

1478

Oak chest of drawers, late 17thC, quarter veneered and crossbanded top, on sliders, parquetry inlay. Richard Wintertons, Burton on Trent. Apr 04. £1,200.

1479

George III mahogany three tier dumb waiter, graduated tiers with raised lid, 123 x 60cm. Rosebery's, London. Mar 04. £1,200.

Hammer Prices £1,200-£1,150

1480

Victorian giltwood and gesso overmantel (mirror). *Lots Road Auctions, Chelsea. Sep 03. £1,200.*

1481

Regency rosewood card table, swivelling top, beechwood column, 92cm wide. *Sworders, Stansted Mount-fitchet. Feb 04. £1,200.*

1482

Early 18thC oak serving base of small proportion, plank top one long drawer, supported on wavy legs, 38.75in wide. *Tring Market Auctions, Herts. May 02. £1,180.*

1483

Set 6 + 2 Edwardian George III style satinwood dining chairs, upholstered seats. *Tring Market Auctions, Herts. Sep 02. £1,180.*

1484

Le Corbusier sofa, black leather, chromed tubular steel supports. *Lots Road Auctions, Chelsea. July 01. £1,150.*

1485

19thC ebonised credenza with brass, string inlay and gilt metal mounts, 85in wide. *Amersham Auction Rooms, Bucks. June 01. £1,150.*

1486

19thC walnut pier cabinet, green marble top, 30.5in wide. *Andrew Hartley, Ilkley. Dec 00. £1,150.*

1487

Sheraton Revival mahog. sideboard. *Peter Wilson, Nantwich. Nov 01. £1,150.*

1488

Victorian walnut loo table, quarter veneered and banded tip up top with parquetry and stringing & central marquetry floral motif. *Andrew Hartley. Ilkley. Oct 01. £1,150.*

1489

19thC figured walnut work & games table by Robert Rough, Cabinet Maker & Upholsterer, Opposite The Mansion House, London, 22.5in wide. *Canterbury Auc. Galleries, Kent. Aug 02. £1,150.*

1490

Edwardian Sheraton revival painted satinwood pembroke table, 79.5cm wide. *Bristol Auc. Rooms. Dec 01. £1,150.*

1491

Victorian teak linen press. *Lambert & Foster, Tenterden. Oct 01. £1,150.*

1492

Victorian rosewood whatnot. *Louis Taylor, Stoke on Trent. Mar 02. £1,150.*

1493

George IV mahog. occasional table, 24 x 18 x 28.5in high. *Canterbury Auc. Galleries, Kent. Aug 02. £1,150.*

1494

Well carved Victorian walnut parlour suite, viz: 3 seat bench, 2 corner chairs and a stool. *Sworders, Stansted Mountfitchet. Apr 01. £1,150.*

1495

Geo. III mahog. bow fronted corner cupboard, 29in wide, 43in high. *Andrew Hartley, Ilkley. Feb 01. £1,150.*

1496

Art Deco burr walnut dining suite, 4 chairs, table, sideboard, table measures 6ft long, 3ft wide. *Sworders, Stansted Mountfitchet. Apr 01. £1,150.*

1497

Edwardian mahogany/inlaid linen press with satinwood banding throughout, 215 x 136cm. *Rosebery's, London. Mar 02. £1,150.*

1498

Edwardian rosewood cylinder bureau, 30.75in wide. *Andrew Hartley, Ilkley. Dec 00. £1,150.*

1499

Arts & Crafts oak desk, 39in wide. *Andrew Hartley, Ilkley. Oct 00. £1,150.*

1500

Victorian walnut swivel top fold over card table, 36in. *Dee, Atkinson & Harrison, Driffield. Sep 00. £1,150.*

1501

Geo. III mahog. bow-fronted sideboard, 67in overall. *Dockree's, Manchester. Feb 01. £1,150.*

1502

Regency rosewood jardinière stand. (Poor condition). *Lots Road Auctions, Chelsea. Nov 03. £1,150.*

1503

Early 18thC japanned and painted hanging corner cupboard with scene of a king on a throne, 19.5in wide. *Tring Market Auctions, Herts. Nov 03. £1,150.*

1504

Oak open dresser, pierced brass drop handles, 77.25in wide. *Andrew Hartley, Ilkley. Feb 04. £1,150.*

> Prices quoted are hammer and exclude the buyer's premium. Adding 15% will give approx. buying price.

1505

George III mahog. open front dwarf bookcase, 37in wide. *Canterbury Auc. Galleries, Kent. Feb 04. £1,150.*

1506

Mid 19thC mahog. wardrobe, 188 x 136cm. *Rosebery's, London. Mar 04. £1,150.*

1507

19thC Pembroke table, satinwood and banded with exotic woods, 112cm extended. *Lots Road Auctions, Chelsea. Oct 02. £1,150.*

1508

Regency mahog. side cabinet. *Eastbourne Auction Rooms, Sussex. Apr 04. £1,150.*

1509

17thC panelled oak chest in 2 sections, plain top, 40in wide. *Canterbury Auc. Galleries, Kent. Feb 04. £1,150.*

1510

Early Victorian mahogany cabinet bookcase, 41in wide. *Amersham Auction Rooms, Bucks. Aug 02. £1,150.*

1511

Victorian walnut loo table, 60in wide. *Andrew Hartley, Ilkley. Feb 04. £1,150.*

1512

George III walnut chequer strung miniature bureau. *Biddle & Webb, Birmingham. May 02. £1,120.*

1513

Set of Edwardian mahogany quartetto tables, satinwood stringing, 19.75in wide. *Andrew Hartley, Ilkley. Oct 00. £1,100.*

1514

Antique giltwood stool with green dralon upholstered top on 4 George I design cabriole legs, 1ft 9in. (legs possibly from a settee). *Gorringes, Lewes. Feb 01. £1,100.*

1515

Edwardian inlaid mahogany quartetto, 21in wide. *Dee, Atkinson & Harrison, Driffield. Dec 00. £1,100.*

Hammer Price £1,100

1516

George III mahogany bureau, 37in wide. *Wintertons Ltd, Lichfield. Mar 01. £1,100.*

1517

Victorian walnut games table, folding top, central marquetry, 28in wide. *Amersham Auction Rms, Bucks. Mar 01. £1,100.*

1518

Pair of William IV mahogany library chairs. *Cheffins, Cambridge. Oct 00. £1,100.*

1519

Mid 19thC mahog. military dressing chest, 36in wide. *Amersham Auction Rooms, Bucks. Mar 01. £1,100.*

1520

George III style oak dresser, 6ft long. *Sworders, Stansted Mountfitchet. Mar 01. £1,100.*

1521

Late 19thC French mahog. and kingwood 2-tier etagere, 2ft 7in. *Gorringes, Lewes. Sep 00. £1,100.*

1522

Early 19thC rosewood console table, 30in wide. *Dockree's, Manchester. Feb 01. £1,100.*

1523

William IV rosewood library table. *Rosebery's, London. Sep 01. £1,100.*

1524

Early 19thC mahog. library table, 39in wide. *Dockree's, Manchester. Feb 01. £1,100.*

1525

Geo. III mahog. linen press, 49in wide. *Hamptons, Godalming. Nov 01. £1,100.*

1526

19thC Dutch mahogany jardiniere, detachable brass liner, 15in wide. *A. Hartley, Ilkley. Feb 01. £1,100.*

1527

George III mahogany traytop commode with frieze drawer, cupboard and base drawer, 1ft 10in. *Gorringes, Lewes. Oct 01. £1,100.*

1528

Queen Anne herringbone banded figured walnut chest on stand, 105cm wide. *Bristol Auction Rooms. Dec 01. £1,100.*

1529

Victorian inlaid rosewood side cabinet, 54in wide. *Sworders, Stansted Mountfitchet. Apr 01. £1,100.*

1530

Geo. III mahogany, drop leaf table. *Lots Road Auctions, Chelsea. Apr 02. £1,100.*

1531

Victorian walnut framed three piece salon suite, sofa 74in wide, 2 arm chairs. *Andrew Hartley, Ilkley. Apr 02. £1,100.*

1532

19thC East European painted pine armoire, 4ft. *Gorringes, Lewes. Mar 01. £1,100.*

1533

George II fruitwood bureau, 35in wide. *Clarke Gammon, Guildford. Apr 02. £1,100.*

1534

Victorian walnut and floral marquetry work table, hinged lid revealing fitted interior, tripod base. *Andrew Hartley, Ilkley. Feb 02. £1,100.*

1535

Geo. III mahog. dumb waiter.
three tiers. Gorringes, Lewes.
July 02. £1,100.

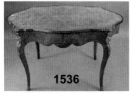

1536

19thC French inlaid walnut
bureau plat, gilt metal mounts
and a single frieze drawer,
48in long. Sworders, Stansted
Mountfitchet. July 01. £1,100.

The numbering system acts
as a reader reference as
well as linking to the
Analysis of each Section

1537

Edward VII Sheraton Revival
painted satinwood bureau,
crossbanded and line inlaid,
medallion of a young woman
to the flap, 69cm wide.
Mellors & Kirk, Nottingham.
Sep 03. £1,100.

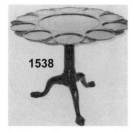

1538

Antique mahog. supper table,
ten sunken wells and carved
shells between, on a fluted
column with bird-cage, 36in
dia. Lambert & Foster,
Tenterden. Dec 02. £1,100.

1539

Pair of Victorian Sheraton
Revival armchairs.
Lots Road Auctions, Chelsea.
Nov 02. £1,100.

1540

Late 19th/early 20thC
bergere sofa, 182cm wide.
Lots Road Auctions, Chelsea.
Feb 03. £1,100.

1541

Early 18thC oak mule chest,
two short drawers and with a
wire hinged cover, 50.5in
wide. Tring Market Auctions,
Herts. Sep 02. £1,100.

1542

Victorian walnut framed
parlour sofa, padded back
and arms, overstuffed seat,
73in wide. Andrew Hartley,
Ilkley. Oct 02. £1,100.

1543

Geo. III mahogany bow front
hanging corner cupboard,
31in wide. Tring Mkt Auctions,
Herts. Nov 02. £1,100.

Hammer Price £1,100

1544

Victorian satinwood string
inlaid walnut pier cabinet,
gilt metal mounts, 32in wide.
Amersham Auction Rooms,
Bucks. July 02. £1,100.

1545

Late 18thC/19thC satinwood
inlaid demi-lune tea table,
30in wide. Amersham Auction
Rms, Bucks. Aug 02. £1,100.

1546

Victorian carved walnut
double chair back settee with
open work back and buttoned
upholstery, 1.78m wide.
Sworders, Stansted Mount-
fitchet. July 03. £1,100.

1547

Queen Anne style burr walnut
bureau bookcase. Gorringes,
Bexhill. Dec 02. £1,100.

1548

George III mahogany card
table, 3ft 6in wide. Gorringes,
Bexhill. Mar 03. £1,100.

1549

Arts & Crafts oak chemist
cabinet, 13 handles missing,
117 x 112cm. Sworders,
Stansted Mountfitchet.
Mar 03. £1,100.

1550

Victorian brass half-tester
bed. Mellors & Kirk,
Nottingham. Feb 03. £1,100.

1551

19thC mahogany telescopic
dining table, 2 leaves, Gillows
style supports, 240 x 120cm
extended. Bristol Auction
Rooms. Sep 03. £1,100.

1552

19thC Milanese centre table,
ebonised and ivory inlaid.
Lots Road Auctions, Chelsea.
May 02. £1,100.

Hammer Prices £1,100-£1,050

Early 20thC mahogany framed bergere suite: settee and two armchairs. *Amersham Auction Rooms, Bucks. Oct 03. £1,100.*

17th/18thC elm stick and rail back carver chair with solid seat. *Denhams, Warnham. Oct 03. £1,100.*

17thC oak chest, turned fruitwood handles, escutcheons in brass, 3ft 1in. *Gorringes, Lewes. Jan 04. £1,100.*

Pair of fauteuils, late 19thC/early 20thC painted and gilt. *Lots Road Auctions, Chelsea. Mar 04. £1,100.*

Oak dresser, 17thC and later, 4ft 7in wide. *Gorringes, Bexhill. Mar 04. £1,100.*

Set of six Victorian mahog. dining chairs, upholstered leather, serpentine seats. *Dee, Atkinson & Harrison, Driffield. Mar 04. £1,100.*

Edwardian mahogany display cabinet, 49.75in wide, 72.5in high. *Andrew Hartley, Ilkley. Feb 04. £1,100.*

19thC Continental carved oak armoire, 4ft 10in wide. *Sworders, Stansted Mountfitchet. July 01. £1,100.*

George III mahog. wine table, replaced turned ebonised stem on period tripod, 1ft 2in. *Gorringes, Lewes. Mar 04. £1,100.*

Painted metal tray top side table, attributed to Tom Parr of Colefax and Fowler, 84cm wide. *Cheffins, Cambridge. Apr 04. £1,100.*

George III oak linen press. *Rupert Toovey, Washington, Sussex. Oct 03. £1,100.*

Victorian bow fronted mahog. chest of drawers. *Sworders, Stansted Mountfitchet. Apr 01. £1,080.*

Geo. III mahog. butler's tray, hinged sides, pierced carrying handles, trestle base, 26in wide. *Tring Market Auctions, Herts. May 02. £1,080.*

George III oak lowboy. *Tring Market Auctions, Herts. Jan 02. £1,050.*

Pair of Aubusson covered fauteuil. *Lots Road Auctions, Chelsea. Nov 00. £1,050.*

Ash kitchen cupboard. *Hamptons, Marlborough. Mar 00. £1,050.*

Victorian davenport, walnut with line and foliate inlays, lidded gallery, writing slides to either side with four side drawers. *Lots Road Auctions, Chelsea. June 01. £1,050.*

Victorian walnut teapoy, fitted interior with pr. of glass bowls and a pair of oval caddies, 20in wide. *Andrew Hartley, Ilkley. Feb 01. £1,050.*

George I walnut wine cooler, three cast gilt metal handles, 12in dia. (restoration required) *Tring Market Auctions, Herts. Mar 02. £1,050.*

Mahogany fold over tea table, c1830, D shaped swivel top, 36in long. *Peter Wilson, Nantwich. Nov 01. £1,050.*

Early 20thC mahogany pedestal desk, 5ft x 3ft 5in. *Sworders, Stansted Mountfitchet. Apr 01. £1,050.*

William IV mahog. tea table, swivel top banded in rosewood with brass line inlay, 36in wide. *Peter Wilson, Nantwich. Nov 01. £1,050.*

Art Nouveau mahog. display cabinet, inlaid in coloured woods with fruiting trees and branches, labelled 'Maples', 60in long. *Peter Wilson, Nantwich. Nov 01. £1,050.*

George III set six elm dining chairs, panel seats. *A. Hartley, Ilkley. June 02. £1,050.*

Victorian flame mahogany cylindrical pot cupboard,. *Rosebery's, London. Mar 02. £1,050.*

19thC sofa cream painted and parcel gilt, 58cm wide. *Lots Road Auctions, Chelsea. Nov 02. £1,050.*

The illustrations are in descending price order. The price range is indicated at the top of each page.

Edwardian bonheur du jour, sliding centre section, green leather writing surface and stationery well, 25.5in wide, stamped Jas. Shoolbred & Co. *Andrew Hartley, Ilkley. Feb 02. £1,050.*

19thC mahog. breakfast table, 131cm wide. *Lots Road Auctions, Chelsea. Nov 02. £1,050.*

Hammer Price £1,050

George III mahog. draughtsman's table, 34in, af. *Sworders, Stansted Mountfitchet. July 01. £1,050.*

Hepplewhite period mahog. serpentine tea table, 3ft wide. *Mervyn Carey, Tenterden. July 02. £1,050.*

Pair of mid 19thC Continental mahogany upholstered library chairs. *Tring Market Auctions, Herts. Sep 02. £1,050.*

Commode, 19thC French rosewood, inset marble top, 51in wide. *Lots Road Auctions, Chelsea. Mar 01. £1,050.*

Regency mahog. card table, 35in. *Lots Road Auctions, Chelsea. Jan 02. £1,050.*

George III mahogany chest on chest with slide, 103cm. *Henry Adams, Chichester. Sep 02. £1,050.*

19thC Biedermeier mahogany cylinder bureau, 110cm wide. *Thos Mawer & Son, Lincoln. Nov 02. £1,050.*

19thC mahog. breakfast table, segment veneered tilt top, 137cm. *Lots Road Auctions, Chelsea. Feb 03. £1,050.*

George IV oak and mahogany crossbanded bookcase, prob. Welsh, 122cm. *Wintertons Ltd, Lichfield. Sep 02. £1,050.*

Hammer Prices £1,050-£1,000

1590

Edwardian mahogany inlaid cylinder writing desk, hinged to reveal drawers and pigeon holes, sliding leather inset, 107cm. Sworders, Stansted Mountfitchet. Feb 04. £1,050.

1591

Victorian mahogany display cabinet, carved with foliate panels and floral swags, 90.5in high. Andrew Hartley, Ilkley. Dec 03. £1,050.

1592

Regency rosewood and brass inlaid card table, 35.75in wide. Andrew Hartley, Ilkley. June 03. £1,050.

1593

Edwardian mahog. satinwood inlaid desk, rising cylinder front, 33in wide. Amersham Auction Rooms, Bucks. Sep 03. £1,050.

1594

19thC Venetian giltwood wall mirror, floral swags, original plate, 99cm. Rosebery's, London. Dec 03. £1,050.

1595

Victorian figured mahogany linen press, 146cm wide. Bristol Auction Rooms, Bristol. Jan 04. £1,050.

1596

Edwardian satinwood display cabinet, walnut veneers, rosewood banding, glazed doors, 183 x 130cm. Rosebery's, London. Mar 04. £1,050.

1597

Edwardian mahogany kidney shaped writing table, stamped Howard & Sons Ltd, Berners St., top inset with red leather panel, 54in wide. Gorringes, Bexhill. June 03. £1,050.

1598

Victorian walnut button back armchair and matching nursing chair. John Taylors, Louth. Jan 04. £1,050.

1599

Queen Anne walnut chest, quarter veneered top with herringbone banding, 87 x 100cm. Rosebery's, London. Mar 04. £1,050.

1600

Early 20thC Boudoir suite, limed maple. Dressing table, bijouterie table and a pair of bergeres, table 150cm wide. Lots Road Auctions, Chelsea. Jan 03. £1,050.

1601

Small size George III mahogany chest, brushing slide. Lots Road Auctions, Chelsea. Mar 03. £1,050.

1602

George III mahogany tray top commode, 24in wide. Tring Market Auctions, Herts. Mar 03. £1,050.

1603

Victorian mahogany three tier buffet, 48in wide. Peter Wilson, Nantwich. Nov 00. £1,040.

1604

Mid 19thC stained oak settle, 76in wide. Peter Wilson, Nantwich. Nov 00. £1,020.

1605

19thC kingwood/tulipwood inlaid vitrine, 33in wide. af. Lots Road Auctions, Chelsea. Apr 01. £1,000.

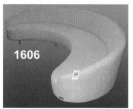

1606

Fendi Sloan sofa, crescent form upholstered in light ecru chenille. Lots Road Auctions, Chelsea. July 01. £1,000.

1607

Regency mahogany Empire style washstand, 32.5in wide. Wintertons Ltd, Lichfield. Nov 00. £1,000.

1608

Harlequin set of 10 + 2 Queen Ann style dining chairs. *Lambert & Foster, Tenterden. June 01. £1,000.*

1609

Set 12 beechwood ladderback dining chairs, rush seats on turned stretchered legs. *Lots Road Auctions, Chelsea. Aug 01. £1,000.*

Prices quoted are hammer and exclude the buyer's premium. Adding 15% will give approx. buying price.

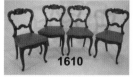

1610

Set four Victorian rosewood carved balloon backed dining chairs on French cabriole supports. *W & H Peacock, Bedford. July 02. £1,000.*

1611

Georgian mahog. bow front chest on chest, 103cm. *Locke & England, Leamington Spa. May 03. £1,000.*

1612

Pair of 17thC style wing chairs, covered in a cream gold silk damask. *Hamptons, Godalming. Sep 01. £1,000.*

1613

Wing armchair, c1900, George II style. *Lots Road Auctions, Chelsea. Nov 01. £1,000.*

1614

Early 18thC oak and walnut veneered chest on stand, 39in wide. *Amersham Auction Rooms, Bucks. Dec 01. £1,000.*

1615

Early 20thC satinwood/ebony inlaid mahogany bureau bookcase, 36in wide. *Amersham Auction Rooms, Bucks. June 01. £1,000.*

Hammer Price £1,000

1616

Titmarsh and Goodwin oak desk, 47in wide. *Amersham Auction Rooms, Bucks. Nov 01. £1,000.*

1617

Pair of Regency mahog. hall chairs, scallop swagged scroll backs, solid seats. *Gorringes, Lewes. Dec 00. £1,000.*

1618

Victorian rosewood card table, rotating, fold over top, 36in wide. *Amersham Auction Rooms, Bucks. Feb 02. £1,000.*

1619

Edwardian satinwood/inlaid desk. *Lots Road Auctions, Chelsea. Apr 02. £1,000.*

1620

Set of 8 1920s Hepplewhite style mahogany dining chairs. *Amersham Auction Rooms, Bucks. Feb 02. £1,000.*

1621

George III mahogany sideboard. *W & H Peacock, Bedford. Dec 02. £1,000.*

1622

William IV rosewood sideboard, 191cm wide. *Lots Road Auctions, Chelsea. June 02. £1,000.*

1623

Geo. I oak chest of drawers, 34in wide. *Hamptons, Godalming. Nov 01. £1,000.*

1624

19thC burr walnut bureau. *Lots Road Auctions, Chelsea. Aug 01. £1,000.*

1625

Mahog. side cabinet, Regency and later. *Lots Road Auctions, Chelsea. May 02. £1,000.*

Hammer Price £1,000

1626

Pair 20thC Bergeres painted in Louis XVI style. *Lots Road Auctions, Chelsea. Nov 02. £1,000.*

1627

Regency mahogany pedestal sideboard by Gillows of Lancaster, 70in wide. (back gallery deficient). *Gorringes, Bexhill. June 03. £1,000.*

1628

19thC walnut framed chaise longue, button upholstered back, 79in wide. *A. Hartley, Ilkley. Feb 03. £1,000.*

1629

19thC walnut and amboyna veneered marquetry foldover card table, 36in wide, 30in high. *Tring Market Auctions, Herts. Nov 02. £1,000.*

1630

George III tray top commode, shaped galleried edge cut out with handle holes, tambour front and converted lower drawer, ovolo moulded legs, 51 x 46 x 74cm. *Hamptons, Godalming. July 02. £1,000.*

1631

Oak lambing chair, late 18th/ early 19thC, 42.5in high. *Andrew Hartley, Ilkley. June 02. £1,000.*

1632

Victorian giltwood/gesso overmantel mirror, 83in x 62in wide. *Lots Road Auctions, Chelsea. Apr 00. £1,000.*

1633

Late 19thC French Louis XV style ebonized boulle serpentine card table, 36 x 35in. *Clarke Gammon, Guildford. Sep 02. £1,000.*

1634

Edwardian mahog. boxwood and ebony line inlaid display cabinet, 4ft 3in. *Gorringes, Bexhill. July 02. £1,000.*

1635

Regency giltwood looking glass, later plate, ebonised reeded slip and sphere decorated frame, 38in. *Lots Road Auctions, Chelsea. Nov 01. £1,000.*

1636

19thC Dutch walnut and marquetry cylinder bureau, 2ft 10in. *Gorringes, Bexhill. Sep 02. £1,000.*

1637

George III mahogany/brass bound cellarette, fitted with carrying handles. *Rosebery's, London. Sep 02. £1,000.*

1638

Late 20thC Maitland & Smith Regency style mahog. 3 tier stand, 16.5in dia. *Amersham Auction Rooms, Bucks. Aug 02. £1,000.*

1639

George III mahog. sideboard, 48in wide. *Andrew Hartley, Ilkley. Dec 03. £1,000.*

1640

George IV mahog. washstand, stamped Gillows, c1825, 99cm high, 138cm wide. *Wintertons Ltd, Lichfield. Mar 03. £1,000.*

1641

Victorian rosewood games table, folding swivel top inlaid for chess/backgammon, 1ft 8in wide. *Gorringes, Bexhill. Mar 03. £1,000.*

1642

Italian marble table top in coloured marbles in a batwing pattern, central rosette, 19thC, 26.75in wide. *Andrew Hartley, Ilkley. Dec 01. £1,000.*

1643

Edwardian mahog. revolving bookcase, banded in satinwood, 19in wide. *P. Wilson, Nantwich. Nov 01. £1,000.*

1644

19thC Sheraton Revival inlaid mahogany dumb waiter, 130cm wide. Mellors & Kirk, Nottingham. Apr 03. £1,000.

1645

19thC Biedermeier figured walnut chest of five drawers, 2ft 7.5in high. Gorringes, Lewes. Jan 04. £1,000.

1646

Regency satinwood/mahogany work table, ebony inlaid anthemion and fleur de lyse motifs, rising top, octagonal silks box, 1ft 9in. Gorringes, Lewes. Apr 01. £1,000.

1647

Concertina games table in mahogany, Georgian design. Lots Road Auctions, Chelsea. Mar 04. £1,000.

1648

Oak dresser, 18thC and later, 4ft 6in wide. Gorringes, Bexhill. Mar 04. £1,000.

1649

Victorian mahog. canterbury, 1ft 7in. Gorringes, Lewes. Sep 03. £1,000.

1650

Early 20thC oak refectory table. Lots Road Auctions, Chelsea. July 01. £1,000.

1651

Regency side cabinet, rosewood and brass mounted with white marble top, 43in wide. Lots Road Auctions, Chelsea. Aug 01. £1,000.

1652

20thC oak gateleg table by Cumper of Salisbury, 83in wide x 54in deep x 30in high. Dee, Atkinson & Harrison, Driffield. Apr 01. £1,000.

1653

Arts & Crafts oak side cabinet, manner of Liberty, blacksmith furniture throughout, 137cm wide. R. Wintertons, Burton on Trent. Jan 04. £1,000.

Hammer Price £1,000

1654

Regency mahog. wine cooler, tin liner, 84cm wide. Sworders, Stansted Mountfitchet. Feb 04. £1,000.

1655

Set of six 19thC painted mahogany dining chairs, overstuffed seats. Cheffins, Cambridge. Apr 04. £1,000.

1656

Victorian burr walnut/satinwood inlaid music cabinet/whatnot. Lambert & Foster, Tenterden. Apr 03. £1,000.

1657

Set of 6 George. III mahog. dining chairs, Country Chippendale design. Canterbury Auc. Galleries, Kent. Aug 03. £1,000.

1658

19thC mahog. salon suite in yellow damask, settee 59in wide, 2 armchairs, 2 elbows. Andrew Hartley, Ilkley. Feb 04. £1,000.

1659

Regency mahog. cellaret of sarcophagus form, 20in high, 23in wide. Amersham Auction Rooms, Bucks. Apr 02. £1,000.

1660

Early 19thC butler's mahog. tray and stand, 35 x 26in. Canterbury Auc. Galleries, Kent. Feb 04. £1,000.

1661

Regency mahog. linen press, 48.5in wide. Andrew Hartley, Ilkley. Aug 03. £1,000.

1662

Arts and Crafts oak dresser. W & H Peacock, Bedford. Dec 02. £1,000.

Section VIII <£1,000 to £750

Quarter cutting produces medullary rays, lines of dense tissue radiating from the centre of a log crossing the annual ring marks. These very desirable 'silver' waves can be seen very frequently in 1930s oak and also in earlier furniture.

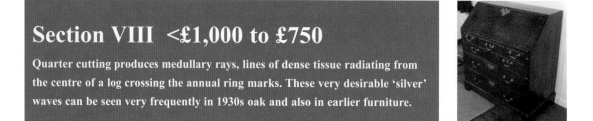

Victorian lots now match those from the Georgian period. The sixteenth and seventeenth centuries have only about sixteen lots but now the twentieth century is represented by more than fifty. It is probable now that the nineteenth century linen press at **1663**, has done no more than hold its own in recent years and notice the lean £950 achieved for a George III mahogany bureau bookcase at **1680**. Now check out the c1935 reproduction George I style walnut card table at **1687**. Then compare it with the genuine George II card table a year later at **1699**, which fetched the same price. Clearly the reproduction is of fine quality. Prices blur as quality takes priority over age. Whilst discussing reproductions it is nevertheless appropriate to point out the rather awkward form of the bookcases at **1690**, the pair reaching £950 in July 2001.They may seem a reasonable price in the context of buying new but are such absurd objects an investment? I doubt it. Better to buy the more sympathetic Gothic Revival occasional table at **1701** for the same money or almost anything else on these pages such as the early eighteenth century Spanish walnut side table at **1709**, which could show a future profit.

You can follow stools through the **Index** but here at **1702** and **1717** are two eighteenth century examples, one in walnut, the other mahogany, which give a fair idea of how much these items fetch. Another linen press at **1754** has fetched much the same as its predecessor **1663** a year earlier. The reader is drawn to our comments in the **Introduction** but should still consider buying providing originality has not been compromised. Now two chests of drawers. The first is seventeenth century English oak, **1733** fetching £900 in 2001. The second, also Jacobean, but with replaced handles fetched the same amount two years later. See **1760**. The reader who is prepared to study the photographs and use the **Index**, will find opportunities to make sound market judgements.

Continental painted pine appears again at **1776**. Notice the similar prices for pieces of this type. At **1808**, a Jacobean chest-on-stand fetches a similar price to the previous Jacobean chests. Now go to the quarter-cut oak bureau, c1755-1775, **1845**, sold at Richard Winterton's, Burton-on-Trent in April 2004. This is an exceptionally fine piece and despite the failing fashion for bureaux offers superb value for money at £820. Quarter cutting produces medullary rays, lines of dense tissue radiating from the centre of a log crossing the annual ring marks.

These very desirable 'silver' waves can be seen very frequently in 1930s oak but it can also be found throughout the oak period but is not so obvious. Could this be because earlier oak has darkened and the medullary rays are difficult to see? At **1846** is another rare piece of furniture, a George IV mahogany open bookcase. Bookcases are very useful additions to home furnishings and they will always hold their price well.

Now at **1858** is another lone piece of pine! The date seems uncertain but the £800 hammer does suggest that buyers considered it a genuine piece. If so then this is quite rare. We certainly don't get many period pine dressers submitted for consideration. Another rare object must be the George III simulated bamboo (probably beech), 4-seater chair-back settee at **1870** which fetched £800 at Locke & England, Leamington Spa in September, 2002. In the Editor's opinion this extremely rare piece of furniture should be in a museum and should have its value tentatively raised at least five-fold if not more? At **1873** is a good quality twentieth century oak suite by Austin & Cumberbirch of Rochdale. This kind of furniture presents exactly the right quality at the right price, in the right material, which is profoundly of much better value than the 'dotcom wonderstock' discussed in our **Introduction**.

Some pieces of Regency furniture are quite extraordinary and can have a twentieth century, modernistic look about them. I had a friendly argument recently with a furniture dealer about a pier table which he had labelled up as Regency and which I considered on sight to be Art Deco! One could be similarly confused by **1901** on page 118. This table has an ethereal or Utopian character which defies dating. Remember the expensive spoon rack? Here now at **1923** is an eighteenth century plate rack which again didn't come cheap considering what is available for £800 or so. However such items are again so rare that they always fine ready buyers. Queen Anne walnut chests of drawers can rarely be bought in this price range but at **1939**, this specimen has a few problems. Are such purchases good value for money or should one always be seeking to buy clean furniture of which there is certainly no shortage. In this case I cannot answer the question but there is certainly furniture on this page and in this price range, of the same period and in near original or original condition which may offer at least a greater feeling of satisfaction.

1663

Mahogany linen press, 19thC,
49.5in wide x 79.75in high.
A. Hartley, Ilkley. Oct 01. £980.

1664

19thC satin birch chiffonier,
by Holland & Son, 4ft 1in
wide, 6ft 3in high. (top of
door bears makers stamp).
*Sworders, Stansted Mount-
fitchet. Apr 01. £980.*

1665

Green shagreen veneered
toilet mirror, shaped cresting
8 x 6in., some damage.
*Canterbury Auc. Galleries,
Kent. Aug 01. £980.*

1666

George III mahog. Pembroke
table, satinwood banded and
line inlaid top. *Henry Adams,
Chichester. Sep 02. £980.*

1667

Regency mahog. canterbury,
single frieze drawer, 46cm.
*Sworders, Stansted
Mountfitchet. Feb 04. £980.*

1668

Late Victorian satinwood
inlaid walnut canterbury, 22in
wide. *Amersham Auction
Rooms, Bucks. Sep 01. £970.*

1669

Edwardian mahogany bow
front china cabinet, 47in
wide. *Amersham Auction
Rooms, Bucks. Apr 02. £970.*

1670

Set of six Regency rosewood
dining chairs, overstuffed
seats. *Amersham Auction
Rooms, Bucks. June 02. £970.*

1671

17th/18thC ebony/satinwood
marquetry, carved oak coffer,
59in wide. *Amersham Auction
Rooms, Bucks. May 03. £970.*

Hammer Prices £980-£950

1672

19thC inlaid walnut veneered
cabinet, ormolu mounts. *John
Taylors, Louth. Apr 01. £960.*

1673

Oak coffer, c1680. *Bristol
Auction Rooms. May 03. £960.*

1674

Georgian mahogany chest of
4 long drawers, brushing
slide, 34in. *Denhams,
Warnham. Aug 03. £960.*

> The numbering system acts
> as a reader reference as
> well as linking to the
> Analysis of each Section.

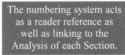

1675

Sofa with a 'lip' shaped back,
chrome cow horn supports.
*Lots Road Auctions, Chelsea.
Apr 01. £950.*

1676

19thC rosewood X frame
stool, overstuffed seat in gros
point, 22in wide. *Andrew
Hartley, Ilkley. Apr 01. £950.*

1677

Georgian mahogany fold over
tea/card table, 33in wide.
*Dee, Atkinson & Harrison,
Driffield. Apr 01. £950.*

1678

Large 19thC Chippendale
style mirror. *Lots Road
Auctions, Chelsea.
Nov 01. £950.*

1679

George I style burr walnut
veneer/crossbanded bureau,
31 x 41in. *David Duggleby.
Scarborough. July 01. £950.*

1680

George III mahogany bureau
bookcase, 44in wide.
*Amersham Auction Rooms,
Bucks. June 01. £950.*

Hammer Price £950

1681

Regency mahogany tea table, 32in wide. Amersham Auction Rooms, Bucks. May 01. £950.

1682

Victorian inlaid walnut davenport, hinged writing slope, 4 side drawers, 22in. Gorringes, Bexhill. Dec 01. £950.

1683

Ebonised and brass inlaid pier cabinet, gilt metal trim and mounts, 19thC, 32in wide. Andrew Hartley, Ilkley. Dec 01. £950.

1684

4 twin panel oak lockers, 19thC, plinth base. Lots Road Auctions, Chelsea. Apr 02. £950.

1685

Dutch late 19thC green heart semanier of typical seven graduated drawer form, 37 x 18 x 56in. Hamptons, Godalming. Jan 02. £950.

1686

Geo. III mahog. linen press, 47in wide. Sworders, Stansted Mountfitchet. Apr 01. £950.

1687

George I style burr walnut card table, c1935, 72 x 84cm. Rosebery's, London. Mar 02. £950.

1688

19thC Biedermeier parcel gilt mahogany dressing table, oval mirror back and swans head supports, 3ft 2in. Gorringes, Lewes. Apr 01. £950.

1689

19thC rosewood foldover card table, raised on four splayed cabriole legs, 37in wide. Tring Market Auctions, Herts. May 02. £950.

1690

Pair mid 20thC walnut bookcases, astragal glazing, each 36in wide x 48in high. Sworders, Stansted Mountfitchet. July 01. £950.

1691

Early 18thC oak low dresser, 3 central drawers flanked by 2 side cupboards, 71.5in wide. Tring Market Auctions, Herts. Sep 02. £950.

1692

George III oak settle. Lots Road Auctions, Chelsea. Oct 03. £950.

1693

19thC yewwood/elm seated 'Yorkshire' Windsor armchair. Canterbury Auc. Galleries, Kent. Aug 03. £950.

1694

Set of four dining chairs, late 18thC Continental, radiating fan splats. Lots Road Auctions, Chelsea. Oct 02. £950.

1695

Early 19thC bowfronted chest, brushing slide, 101cm wide. Lambert & Foster, Tenterden. Jan 03. £950.

1696

French walnut table, c1890, fold over top, four telescopic action carved cabriole legs with hoof feet, extending to 159cm. Lots Road Auctions, Chelsea. Apr 03. £950.

1697

Georgian inlaid and crossbanded mahogany bowfront chest. W & H Peacock, Bedford. June 03. £950.

1698

19thC library chair, padded back, arms and cushion seat. Cheffins, Cambridge. Sep 03. £950.

1699

George II mahogany card table, c1750. Wintertons Ltd, Lichfield. Nov 03. £950.

1700

William IV mahog. linen press, 128 x 130cm. Rosebery's, London. Dec 03. £950.

1701

Victorian Gothic Revival oak occasional table. Rupert Toovey, Washington, Sussex. Jan 04. £950.

1702

George I period walnut stool with drop in upholstered seat. Mervyn Carey, Tenterden. Feb 04. £950.

1703

20thC side cabinet, mahogany and kingwood banded, 92cm wide. Lots Road Auctions, Chelsea. Apr 04. £950.

1704

19thC convex mirror, 64cm wide. Lots Road Auctions, Chelsea. Feb 03. £950.

1705

Early Victorian mahogany library pier cabinet, hinged adjustable top with book rest, 5 drawers, 24in wide. Andrew Hartley, Ilkley. Apr 04. £950.

> The illustrations are in descending price order. The price range is indicated at the top of each page.

1706

Regency gilt gesso convex wall mirror, eagle surmount, ball frieze, 27in wide. Gorringes, Lewes. Apr 01. £950.

1707

George III mahogany chest of drawers, probably Irish. Bristol Auction Rooms, Bristol. Jan 03. £940.

1708

Rosewood chiffonier, c1840, 119.5cm wide. Bristol Auction Rooms, Bristol. Nov 01. £940.

1709

Early 18thC Spanish walnut side table. Tring Market Auctions, Herts. Jan 02. £940.

1710

Oak panelled chest, fascia with 4 fielded panels over 3 drawers, 60in wide. Andrew Hartley, Ilkley. Apr 04. £940.

1711

Pair of 19thC fruitwood/elm wheel back Windsor arm-chairs. Canterbury Auction Galleries, Kent. Aug 02. £940.

1712

Late 17thC yew wood miniature floral and insect marquetry bureau, 19.5in wide. Tring Market Auctions, Herts. Nov 02. £940.

1713

Regency mahog. chiffonier, 2 drawers, double cupboard, grilled panelled doors, 37in. Denhams, Warnham. June 04. £940.

1714

Adzed oak arm chair by Robert 'Mouseman' Thompson, bowed arm rail with arched back, padded seat. Andrew Hartley, Ilkley. June 04. £925.

1715

Victorian brass bedstead of railed construction, 60in. David Duggleby, Scarborough. July 01. £920.

1716

Victorian burr walnut loo table, 57in x 43in x 28in. Hamptons, Godalming. Sep 01. £920.

1717

18thC mahogany stool, c1880. Richard Wintertons, Burton on Trent. Feb 02. £920.

Hammer Prices £920-£900

1718

Regency mahogany small chest of drawers, 78cm wide. Bristol Auction Rooms, Bristol. July 02. £920.

1719

Early Victorian rosewood card table, 3ft. Gorringes, Bexhill. Oct 02. £920.

1720

Brass club fender, leather covered button seat, 204cm wide. Cheffins, Cambridge. Apr 04. £920.

1721

19thC mahogany double back chair settee, 49in wide. Sworders, Stansted Mount fitchet. Apr 01. £920.

1722

Waring & Gillows Georgian style mahogany bureau bookcase, 2 astragal glazed doors, fitted drawer, 43in wide. Sworders, Stansted Mountfitchet. Apr 01. £920.

1723

Regency mahogany pedestal pembroke table, 79 x 87cm. Rosebery's, London. Mar 02. £920.

1724

George III style white painted settee, arched padded back, scrolling arms and cushion seat, 205cm wide. Cheffins, Cambridge. Apr 04. £920.

1725

Late 18th/19thC Dutch walnut and floral marquetry centre table, inlaid bone and mother of pearl ornament, 40in wide. Amersham Auction Rooms, Bucks. Sep 03. £920.

1726

19thC mahogany satinwood/kingwood veneered commode, 51in wide. Amersham Auction Rooms, Bucks. Apr 01. £920.

1727

Edwardian inlaid mahogany square revolving bookcase, 21in. Denhams, Warnham. Aug 03. £920.

1728

Edwardian mahogany and boxwood line inlaid salon suite, 126cm wide, two armchairs. Rosebery's, London. Dec 03. £920.

1729

19thC teak 2 part campaign chest with 'Army & Navy O.S.L. Makers' mark, 99cm wide. Bristol Auction Rooms, Bristol. May 03. £920.

1730

Sheraton style inlaid mahog. 4 poster bed, internal 191 x 120cm. Bristol Auction Rooms. Jan 02. £920.

1731

Edwardian rosewood Carlton House style writing desk stamped Maple and Co., 36 x 19 x 40in. Hamptons, Godalming. Mar 02. £920.

1732

Early 19thC rosewood tea table, fold over top, 36in wide. Amersham Auction Rooms, Bucks. Aug 01. £920.

1733

Chest of drawers, 17thC English oak, 33in wide. Lots Road Auctions, Chelsea. Nov 01. £900.

1734

William IV mahog. sideboard, top having a low upstand with scroll carved decoration, 52in wide. Amersham Auction Rooms, Bucks. Dec 01. £900.

1735

Commode, Louis Philippe burr elm and fruitwood, 50in wide. Lots Road Auctions, Chelsea. Mar 01. £900.

1736

19thC gilt wood overmantel mirror, 55in long, 35.5in high. Andrew Hartley, Ilkley. Apr 01. £900.

1737

Victorian mahog. desk, fitted 3 frieze drawers, two baluster turned supports, rear comprising a series of cupboards and drawers, 32in wide x 58.25in long. Wintertons Ltd, Bakewell. Oct 01. £900.

Set of 5 + 1 Geo. III mahog. chairs, Sheraton style. *Andrew Hartley, Ilkley. Oct 01. £900.*

Victorian walnut folio cabinet, standing on cavetto moulded plinth, 24in wide. *Hamptons, Godalming. Sep 01. £900.*

Prices quoted are hammer and exclude the buyer's premium. Adding 15% will give approx. buying price.

19thC gilt framed overmantel mirror, 65in high, 56in wide. *Fellows & Sons, Hockley, Birmingham. July 03. £900.*

George III mahogany secretaire chest, fitted drawer, and later bookcase top, 107in wide, 84in high. *Sworders, Stansted Mountfitchet. Apr 01. £900.*

19thC' Louis XV style king-wood and rosewood poudreuse. *Tring Market Auctions, Herts. Jan 02. £900.*

George III oak mule chest, 56in wide. *Sworder & Sons, Stansted Mountfitchet. Apr 01. £900.*

Edwardian walnut writing desk. *Sworders, Stansted Mountfitchet. Apr 01. £900.*

Early 19thC mahogany secretaire bookcase, 125cm wide x 237cm high. *Henry Adams, Chichester. July 02. £900.*

19thC rosewood/marquetry sideboard. *Lambert & Foster, Tenterden. May 02. £900.*

Hammer Price £900

Victorian burr oak open bookcase, 2 adjustable shelves, 148cm wide, 32cm deep. *Thos Mawer & Son, Lincoln. Apr 02. £900.*

French Louis XVI style marble top centre table, 110cm wide. *Bristol Auction Rooms, Bristol. Jan 02. £900.*

Late regency mahogany tea table, oak crossbanded edge with white line inlay, 94 x 46cm. *Hamptons, Godalming. July 02. £900.*

Pair Victorian walnut framed parlour chairs of spoonback form. *Andrew Hartley, Ilkley. Feb 02. £900.*

19thC figured rosewood 'D' swivel top tea table, 33.5in wide. *Dockree's, Manchester. Feb 01. £900.*

Early 19thC carved/painted wall mirror, fruiting vine surround, 128 x 103cm. *Rosebery's, London. June 04. £900.*

Victorian figured walnut worktable. *Clevedon Salerooms, Bristol. Mar 01. £900.*

Victorian mahogany linen press, 122cm. *Henry Adams, Chichester. July 02. £900.*

Victorian walnut work/games table, inlaid hinged rising top enclosing a leather inset adjustable writing surface, 20.5in wide. *Clarke Gammon, Guildford. Apr 02. £900.*

Hammer Price £900

1756

Edwardian satinwood and rosewood collectors cabinet, 26in. Gorringes, Lewes. Oct 02. £900.

1757

Set of six William IV mahogany framed dining chairs. Amersham Auction Rooms, Bucks. Oct 02. £900.

1758

19thC lamp table, birds eye maple satinwood cross-banding, 55cm wide. Lots Road Auctions, Chelsea. Oct 02. £900.

1759

Edwardian Sheraton revival inlaid and cross banded mahogany display cabinet. W & H Peacock, Bedford. Dec 02. £900.

1760

Jacobean oak 2 section chest of drawers, replaced handles, 38in. Gorringes, Lewes. Mar 03. £900.

1761

Edwardian Hepplewhite style satinwood armchair, back painted with Prince of Wales' feathers. Clarke Gammon, Guildford. Dec 02. £900.

1762

19thC Trumeau (pier glass, mirror), painted, gilt, 127in high. Lots Road Auctions, Chelsea. Sep 03. £900.

1763

George III mahog. bookcase on table stand, fitted drawer, 38in wide. Sworders, Stansted Mountfitchet. July 01. £900.

1764

19thC walnut upholstered armchair, floral crest. Tring Market Auctions, Herts. Mar 03. £900.

1765

Victorian rosewood side cabinet, 190cm high, 137cm wide. Mellors & Kirk, Nottingham. Apr 03. £900.

1766

Regency mahogany work table. (bag missing), Lots Road Auctions, Chelsea. May 03. £900.

1767

Big Brother diary room red upholstered chair from Series 3, originally designed by Gaetano Pefco in 1969, B&B Italia manufactured this modern version. Richard Wintertons, Burton on Trent, Staffs. Feb 03. £900.

1768

Pair of armchairs, early 20thC Swedish, satin birch with maple front tablets. Lots Road Auctions, Chelsea. July 04. £900.

1769

19thC walnut and satinwood inlaid, serpentine shaped fold over card table, 37in wide. Amersham Auction Rooms, Bucks. May 02. £900.

1770

George II mahogany lowboy, 30in wide. Clarke Gammon, Guildford. June 04. £900.

1771

Charles II oak gateleg table, oval top and frieze drawer on bobbin legs, 3ft 6in. Gorringes, Lewes. Jan 04. £900.

1772

George III mahogany chest of drawers. Rupert Toovey, Washington, Sussex. Oct 03. £900.

Hammer Prices £900-£880

1773

Set of 4 Victorian oak chairs, on X frame supports, label Simpson & Sons Ltd, Halifax. *Locke & England, Leamington Spa. Sep 03. £900.*

1774

19thC French amboyna work table, 21in wide. *Gorringes, Bexhill. Sep 03. £900.*

> The numbering system acts as a reader reference as well as linking to the Analysis of each Section

1775

French Empire mahogany and gilt brass mounted commode, white/grey marble top, 48in wide. *Hampton & Littlewood, Exeter. Apr 04. £900.*

1776

Austrian painted pine armoire, early 19thC, 146cm wide. af. *Lots Road Auctions, Chelsea. Mar 04. £900.*

1777

Edwardian mahogany display cabinet, bow fronted with stringing/parquetry banding, 47.25in wide. *Andrew Hartley, Ilkley. Apr 04. £900.*

1778

George IV library armchair, c1830, with later drop in seat and back cushion, 38in high. *Wintertons Ltd, Lichfield. Mar 02. £880.*

1779

Victorian walnut sewing table, fitted frieze drawer, brass loop handles over sliding basket, 25.75in wide. *Dee, Atkinson & Harrison, Driffield. Mar 04. £880.*

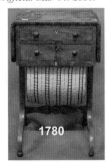

1780

William IV figured walnut wood drop flap work table, 17in. *Denhams, Warnham. Aug 03. £880.*

1781

Late 19thC, George II style mahogany card table, fold over top, single drawer frieze, 73 x 75cm. *Rosebery's, London. June 04. £880.*

1782

Georgian bow fronted corner cupboard. *John Taylors, Louth. Mar 01. £880.*

1783

William IV walnut framed salon chair, arched button upholstered back. *Andrew Hartley, Ilkley. Dec 01. £880.*

1784

Oak bookcase by Robert 'Mouseman' Thompson. *Rupert Toovey, Washington, Sussex. Aug 03. £880.*

1785

George IV mahogany low boy, 2ft 6in. *Gorringes, Lewes. July 03. £880.*

1786

George III red walnut chest, 33in wide. *Wintertons Ltd, Lichfield. May 01. £880.*

1787

Early reproduction mahogany Carlton House desk, 38in wide. *Lambert & Foster, Tenterden. Aug 01. £880.*

1788

Compact Regency mahogany bow front chest, 37.5 x 41.25in. *David Duggleby, Scarborough. July 01. £880.*

1789

Carved oak settle, pewter decoration of cherubs etc, inscribed 'Rest and Be Thankful', solid seat, 134cm wide. af. *Lambert & Foster, Tenterden. Feb 04. £880.*

111

Hammer Prices £875-£850

1790

Kingwood/floral marquetry work table, hinged lid with mirror, interior with lift out tray, 19thC French. *Andrew Hartley, Ilkley. Apr 03. £875.*

1791

19thC boxwood string inlaid mahogany centre table, top with central floral marquetry decoration, 46in wide. *Amersham Auction Rooms, Bucks. June 01. £870.*

1792

Set of 3 nesting, late 19thC walnut occasional tables, largest 27in high x 21in wide. *Amersham Auction Rooms, Bucks. May 01. £870.*

1793

William IV string inlaid and crossbanded walnut work box, quarter veneered top, fabric interior, concealed castors, 18.5in wide. *Amersham Auction Rooms, Bucks. Feb 04. £870.*

1794

Edwardian satinwood and boxwood inlaid mahogany desk, green leather scriber, 42in wide. *Amersham Auction Rooms, Bucks. Sep 03. £870.*

1795

Set six William IV rosewood framed dining chairs. *Amersham Auction Rooms, Bucks. Aug 01. £870.*

1796

Pair of armchairs, early 20thC Swedish, satin birch with maple front tablets. *Lots Road Auctions, Chelsea. July 04. £860.*

1797

Victorian satinwood writing table, by Holland & Sons, 42in. *Denhams, Warnham. Nov 03. £860.*

1798

Georgian mahogany bow fronted corner cupboard. *John Taylors, Louth. Apr 01. £860.*

1799

Mahogany 4 poster bedstead, cotton drapes, 19thC and later, 42in wide. *Andrew Hartley, Ilkley. Apr 03. £860.*

1800

Victorian mahog. extending dining table, with two extra leaves, 5ft 7in fully extended. *Sworder & Sons, Stansted Mountfitchet. Apr 01. £860.*

The illustrations are in descending price order. The price range is indicated at the top of each page.

1801

19thC mahogany chiffonier, 54in wide. *Andrew Hartley, Ilkley. Feb 01. £860.*

1802

Late Victorian satinwood oval tray topped two tier etagere, central fan motif, 27 x 19 x 31in high. *Canterbury Auction Galleries, Kent. Feb 04. £860.*

1803

Georgian mahog. demi-lune fold over tea table, 35in wide. *Dee, Atkinson & Harrison, Driffield. Apr 01. £850.*

1804

19thC rosewood occasional table, top with scrolled frieze, 19.75in wide. *Andrew Hartley, Ilkley. Apr 01. £850.*

1805

Barcelona chair, Mies van der Rohe design, button back leather. *Lots Road Auctions, Chelsea. Nov 01. £850.*

1806

William IV rosewood card table, 36in wide. *Wintertons Ltd, Lichfield. July 01. £850.*

1807

William IV mahog. bow front chest of drawers. *Tring Mkt. Auctions, Herts. Jan 02. £850.*

Antique chest on stand of Jacobean origin. Locke & England, Leamington Spa. Nov 02. £850.

Queen Anne style walnut double dome bookcase top, 40in wide. Sworders, Stansted Mountfitchet. July 01. £850.

Geo. IV rosewood chiffonier, centre panels now covered with floral needlework, 37in wide. Canterbury Auction Galleries, Kent. Aug 03. £850.

Edwardian mahogany display cabinet, satinwood banded, 3ft 6in wide. Gorringes, Bexhill. July 03. £850.

William & Mary walnut frame pier glass (mirror), later oblong plate, oyster veneer with stringing, 31.5 x 26in. Andrew Hartley, Ilkley. Dec 03. £850.

Miniature mahogany and oak bureau, 9.5in high. Kivell & Sons, Bude. Dec 02. £850.

Regency rosewood/satinwood banded swivel turnover top card table, 92cm wide. Locke & England, Leamington Spa. Jan 03. £850.

Set 6 early 19thC mahogany dining room chairs, good original colour. Hamptons, Godalming. Mar 02. £850.

Edwardian mahogany and marquetry wardrobe in Sheraton revival manner, 182cm wide. Lots Road Auctions. July 04. £850.

Hammer Price £850

Pair of late 19thC giltwood fauteuils, in Louis XVI style. Lots Road Auctions, Chelsea. Oct 02. £850.

William IV rosewood chaise longue, carved decoration. Sworders, Stansted Mountfitchet. Apr 01. £850.

Late Victorian Maple & Co oak desk, reeded decoration, 102 x 114cm. Rosebery's, London. Mar 02. £850.

French Louis XV style kingwood and tulipwood serpentine bombe commode, 28in wide. Clarke Gammon, Guildford. June 02. £850.

William IV mahogany buffet. Eastbourne Auction Rooms, Sussex. Mar 02. £850.

Regency rosewood foldover card table. W & H Peacock, Bedford. Mar 03. £850.

Victorian walnut oval centre table, top quarter veneers in burred effect, 143 x 111cm. Locke & England, Leamington Spa. May 03. £850.

William IV mahogany open library bookcase, 183.5cm wide. Sworders, Stansted Mountfitchet. Dec 03. £850.

19thC mahogany/brass bound 2 section military chest, 39in wide. Canterbury Auction Galleries, Kent. Feb 04. £850.

Victorian mahogany chiffonier. John Taylors, Louth. May 04. £850.

Hammer Prices £850-£820

1827

Victorian walnut games table, drop flap top inlaid with a chessboard, 2 frieze drawers, 1ft 7in. *Gorringes, Lewes. Mar 04. £850.*

1828

Victorian walnut credenza, inlaid satinwood arabesques, gilt bronze mounts, glazed doors, 58in wide. *Gorringes, Bexhill. Mar 04. £850.*

1829

Victorian carved oak two drawer writing table, leather lined top, 51in wide. *Sworders, Stansted Mountfitchet. July 01. £840.*

1830

Edwardian Sheraton style mahogany display cabinet, 33in wide. *Maxwells, Wilmslow. Sep 02. £840.*

114

1831

Geo III mahog. canterbury, 18 x 13 x 19in high. (formerly on castors, one side rail missing). *Canterbury Auction Galleries. Kent. Aug 02. £840.*

1832

Mahogany framed window seat, velvet covering, early 20thC, 73.5in long. *Andrew Hartley, Ilkley. June 04. £840.*

1833

Victorian figured rosewood card table, baize lined folding top, 36in wide. *Canterbury Auction Galleries, Kent. Dec 03. £840.*

1834

Pair 19thC ash/elm windsor chairs, crinoline stretchers. *Sworders, Stansted Mountfitchet. Apr 01. £830.*

1835

Late Regency, rosewood veneered, apprentice piece chiffonier, 41in high, 57in wide. *Amersham Auction Rooms, Bucks. Sep 01. £830.*

1836

Late 18th early 19thC Italian commode in walnut, shaped marble top, 84cm wide. *Lots Road Auctions, Chelsea. Mar 03. £820.*

1837

Victorian teak two-part campaign chest. *Bristol Auction Rooms. Sep 01. £820.*

1838

Leather button back Edwardian chesterfield. *Hogben Auctioneers, Folkestone. Apr 01. £820.*

1839

Geo. II mahog. tea table, fold over top, inverted breakfront, claw and ball legs, 30.5in wide. *Sworders, Stansted Mountfitchet. Apr 01. £820.*

1840

19thC rosewood pier cabinet bookcase, twin glazed doors, 114cm wide. *Bristol Auction Rooms, Bristol. Jan 04. £820.*

1841

Late Regency mahogany chiffonier with mirror back, 92cm. *Henry Adams, Chichester. July 02. £820.*

1842

Geo. III mahog. night table, galleried top, long drawer, pair panelled doors, commode drawer, 2ft wide. *Gorringes, Bexhill. Oct 01. £820.*

1843

Regency rosewood card table, foldover top, baize lined, 35.5in wide. *Amersham Auction Rooms, Bucks. June 03. £820.*

1844

Arts & Crafts copper, brass, boxwood inlay mahog. display cabinet, lead glazed doors, 36in wide. *Amersham Auction Rooms, Bucks. Mar 04. £820.*

1845

Quarter cut oak bureau, C1755-1775, flap opening to an arrangement of pigeon holes, 92cm wide. Richard Wintertons, Burton on Trent, Staffs. Apr 04. £820.

1846

George IV mahogany open bookcase, 53in wide. af. Sworders, Stansted Mountfitchet. Apr 01. £820.

Prices quoted are hammer and exclude the buyer's premium. Adding 15% will give approx. buying price.

1847

Small George III mahogany chest. Tring Market Auctions, Herts. Nov 03. £820.

1848

Early 19thC mahogany chest, parquetry banded top, 37in wide. Andrew Hartley, Ilkley. Apr 04. £820.

1849

Oak hall seat in the gothic style, 43in wide. Andrew Hartley, Ilkley. Apr 04. £820.

1850

Victorian button back settee. John Taylors, Louth. July 02. £810.

1851

Small George III mahogany chest with re-arrangements, faults, 79cm wide. Dockree's, Manchester. June 01. £800.

1852

Small 18thC red walnut fold-over tea table, 72cm wide, (leg restored). Dockree's, Manchester. June 01. £800.

1853

Regency giltwood and gesso convex wall mirror. D M Nesbit & Company, Southsea. Feb 03. £800.

1854

Set of 4 + 2 Sheraton Revival mahog. chairs. Thos Mawer & Son, Lincoln. Apr 02. £800.

1855

Late 19thC cheval mirror, Empire Revival fruitwood, giltwood and metal mounted, 195cm by 116cm wide. Lots Road Auctions, Chelsea. Feb 03. £800.

1856

Gordon Russell oak boot cupboard with hand written paper label, dated 1923. Sworders, Stansted Mountfitchet. Sep 01. £800.

1857

Antique oak chest on chest, 88cm wide, 152cm high. Lambert & Foster, Tenterden. June 04. £800.

1858

Antique pine dresser base. Crows, Dorking. May 01. £800.

1859

18thC Italian wall mirror, giltwood, 96cm high, 86cm wide, af. Lots Road Auctions, Chelsea. Nov 2. £800.

1860

Mahogany wine cooler base, c1810, brass bound, 65cm wide. R. Wintertons, Burton on Trent, Staffs. Jan 02. £800.

1861

Late 18thC oak cricket table, plank constructed top, raised on turned, block legs, 24in high. Amersham Auction Rooms, Bucks. Apr 01. £800.

1862

Victorian rosewood framed salon chair. (upholstery af). Sworders, Stansted Mountfitchet. Apr 01. £800.

Hammer Price £800

1863

Edwardian mahogany vitrine, Sheraton Revival design, parquetry inlay, 115cm wide. *Richard Wintertons, Burton on Trent, Staffs. Dec 01. £800.*

1864

Victorian inlaid walnut sutherland table, 35.5in wide. *Sworders, Stansted Mountfitchet. Feb 02. £800.*

1865

Edwardian inlaid mahogany display cabinet, 65in high. *Sworders, Stansted Mountfitchet. Apr 01. £800.*

1866

19thC inlaid walnut cabinet, gilt metal mounts, 33in wide x 42.5in. *Sworders, Stansted Mountfitchet. Apr 01. £800.*

1867

Mid Victorian mahogany dining table, parquetry top, 134cm dia. *Thos Mawer & Son, Lincoln. Apr 02. £800.*

1868

George IV mahogany double scroll-end sofa, upholstered in gold floral damask, 84in wide. *Clarke Gammon, Guildford. Apr 02. £800.*

1869

Georgian style walnut chest, quarter veneered hinged top with herringbone border, 81 x 54cm. *Rosebery's, London. Mar 02. £800.*

1870

George III simulated bamboo four seater chair back settee, original state, in need of restoration. *Locke & England, Leamington Spa. Sep 02. £800.*

1871

George III mahogany bureau, sloping fall, fitted interior, 104cm wide. *Lots Rd Auctions, Chelsea. Sep 02. £800.*

1872

Set of 4 + 1 mahog. Sheraton revival dining chairs, over-stuffed seats in woolwork, on wrythen turned tapering front legs. *Andrew Hartley, Ilkley. June 02. £800.*

1873

Austin and Cumberbirch (of Rochdale) oak suite: sideboard, side and dining tables, eight leather upholstered chairs. *Sworders, Stansted Mountfitchet. July 01. £800.*

1874

Early 20thC mahogany show frame window seat, 126cm wide. *Dreweatt Neate, Newbury. Nov 02. £800.*

1875

Regency rosewood card table, rotating fold-over top, blue baize lined surface, 36in wide. *Amersham Auction Rooms, Bucks. Sep 02. £800.*

1876

Regency mahog. sarcophagus cellaret. *W & H Peacock, Bedford. Mar 03. £800.*

1877

20thC Louis XVI style 7 piece drawing room suite: 3 seater canape, 4 armchairs, coffee table and 2 occasional tables, black marble top. *Maxwells, Wilmslow. Sep 02. £800.*

1878

Regency mahog. washstand in the manner of Gillows. *Bristol Auction Rooms, Bristol. Sep 02. £800.*

1879

Edwardian rosewood and marquetry envelope card table. *Lambert & Foster, Tenterden. May 02. £800.*

1880

19thC burr walnut whatnot, centre drawer, 61cm wide. *Lots Road Auctions, Chelsea. Oct 02. £800.*

1881

19thC burr walnut table cabinet, fitted central cupboard and 15 drawers inlaid with coloured woods, 25 x 19.25in high. Lambert & Foster, Tenterden. Apr 03. £800.

1882

19thC design mahogany four poster bed, hung with foliate printed curtains and tie backs. Locke & England, Leamington Spa. May 03. £800.

The numbering system acts as a reader reference as well as linking to the Analysis of each Section

1883

Victorian satinwood two stage Sutherland table, 73cm high. Mellors & Kirk, Nottingham. June 03. £800.

1884

Victorian satinwood/boxwood inlaid rosewood envelope card table, top with marquetry urn motifs, baize lined interior, 22in wide. Amersham Auction Rooms, Bucks. Nov 03. £800.

1885

Regency rosewood 3-tier whatnot, reeded knop finials, base drawer, 18in. Gorringes, Lewes. Jan 04. £800.

1886

Edwardian mahogany nest of 4 tables. Lambert & Foster, Tenterden. Dec 03. £800.

1887

Late 19thC walnut and oak framed settle, 42in wide. Amersham Auction Rooms, Bucks. June 03. £800.

1888

Georgian mahogany bureau bookcase, associated later top, 40in. Denhams, Warnham. Dec 03. £800.

Hammer Price £800

1889

Geo. III mahog. bowfront sideboard, 94 x 168cm. Rosebery's, London. Sep 03. £800.

1890

Set of six Victorian walnut balloon back dining chairs, carved foliage, stuff over seats. Sworders, Stansted Mountfitchet. July 03. £800.

1891

Regency mahog. low bookcase, tulipwood crossbanded, boxwood/ebony line inlaid, later galleried back, 3ft 5in wide. Gorringes, Bexhill. Feb 04. £800.

1892

19thC walnut framed settee, button upholstered in a green linen, 79in wide. Andrew Hartley, Ilkley. Feb 04. £800.

1893

Regency mahogany chest of drawers, crossbanded top, brass 'Sphinx' handles, 87cm. Sworders, Stansted Mountfitchet. Feb 04. £800.

1894

Charles II oak side table, 2ft 10in. Gorringes, Lewes. Jan 04. £800.

1895

19thC rosewood davenport, real and dummy opposing drawers, 1ft 10in. Gorringes, Lewes. Mar 04. £800.

1896

Nest of 19thC 'Gonzalo Alvez' interfitting coffee tables, 21in. Denhams, Warnham. Mar 04. £800.

1897

19thC walnut davenport, burrwood banding, boxwood stringing, interior veneered in birdseye maple, music cabinet under fitted shelves, 24in wide. Canterbury Auction Galleries, Kent. Feb 04. £800.

Hammer Prices £800-£770

1898

19thC Italian yewwood centre table, turned carved supports, 150cm. af. *Lots Rd Auctions, Chelsea. Mar 04. £800.*

1899

George II oak mule chest on stand, initials 'A.T.' and the date '1764', 56in wide. *Clarke Gammon, Guildford. Apr 04. £800.*

1900

19thC figured walnut davenport, slope and dome topped stationery cabinet inlaid with burrwood banding, boxwood and ebonised stringings, 21in wide. *Canterbury Auction Galleries, Kent. Apr 04. £800.*

1901

Regency mahogany hall table, 2 frieze drawers, H stretcher, 3ft 8in. *Gorringes, Lewes. Mar 04. £800.*

1902

Italian walnut and parquetry banded cassone, 16th/17thC, now with lime wash finish, 166cm wide. *Bristol Auction Rooms, Bristol. Jan 02. £790.*

118

1903

18thC oak settle, rising seat reveals void interior, 137 x 53 x 57cm. *Hamptons, Godalming. July 02. £780.*

1904

Early 19thC mahogany card table, satinwood and rosewood banding, 36in wide. (top leaf warped). *Sworders, Stansted Mountfitchet. Apr 01. £780.*

1905

Pair of 19thC French cream painted and gilt oval girandoles, plain mirror plate, 24 x 14.5in. *Canterbury Auction Galleries, Kent. Aug 03. £780.*

1906

18thC oak gateleg dining table, 3ft 10in. *Gorringes, Bexhill. Oct 01. £780.*

1907

Mid Victorian mahogany hall stand, one arm replaced, 206 x 95cm. *Rosebery's, London. Mar 02. £780.*

1908

Victorian rosewood Davenport desk. *Denhams, Warnham. Aug 03. £780.*

1909

Edwardian mahogany breakfront bookcase, 4 astragal glazed doors, length 70in. *Fellows & Sons, Hockley, Birmingham. Oct 03. £780.*

1910

Set 4 Georgian style ribbon back dining chairs, c1900, 106cm. *Bristol Auction Rooms. Nov 03. £780.*

1911

French Napoleon III console table and mirror in rosewood, 272 x 113cm. *Lots Rd Auctions, Chelsea. Mar 03. £780.*

1912

Regency mahogany pedestal sideboard, 2 cellarets, cupboards either side. *Sworders, Stansted Mountfitchet. Dec 03. £780.*

1913

Victorian rosewood framed chaise longue, orange button upholstered, 80in long. *Dee, Atkinson & Harrison, Driffield. Mar 04. £780.*

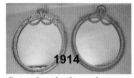

1914

Pair of oval giltwood mirrors, lions mask crestings, early 20thC, 36in high x 26in wide. *Sworders, Stansted Mountfitchet. Apr 01. £780.*

1915

Victorian rosewood folding card table, D shaped top, 36in wide. *Andrew Hartley, Ilkley. Dec 01. £775.*

1916

19thC walnut davenport, panelled flank cupboard door, enclosing 4 graduated drawers, facsimiles on the reverse and a secret pen drawer, 22in wide. *Amersham Auction Rooms, Bucks. June 03. £770.*

1917

19thC Spanish/Portuguese ebonised centre table inlaid with etched and inked bone, 47in wide. *Amersham Auction Rooms, Bucks. May 03. £770.*

1918

Mid Victorian mahogany and ebonised folio stand, 36in wide. *Amersham Auction Rooms, Bucks. Mar 01. £770.*

The illustrations are in descending price order. The price range is indicated at the top of each page.

1919

Victorian walnut framed spoon back open arm easy chair, rose striped cloth. *Canterbury Auc. Galleries, Kent. Dec 03. £760.*

1920

18thC oak press. *John Taylors, Louth. Feb 01. £760.*

1921

Victorian mahogany show frame gentleman's chair. *Peter Wilson, Nantwich. July 02. £760.*

1922

Oak coffer, moulded edge, right handed till, fascia with leaf carved frieze, moulded uprights and stiles, 53.5in wide. *Andrew Hartley, Ilkley. June 02. £760.*

1923

18thC plate rack. *John Taylors, Louth. Mar 01. £760.*

1924

19thC mahogany canterbury. *Biddle & Webb, Birmingham. Jan 02. £760.*

1925

George III inlaid mahogany oval pembroke table, line inlaid top over curved front, 85cm wide. *Bristol Auction Rooms, Bristol. Sep 03. £760.*

Hammer Prices £770-£750

1926

Set of six Victorian mahogany dining chairs. *John Taylors, Louth. May 01. £760.*

1927

19thC mahogany sideboard, with three drawers, 6ft long. *Sworders, Stansted Mountfitchet. Apr 01. £760.*

1928

19thC walnut occasional table, top carved with scroll work, hexagonal carve column signed Lawrence, 19in dia. x 18.5in high. *Canterbury Auc. Galleries, Kent. Feb 04. £760.*

1929

19thC yew wood/elm seated 'Yorkshire' Windsor armchair, (slightly damaged). *Canterbury Auction Galleries, Kent. Aug 03. £760.*

1930

Pair of 19thC mahogany and Dutch marquetry inlaid side chairs. *Crows, Dorking. Feb 01. £750.*

1931

Early 19thC mahogany bow fronted chest of drawers, 42.5in wide. *Dockree's, Manchester. Feb 01. £750.*

1932

Early Victorian mahogany linen press, 84in high, 55in wide. *Amersham Auction Rooms, Bucks. Apr 01. £750.*

1933

19thC figured mahogany rent desk, 23in wide. *Dee, Atkinson & Harrison, Driffield. Apr 01. £750.*

Hammer Price £750

1934

Pair of Italian giltwood pedestals, with carved frieze detail. Lots Road Auctions, Chelsea. Aug 01. £750.

1935

Oak drawleaf refectory table, early 18thC style, (8ft 6in extended). Lots Road Auctions, Chelsea. Aug 01. £750.

1936

18thC elm lowboy, planked top, frieze drawer, 39.75in wide. Wintertons Ltd, Bakewell. Oct 01. £750.

1937

19thC rosewood chiffonier, 51in wide. Peter Wilson, Nantwich. Nov 01. £750.

1938

19th/early 20thC mahogany bookcase cabinet, 83 x 234 x 27cm. Locke & England, Leamington Spa. Sep 02. £750.

1939

Queen Anne walnut chest of drawers, later feet, (some damage, restoration) 40.5in wide. Sworders, Stansted Mountfitchet. July 01. £750.

1940

Victorian mahogany buffet, 34in wide. Sworders, Stansted Mountfitchet. Apr 01. £750.

1941

Oak hall settle, foliate design, initialled RC and dated 1699, 150cm wide. Thos Mawer & Son, Lincoln. Nov 02. £750.

1942

Early Victorian rosewood canterbury. Gorringes, Lewes. Oct 02. £750.

1943

George III mahogany/satinwood inlaid dressing chest, secretaire drawer front with fitted interior, 42in wide. Amersham Auction Rooms, Bucks. June 02. £750.

1944

19thC burr walnut canterbury, with a gilt metal pierced gallery. Thos Mawer & Son, Lincoln. Apr 02. £750.

1945

17thC oak Wainscot armchair, panelled back carved with tulips and leaf scrolls. (seat replaced). Gorringes, Lewes. Mar 02. £750.

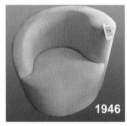

1946

Nautilus chair designed by Vladimir Kagan, cream chenille upholstered, swivel action. Lots Road Auctions, Chelsea. July 01. £750.

1947

Regency mahog. chiffonier, 2 tiered shelves, 3 small in line drawers, latticed metal doors, linen backcloths, 44in wide. Amersham Auction Rooms, Bucks. June 02. £750.

1948

Regency rosewood chiffonier. Locke & England, Leamington Spa. Nov 02. £750.

1949

17thC oak joined stool, branded 'TS', 17in. Gorringes, Bexhill. May 02. £750.

1950

Carved oak bureau bookcase, c1910. Hogben Auctioneers, Folkestone. Mar 01. £750.

1951

18thC mirror, mahogany veneered frame, original bevelled plate to a cusp top moulded inner border, 42.5in x 22in. Woolley & Wallis, Salisbury. Aug 00. £750.

1952

Mid Victorian rosewood centre table, 28in high, 44in wide. *Amersham Auction Rooms, Bucks. Oct 02. £750.*

1953

Regency mahogany chaise longue. *Henry Adams, Chichester. Jan 03. £750.*

1954

Georgian mahogany sideboard. *W & H Peacock, Bedford. Mar 03. £750.*

Prices quoted are hammer and exclude the buyer's premium. Adding 15% will give approx. buying price.

1955

Louis XVI canapé painted beechwood with original Aubusson covers, 91cm wide. *Lots Road Auctions, Chelsea. Apr 03. £750.*

1956

George III mahog. twinflap dining table, 41.5in wide. *Tring Market Auctions, Herts. Nov 03. £750.*

1957

Oak panelled coffer, late 17th/18thC, 37.25in wide. *Andrew Hartley, Ilkley. Feb 04. £750.*

1958

19thC mahog. library table, 135cm wide. *Lots Rd Auctions, Chelsea. Aug 03. £750.*

1959

Walnut and parcel gilt wall mirror, c1900, moulded edge and central leaf surmount, triple bevelled plate, 138 x 94cm. *Rosebery's, London. June 04. £750.*

1960

Pair 20thC Continental beech framed footstools, serpentine tops upon scallop and rococo foliate carved apron and cabriole supports. *Rosebery's, London. June 04. £750.*

1961

Art Nouveau mahogany and inlaid display cabinet, c1910, 125cm wide. *Wintertons Ltd, Lichfield. May 03. £750.*

Hammer Price £750

1962

Victorian mahogany tray top commode, 21.5in. *Gorringes, Lewes. Mar 04. £750.*

1963

Regency giltwood pier mirror. *Kidson Trigg Auctions, Swindon. May 04. £750.*

1964

Georgian tilt top mahogany occasional table, top divided by acanthus carving, 90cm dia. *Rosebery's, London. Dec 03. £750.*

1965

Victorian walnut pedestal. *Eastbourne Auction Rooms, Sussex. Apr 04. £750.*

1966

Geo. III mahog. tripod table, 75cm. *Sworders, Stansted Mountfitchet. Feb 04. £750.*

1967

Edwardian rosewood Davenport, line and urn inlay and fitted interior. *Biddle & Webb, Birmingham. Apr 04. £750.*

1968

French Louis XV style gilt metal mounted tulipwood and kingwood bureau de dame, 35in wide. *Clarke Gammon, Guildford. Feb 03. £750.*

1969

Austrian Biedermeier walnut armoire, c1840, 123cm wide. *Lots Road Auctions, Chelsea. Apr 03. £750.*

121

Section IX <£750 to £500

The reader should be aware that the continuation of, and the reproduction of styles, complicated by regional variations means that at times we are going to have to allow a considerable time window when making attributions.

Seventeenth and eighteenth century furniture remains available. Whilst age is a criterion, quality remains important. Certain market conditions might produce serious bargains or conversely competition drive prices beyond their reasonable limit. Here the seventeenth century accounts for over a dozen lots and the Georgian period for over 130. Victorian exceeds 160, with the twentieth century now showing well.

Readers with an interest in the early period still have some choice. Inevitably in this price range one finds the usual oak or elm coffers. However, there is a good looking dressing chest at **2158**, which went for £600 and a chest of drawers at **2253**, which fetched £550 at Clarke Gammon, Guildford in June 2003. Incidentally, don't miss the twentieth century reproduction of a Carolean oak side table at **2237**. There is a mystery about **2268**. This carved oak chair is dated 1612 but the description reads early eighteenth century. Let us stick our necks out and suggest that as this chair appears to have all the characteristics of the early seventeenth century that this may be a cataloguing error. The reader however should be aware that the continuation of, as well as the reproductions of styles, complicated by regional variations means that at times we are going to have to allow a considerable time window when making attributions. Nor is it unusual for a cataloguer to play safe by suggesting the latest rather than the earliest attribution. Here still you can find a genuine late seventeenth century oak side table, **2306**, for £520, or a quite rare seventeenth century single caned chair, **2336**, for £500. In my opinion such a chair is a very nice find.

Here are many examples of reproductions, or conversions, or lots which have been made up. See **2008**, **2027** and **2038** for lots that are not all they appear. Turning to reproduction, would you be able to 'spot' **2063**, **2065** and **2077** on page 128? After all these lots were reproduced over a 100 years ago. The auctioneers' labelling is clear. We have already mentioned **2237**, the 'Carolean' oak side table, but see also **2299** and **2333**. Now let us return to **2025**, a nice pair of tub chairs in green leather from the earlier twentieth century. Often the leather is the worse for wear on these chairs. However tempting, try to avoid renewing the leather. Not only is it expensive, particularly if you buy good leather, but you are also likely to devalue the chair. Remember the concept of the well-worn look discussed in *Section 5*?

You don't have to pay thousands for a Georgian oak dresser. See **2041** for a £700 Lancashire example. Observe the nice pair of solid mahogany pedestal bedside cabinets, **2139**, which fetched £620 at Denhams in Warnham in March 2004. Walk around any new furniture store. Single bedside cabinets are typically over £250 each and doubles over £500. And they are not even wood! In preparation for this analysis I asked a salesman of new furniture if he could actually show me any solid wood, or even veneered examples. "Sir," he replied, "if I could, you wouldn't be able to afford them." Ignoring the unintended insult I felt smug in the knowledge that our home is full of solid mahogany furniture. It is all antique and has served generations of families before it graced our home. And it was all bought for much less than it would have cost to furnish new!

Yet again only a single item of pine can be found, a Georgian painted pine corner cabinet, **2141**, which fetched £620 at Lambert and Foster in Tenterden, Kent in 2002. This should have increased in value. At **2170**, are two dining table 'D' ends which fetched £600 at Sworders in Essex in 2001. Readers could research this table type and how they are extended by additional boards/tables which fit between the 'D' ends. When not in use the 'D' ends can sit against walls. When complete, such a table, in good condition, with an original faded patina, should fetch about £2,000-3,000 retail and probably less at auction. See **804** on page 54 at £2,100.

Don't miss the George III Irish, mahogany Chippendale style dining chair, **2202**, dating from about 1760. This example is inexpensive at £600 in 2004. Affording a set of six or eight would be beyond the reach of most of us at say £8,000-10,000. It is possible to collect singles and thus make up a harlequin set for much less than half the price. Note the occasional table at **2251** on page 138. These are invariably Edwardian or later and about £70-£100. Would you be able to spot a Georgian example worth £500 or more? Go to page 141 and the Titchmarsh & Goodwin Jacobean style court cupboard, **2312**. This is modern but being secondhand and of fine quality offers good value at only £520. A Titchmarsh & Goodwin oak desk can be found on page 101 which fetched £1,000 in 2001. Finally note the excellent value of a nineteenth century breakfront four door wardrobe, **2341**, on page 143 at only £500. This fine example is bound to go up in value in the next few years. At this price, buy!

Hammer Prices £740-£720

1970

Victorian mahogany chiffonier, 59in wide. *Sworders, Stansted Mountfitchet. Apr 01. £740.*

1971

Victorian walnut Davenport with carved scrolled supports, 22in wide. *Sworders, Stansted Mountfitchet. July 01. £740.*

The numbering system acts as a reader reference as well as linking to the Analysis of each Section

1972

Mid Georgian joined oak settle, 190cm wide. *Bristol Auction Rooms, Bristol. Jan 03. £740.*

1973

1930s black lacquered chinoiserie style bureau, upper section with bevel plate shaped dressing mirror, fall front with well fitted interior, 28in. *Denhams, Warnham. June 04. £740.*

1974

19th C rosewood work table, basket slide (basket missing), 16.75in wide. *A. Hartley, Ilkley. Feb 02. £725.*

1975

George III mahogany chest, 31 x 30in. *David Duggleby, Scarborough. July 01. £720.*

1976

Oak twin pedestal partners desk, drawers one side and cupboards on the other, 6ft long. *Sworders, Stansted Mountfitchet. Apr 01. £720.*

1977

Set 4 late 18thC chairs in the Sheraton manner, original colour, seat rails stamped 'M.B.', 32in. *Hamptons, Godalming. Mar 02. £720.*

1978

Edwardian strung mahogany cheval mirror, 63in high. *Sworders, Stansted Mountfitchet. Apr 01. £720.*

1979

19thC serpentine red boulle and ormolu fold over card table, baize lined interior, 36in wide. *Maxwells, Wilmslow. Sep 02. £720.*

1980

Set 6 19thC oak dining chairs, Charles II style, label, Druce & Co., London. *Cheffins, Cambridge. June 01. £720.*

1981

Georgian mahogany & brass cellaret on tripod stand, 36cm dia, 65cm high. *Rosebery's, London. Mar 02. £720.*

1982

Edwardian mahogany display cabinet inlaid in art nouveau style with coloured woods, pewter and copper, 92cm wide. *Peter Wilson, Nantwich. July 02. £720.*

1983

Six Victorian balloon back dining chairs. *Sworders, Stansted Mountfitchet. July 01. £720.*

1984

Victorian walnut Davenport, pierced gallery cushion shape stationery compartment, 56cm. *Locke & England, Leamington Spa. May 03. £720.*

1985

Edwardian mahogany folio stand. *Sworders, Stansted Mountfitchet. Apr 01. £720.*

1986

19thC mahog. bow front chest of drawers, bracket feet, 43in wide. *Sworders, Stansted Mountfitchet. July 01. £720.*

1987

Geo. III mahog. tilt top tripod table. *Sworders, Stansted Mountfitchet. Feb 04. £720.*

Hammer Prices £720-£700

1988

Late 19thC Louis XVI style fauteuil. *Amersham Auction Rooms, Bucks. Mar 04. £720.*

1989

Victorian mahogany inlaid chiffonier, 52in wide. *Dee, Atkinson & Harrison, Driffield. Mar 04. £720.*

1990

Mahog. bookstand by Gillow & Co, Lancaster, 19.75in wide, stamped mark and label for Denby & Spink, Leeds, late 19th/20thC. *A. Hartley, Ilkley. Dec 03. £720.*

1991

Victorian mahog. extending dining table, with single leaf, 68 x 48in extended. *Dee, Atkinson & Harrison, Driffield. Mar 04. £720.*

1992

Geo. III style partner's desk, inverted breakfront kneeholes, 152 x 76 x 106cm. *Hobbs Parker, Ashford, Kent. June 04. £720.*

1993

Victorian oval inlaid walnut worktable, 55 x 43cm. *Lambert & Foster, Tenterden. Apr 04. £720.*

1994

Victorian brass bed. *John Taylors, Louth. Apr 01. £710.*

1995

Figured walnut cabinet on stand by Beresford & Hicks, of late 17thC style, 55.5in wide. *Morphets, Harrogate, N Yorks. Mar 01. £700.*

1996

Regency rosewood pembroke work table, brass line inlaid, 2 drawers, 19in. *Gorringes, Bexhill. Dec 01. £700.*

1997

Mid Victorian chaise longue, polished walnut frame. *Thos Mawer & Son, Lincoln. Apr 02. £700.*

1998

George III elbow chair, rope twist top rail. (some new timber). *Gorringes, Lewes. June 01. £700.*

1999

Mid Victorian figured walnut breakfast table. *Tring Market Auctions, Herts. Jan 02. £700.*

2000

18thC gateleg table in untouched condition. *Richard Wintertons, Burton on Trent. Apr 02. £700.*

2001

Set of ten mahogany dining chairs, Hepplewhite design. *Lots Road Auctions, Chelsea. Aug 01. £700.*

2002

Edwardian satin beech bookcase/display cabinet, fitted two oval bar glazed doors and three small drawers, 36in wide, 80.5in high. *Wintertons Ltd, Bakewell. Oct 01. £700.*

2003

Mid 19thC musical hall chair. (possibly Swiss). *Lots Road Auctions, Chelsea. Feb 02. £700.*

2004

Gilt/gesso wall mirror, Adam style, 117cm high. *Cheffins, Cambridge. Oct 00. £700.*

2005

18th/19thC Irish, Chippendale design, mahog. open armchair. *Amersham Auction Rooms, Bucks. Feb 02. £700.*

2006

Geo. IV mahog. fold over card table, 3ft wide. Sworders, Stansted Mountfitchet. Apr 01. £700.

2007

Set 6 19thC mahog. dining chairs, each with inverted crest. Amersham Auction Rooms, Bucks. Mar 02. £700.

2008

Antique timbered oak chest of 9 drawers, fronts later carved male/female portraits, 189cm. Locke & England, Leamington Spa. May 03. £700.

The illustrations are in descending price order. The price range is indicated at the top of each page.

2009

Victorian mahogany three tier buffet, 154cm wide. Thos Mawer & Son, Lincoln. Apr 02. £700.

2010

Robert 'Mouseman' Thompson, oak work box, 50cm wide. Richard Wintertons, Burton on Trent. July 03. £700.

2011

Georgian wall mirror, mahogany and parcel gilt. Lots Road Auctions, Chelsea. Apr 02. £700.

2012

Georgian mahogany chest of 2 short and 3 long drawers, 91cm wide. Thos Mawer & Son, Lincoln. Apr 02. £700.

2013

Victorian mahogany parlour suite: two seat settee, 2 elbow chairs and 4 single chairs. Sworders, Stansted Mountfitchet. July 01. £700.

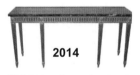
2014

20thC Neo classical style giltwood, marble top serving table, 190cm wide. Lots Rd Auctions, Chelsea. Feb 03. £700.

2015

Late Regency Brazilian rosewood work table, 'S' scroll supports, 17 x 14.5 x 32.5in. Hamptons, Godalming. Jan 02. £700.

Hammer Price £700

2016

George III mahogany chest of drawers, fluted canted corners, 44in wide. Sworders, Stansted Mountfitchet. July 01. £700.

2017

Set 10 10thC mahog. balloon back dining chairs. Locke & England, Leamington Spa. July 03. £700.

2018

18thC oak mule chest, two base drawers, 52in wide. Sworders, Stansted Mountfitchet. July 01. £700.

2019

19thC Scandinavian salon suite: settee and two chairs, mahog. and parcel gilt, rush seats. Lots Road Auctions, Chelsea. Mar 03. £700.

2020

Pair of mahog. library steps, 41in high. Sworders, Stansted Mountfitchet. July 01. £700.

2021

George II oak lowboy, 32in wide. Amersham Auction Rooms, Bucks. Sep 02. £700.

2022

William IV mahogany crested armchair, c1830. Wintertons Ltd, Lichfield. July 03. £700.

2023

Edwardian inlaid mahogany display cabinet, dentil frieze over double astragal glazed doors, lower section fitted Globe Wernicke style inlaid panel, 100cm wide. Ambrose, Loughton. Mar 02. £700.

2024

Geo. III mahog. cabinet on chest, upper part with twin panelled doors, fitted as a secretaire with fall front, 3 drawer base, 34in wide. Amersham Auction Rooms, Bucks. June 02. £700.

Hammer Price £700

2025

Pair 20thC tub chairs, green leather. Lots Road Auctions, Chelsea. Sep 03. £700.

2026

19thC ebonized/gilt sofa, in green damask, 151cm. Locke & England, Leamington Spa. Sep 03. £700.

2027

Pair mahog. pot cupboards made from a 19thC washstand. Sworders, Stansted Mount-fitchet. Sep 03. £700.

2028

Victorian mahogany linen press, 48in wide. Fellows & Sons, Hockley, Birmingham. Oct 03. £700.

2029

20thC French kingwood bombe commode, rouge marble top, 39in. Gorringes, Lewes. Dec 03. £700.

2030

Late 19thC painted satinwood domed top box on stand of Sheraton design, 18 x 12 x 35.5in high. Canterbury Auc. Galleries, Kent. Dec 03. £700.

2031

19thC carved pine console table, green marble top, satyr mask and hoof front legs, plinth base, 4ft 5in. Gorringes, Lewes. Apr 04. £700.

2032

Set of 2 + 2 Regency dining chairs, Sheraton manner. Andrew Hartley, Ilkley. Feb 04. £700.

2033

Late George III mahogany dumb waiter, c1820. Wintertons Ltd, Lichfield. Nov 03. £700.

2034

Regency mahogany chiffonier, 2 frieze drawers, brass grill doors, 3ft 5in. Gorringes, Lewes. Dec 03. £700.

2035

Regency mahog. bow fronted chest, top with ebony and boxwood barber pole inlay, 2ft 9in wide. Gorringes, Bexhill. Mar 04. £700.

2036

Lady's 19thC Flemish, cross-banded kingwood, walnut veneered and marquetry desk, secretaire drawer, 25in wide. Amersham Auction Rooms, Bucks. Mar 04. £700.

2037

Late Geo. III mahog. four tier whatnot, 17.5in, 61.5in high, 2 central tiers, later side rails. Canterbury Auc. Galleries, Kent. Feb 04. £700.

2038

Originally an 18thC oak kist, a conversion: once rising top over 2 drawers and panelled cupboard doors enclosing later slides, 58in wide. Dee, Atkinson & Harrison, Driffield. Mar 04. £700.

2039

Regency mahogany D shaped two tier washstand, ebony inlaid, 28in wide. Gorringes, Bexhill. Mar 04. £700.

2040

Victorian satinwood bedside cupboard, latticework panel door, 45cm wide. Sworders, Stansted Mountfitchet. Feb 04. £700.

2041

George III Lancashire oak dresser, moulded edged hinged lid, cupboard door with star inlay, 61.25in wide. Andrew Hartley, Ilkley. June 04. £700.

2042

George III mahog. pembroke table, rosewood banding, 35.5in wide. Andrew Hartley, Ilkley. Apr 04. £700.

2043

Early 19thC colonial work table. Hamptons, Godalming. Mar 02. £700.

2044

George III yew wood corner chair. Sworders, Stansted Mountfitchet. Apr 01. £700.

2045

Regency ebony inlaid mahog. wine cooler, zinc liner, 15in wide. Amersham Auction Rooms, Bucks. Mar 04. £700.

2046

19thC floral inlaid rosewood bureau de dame, 2ft 2in. Gorringes, Lewes. Mar 04. £700.

2047

Mahogany Pembroke table 19thC, 20in wide. Andrew Hartley, Ilkley. Feb 04. £700.

2048

Late 19thC gilt decorated landscape overmantel mirror, 4ft 3.75in. Woolley & Wallis, Salisbury. Aug 00. £680.

2049

17thC oak chair table of plain country origin, scroll carved open arms, (one damaged) hinged plank table top 27in wide. Tring Market Auctions, Herts. Sep 02. £680.

Prices quoted are hammer and exclude the buyer's premium. Adding 15% will give approx. buying price.

2050

Regency rosewood library bergere armchair, 90cm high. Bristol Auction Rooms, Bristol. Sep 03. £680.

2051

Set of six George III mahog. dining chairs, 2 with extensive repairs. Canterbury Auction Galleries, Kent. Apr 04. £680.

Hammer Prices £700-£670

2052

William IV wine cooler, sarcophagus shape, recessed brass castors, 53cm high. Mellors & Kirk, Nottingham. June 03. £680.

2053

19thC teak brass mounted campaign chest, removable legs, 38in wide. Gorringes, Bexhill. July 03. £680.

2054

Victorian walnut loo table, tilt top crossbanded, shaped frieze, knurled feet, 136cm. Locke & England, Leamington Spa. Jan 03. £680.

2055

4 + 2 Chippendale style mahogany dining chairs, drop in seats. Sworders, Stansted Mountfitchet. Oct 01. £680.

2056

Victorian rosewood worktable, two drawers and a basket, 18in wide. af. Sworders, Stansted Mountfitchet. July 01. £680.

2057

Geo. III mahog. and boxwood strung tray top commode, c1785. Wintertons Ltd, Lichfield. Nov 03. £680.

2058

19thC Orkney chair of joined ash and pine construction, solid seat and box base with drawer, 104cm. Bristol Auction Rooms. Jan 04. £680.

2059

Early/mid 18thC joint stool, overstuffed, crushed fabric upholstered seat, 20in high. Amersham Auction Rooms, Bucks. June 03. £670.

2060

Early Victorian mahogany framed and part buttoned green hide upholstered chair. Amersham Auction Rooms, Bucks. Mar 02. £670.

Hammer Prices £670-£650

2061

Mid Victorian carved walnut show wood framed ottoman, comprising four outward facing conjoined quadrant seats. *Amersham Auction Rooms, Bucks. Nov 01. £670.*

2062

Art Nouveau marquetry inlaid mahogany kneehole desk, 42in wide. *Amersham Auction Rooms, Bucks. June 01. £670.*

2063

Late 19thC repro of a George III mahogany serpentine front sideboard, 47in wide. *Amersham Auction Rooms, Bucks. Apr 01. £670.*

2064

19thC mahogany Canterbury, 3 divisions with X divides and turned bars. *Rosebery's, London. Mar 02. £660.*

2065

19thC oak lowboy, 75cm wide. *Marilyn Swain Auctions, Grantham. Dec 03. £660.*

2066

Regency carved and gilt wood wall mirror, 47in high, 30.25in wide. *Andrew Hartley, Ilkley. Dec 01. £660.*

2067

19thC mahog. 3 fold screen, canvas panels painted with Kingfishers, owls and heron, 78in high. *Sworders, Stansted Mountfitchet. Apr 01. £660.*

2068

Edwardian mahog. Pembroke table with satinwood banding and stringing, 19.25 x 33in. (extended). *Andrew Hartley, Ilkley. Dec 01. £660.*

2069

Edwardian display cabinet. *John Taylors, Louth. Mar 01. £660.*

2070

Set 6 mid Victorian mahogany framed balloon back dining chairs. *Amersham Auction Rooms, Bucks. June 01. £650.*

2071

William IV mahog. fold over tea table, 36in wide. *Dee, Atkinson & Harrison, Driffield. Aug 01. £650.*

2072

Small 19thC painted canapé of Louis XVI design in blue cord. *Lots Road Auctions, Chelsea. Oct 01. £650.*

2073

Victorian mahogany buffet, 109 x 122cm. *Rosebery's, London. Mar 02. £650.*

2074

Regency period Barrel back easy chair in need of upholstery. *Hogben Auctioneers, Folkestone. Sep 01. £650.*

2075

Edwardian inlaid mahogany sideboard, 60in wide. *Sworders, Stansted Mountfitchet. Apr 01. £650.*

2076

19thC walnut boxwood strung and cross-banded Davenport desk. *Thos Mawer & Son, Lincoln. Apr 02. £650.*

2077

Set 4 walnut George I style dining chairs, c1900, labels, 'W F Greenwood & Sons, 24 Stonegate, York'. *Sworders, Stansted Mountfitchet. Feb 02. £650.*

2078

Geo. III mahog. chest, 124cm. *Locke & England, Leamington Spa. Sep 02. £650.*

2079

Inlaid mahogany escritoire, fitted frieze drawer to top, 36in wide. *Lambert & Foster, Tenterden. Apr 02. £650.*

2080

Set of six William IV mahog. dining chairs, with canted upholstered drop in seats. *Wintertons Ltd, Lichfield. Sep 02. £650.*

2081

George III mahog. bow front
chest, 106cm. *Rosebery's,
London. Mar 02. £650.*

2082

Early George III mahogany
bureau, fall front having
mitred corners and moulded
edge, with fitted interior, over
twin lopers and 4 graduated
long drawers, 36in wide.
*Amersham Auction Rooms,
Bucks. May 02. £650.*

2083

Edwardian Sheraton Revival
table vitrine, 66cm. *Locke &
England, Leamington Spa.
Sep 02. £650.*

2084

Wrought iron framed rocking
chair, slung button padded
seat. *Cheffins, Cambridge.
Sep 03. £650.*

2085

George III oak settle, loose
cushion, 160cm. *Locke &
England, Leamington Spa.
Sep 03. £650.*

2086

Late George II oak lowboy,
c1750, 77cm wide. *Wintertons
Ltd, Lichfield. Sep 02. £650.*

2087

Pair 20thC style armchairs.
*Lots Road Auctions, Chelsea.
May 03. £650.*

2088

Painted Italian console table
with shaped mirror top.
*Lots Road Auctions, Chelsea.
Oct 02. £650.*

2089

19thC tester bed, 168cm
wide. af. *Lambert & Foster,
Tenterden. Dec 02. £650.*

2090

Early 18thC walnut chest, on
later bracket feet, 40in wide.
(formerly the upper part of a
chest on chest). *Gorringes,
Bexhill. June 03. £650.*

2091

Early 20thC beechwood
armchair. *Lots Rd Auctions,
Chelsea. Jan 03. £650.*

2092

Set of six oak Gothic Revival
side chairs, mid 19thC, in the
manner of A.W. N. Pugin.
*Richard Wintertons, Burton
on Trent. July 03. £650.*

2093

Yew Windsor armchair.
*Andrew Hartley, Ilkley.
Feb 03. £650.*

2094

George III mahogany chest,
hinged rising and line inlaid
top, 138cm. *Henry Adams,
Chichester. Jan 03. £650.*

2095

Regency mahogany folding
card table, crossbanded D
shaped turnover top, 88.5cm.
*Locke & England, Leaming-
ton Spa. Jan 03. £650.*

2096

William IV figured mahogany
wine cellarette, interior
converted, 23in wide.
*Tring Market Auctions, Herts.
Mar 03. £650.*

2097

Early 17thC six plank oak
coffer, carved lunettes and
roundels, 49.5in. *Gorringes,
Lewes. Jan 04. £650.*

2098

French walnut dressing table,
gilt metal mounts, secret
drawer over slide, 19thC,
31.5in wide. *Andrew Hartley,
Ilkley. Dec 03. £650.*

Hammer Prices £650-£640

2099

Edwardian satinwood inlaid, mahogany display cabinet, 36in wide. *Amersham Auction Rooms, Bucks. Sep 03. £650.*

2100

Art Deco walnut demi-lune cocktail cabinet, 94cm wide. *Ambrose, Loughton. Feb 02. £650.*

2101

Gothic Revival oak box seat settle, c1900, triple panel back carved with tracery, leaves and fruit, stamped 4893F, 55in. *Peter Wilson, Nantwich. Nov 01. £650.*

2102

Geo. IV rosewood music chair, adjustable seat. *Gorringes, Bexhill. Mar 04. £650.*

130

2103

Late Victorian rosewood needlework/games table, 25in wide. *Tring Market Auctions, Herts. Nov 03. £650.*

2104

Georgian mahogany chest of drawers. *John Taylors, Louth. Mar 04. £650.*

2105

c1920s oak dining room table converting to snooker table, by Riley. *Hogben Auctioneers, Folkestone. Aug 01. £650.*

2106

George III mahog. Pembroke table, 39in wide x 29in high. *Dee, Atkinson & Harrison, Driffield. Apr 01. £650.*

2107

19thC yew/elm Windsor wheel back armchair. *Gorringes, Bexhill. Mar 04. £650.*

2108

Edwardian inlaid mahogany settee, pale green draylon. *Lambert & Foster, Tenterden. Oct 01. £650.*

2109

William IV rosewood tea table, 35 x 35in. *Clarke Gammon, Guildford. Apr 01. £650.*

2110

17thC design chair back settee, caned back panels and seats, carved stretcher rails, 114cm wide. *Lambert & Foster, Tenterden. Apr 04. £650.*

2111

Adzed oak plant trough by Robert 'Mouseman' Thompson, carved mouse trademark, 118in long, 11.5in wide. *Andrew Hartley, Ilkley. Feb 04. £640.*

2112

Victorian rosewood and marquetry envelope card table, 1ft 10in. *Gorringes, Bexhill. Dec 01. £640.*

2113

19thC oak windout dining table, 2 leaves, max 69in x 48in. *Sworders, Stansted Mountfitchet. Apr 01. £640.*

2114

George I style walnut wing armchair upholstered in peach fabric. *Rosebery's, London. Sep 03. £640.*

2115

Regency ebony line inlaid mahogany small side table, 50.5cm wide. *Bristol Auction Rooms, Bristol. Jan 04. £640.*

2116

Edwardian mahog. quartetto of occasional tables, string inlay, 59cm wide. *Richard Wintertons, Burton on Trent. Feb 04. £640.*

2117

William IV mahog. chiffonier, 46.5in wide. *Canterbury Auction Galleries, Kent. June 01. £640.*

2118

Lady's Regency writing table, top with beaded edging, trestle base, 25in wide. *Andrew Hartley, Ilkley. June 04. £640.*

2119

19thC mahogany and walnut finished miniature Wellington chest. *Biddle & Webb, Birmingham. May 02. £640.*

The numbering system acts as a reader reference as well as linking to the Analysis of each Section

2120

Pair of William IV mahogany hall chairs. *Bristol Auction Rooms, Bristol. Sep 02. £630.*

2121

19thC fruitwood lambing chair. *David Duggleby, Scarborough. July 01. £625.*

2122

Edwardian neo-classical design mahogany display cabinet, 154cm wide. *Thos Mawer & Son, Lincoln. June 04. £625.*

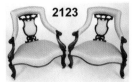

2123

Pair of Victorian walnut framed corner chairs. *Clevedon Salerooms, Bristol. June 01. £620.*

2124

Late Victorian walnut and marquetry pier cabinet, 33in wide. *Amersham Auction Rooms, Bucks. June 01. £620.*

2125

William IV rosewood foldover card table, 36in wide. *Tring Market Auctions, Herts. Sep 02. £620.*

2126

Victorian carved stained wood cigar cabinet, 25in wide. *Andrew Hartley, Ilkley. Aug 02. £620.*

Hammer Prices £640-£620

2127

Chromium and tan leather tubular armchair designed by Marc Brewer, and retailed by Heals. *Gorringes, Bexhill. Oct 01. £620.*

2128

Victorian burr walnut canterbury with a single drawer. *Sworders, Stansted Mountfitchet. Apr 01. £620.*

2129

Victorian walnut metamorphic library chair, pierced Gothic arches, quatrefoils. *Rosebery's, London. Mar 02. £620.*

2130

Regency style convex gilt framed wall mirror, eagle and acanthus decoration, 40in high. *Fellows & Sons, Hockley, Birmingham. July 03. £620.*

2131

Victorian walnut card table, folding figured top with 'D' ends, inlaid and carved foliate decoration, 35 x 36in overall. *Clarke Gammon, Guildford. Sep 02. £620.*

2132

Victorian walnut Canterbury whatnot, serpentine outline, 103 x 56cm. *Rosebery's, London. Sep 02. £620.*

2133

George III mahog. pedestal table, tip top having a later carved foliate border, 32in dia. *Amersham Auction Rooms, Bucks. Aug 02. £620.*

2134

Edwardian Sheraton Revival lady's desk, 62.5cm. *Locke & England, Leamington Spa. Jan 03. £620.*

Hammer Prices £620-£600

2135

George III Sheraton Revival inlaid mahogany bureau. Kidson Trigg Auctions, Swindon. May 04. £620.

2136

Victorian mahogany cheval mirror. John Taylors, Louth. Oct 03. £620.

2137

Georgian mahogany 3 tier whatnot, 17.5in, one leg replaced. Denhams, Warnham. May 04. £620.

2138

19thC Oriental pierced hardwood Fujiama cabinet with gilt and lacquered panels, 42in. Denhams, Warnham. Mar 04. £620.

2139

Pair 19thC mahog. pedestal bedside cabinets, 17in. Denhams, Warnham. Mar 04. £620.

2140

Set of six Victorian rosewood balloon back dining chairs. Canterbury Auc. Galleries, Kent. Apr 04. £620.

2141

2142

Early 19thC cream painted pine corner cabinet, 92cm wide. Lambert & Foster, Tenterden. Dec 02. £620.

18thC and later carved oak cupboard on stand, 171 x 79cm. Rosebery's, London. June 03. £620.

2143

Georgian oak hanging corner cupboard, 33in wide. Dee, Atkinson & Harrison, Driffield. Apr 01. £600.

2144

Late 19thC mahogany pedestal desk, 48in wide. Sworders, Stansted Mountfitchet. July 01. £600.

2145

Victorian mahog. breakfront chiffonier, 59in wide. Dee, Atkinson & Harrison, Driffield. Apr 01. £600.

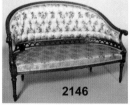

2146

Late 19thC stained beech parlour settee. Amersham Auction Rooms, Bucks. May 01. £600.

2147

19thC giltwood window seat in Louis XVI style. Cheffins, Cambridge. June 01. £600.

2148

Victorian walnut miniature loo table, 11in long x 7in high. Sworders, Stansted Mountfitchet. May 01. £600.

2149

Victorian mahog. chiffonier, 48in wide. Lambert & Foster, Tenterden. Apr 01. £600.

2150

19thC walnut chaise longue, foliate carved moulded frame, buttoned upholstery, fitted ceramic castors. Gorringes, Lewes. July 01. £600.

2151

1920s walnut veneered kneehole writing table, 48in wide. Amersham Auction Rooms, Bucks. June 01. £600.

2152

Late 18th/19thC Colonial mahogany dressing chest, 38in wide. Amersham Auction Rooms, Bucks. June 01. £600.

2153

Pair of 19thC girandoles (mirrors), in oval gilt gesso frames, three candle branches with cartouche cresting, 37in high. *Lots Road Auctions, Chelsea. July 01. £600.*

2154

George IV mahogany chest of drawers. *Gorringes, Bexhill. Sep 01. £600.*

The illustrations are in descending price order. The price range is indicated at the top of each page.

2155

19thC carved mahogany open arm elbow drawing room chair. *Mervyn Carey, Tenterden. July 01. £600.*

2156

Anglo Indian hardwood four door cabinet with shelving, 4ft wide. *Sworders, Stansted Mountfitchet. Apr 01. £600.*

2157

Georgian oak dresser, 18thC. *Andrew Hartley, Ilkley. Oct 01. £600.*

2158

Late 17thC oak dressing chest, 36in high x 39.5in wide. *Amersham Auction Rooms, Bucks. Sep 01. £600.*

2159

Rosewood dining table, c1835, 130cm dia. *Richard Wintertons, Burton on Trent. Dec 01. £600.*

2160

Late 18thC country made oak pedestal tip top table, 33.5in diameter. *Amersham Auction Rooms, Bucks. Nov 01. £600.*

2161

Geo. III mahogany oval drop leaf table, club legs, 44in extended. *Sworders, Stansted Mountfitchet. Apr 01. £600.*

Hammer Price £600

2162

Edwardian mahogany string inlaid cabinet, 37.5in wide. *Dee, Atkinson & Harrison, Driffield. Apr 01. £600.*

2163

Louis IV walnut side chair upholstered in floral needlework. *Hamptons, Godalming. Jan 02. £600.*

2164

Edwardian mahogany bureau bookcase, fall front enclosing drawers, pigeon holes, 42in. *Dee, Atkinson & Harrison, Driffield. Mar 04. £600.*

2165

Quartetto nest of of string inlaid mahogany tables. *Dockree's, Manchester. June 01. £600.*

2166

William IV gilt framed over-mantel mirror, three bevelled plates, 56 x 25in. *Canterbury Auction Galleries, Kent. Aug 02. £600.*

2167

Victorian walnut bookcase, 53in wide. *Peter Wilson, Nantwich. Nov 01. £600.*

2168

Victorian rosewood music cabinet, grained decoration, 21in wide. *Sworders, Stansted Mountfitchet. Apr 01. £600.*

2169

Geo. III barrel shaped wing armchair. af. *Sworders, Stansted Mountfitichet. Apr 01. £600.*

2170

Pair of George III mahogany dining table D ends, 45in wide. *Sworders, Stansted Mountfitchet. Apr 01. £600.*

Hammer Price £600

George II mahogany low boy, 80cm wide. *Ambrose, Loughton. Mar 02. £600.*

Regency mahog. side cabinet, 87cm wide. *Peter Wilson, Nantwich. July 02. £600.*

Early 19thC bowfront mahog. chest of drawers, 107 x 54 x 108cm. *Hamptons, Godalming. July 02. £600.*

George III mahogany chest of five drawers, 41in wide. *Sworders, Stansted Mountfitchet. July 01. £600.*

Sheraton revival satinwood sofa table, 3ft 7in. (some faults). *Gorringes, Bexhill. Dec 02. £600.*

George III mahogany secretaire chest, 46in wide, af. *Sworders, Stansted Mountfitchet. July 01. £600.*

Regency rosewood breakfast table, cushion moulded edge, tapered, octagonal column, triform platform, 48in dia. *Amersham Auction Rooms, Bucks. June 02. £600.*

George II style mahogany armchair. *Lots Road Auctions, Chelsea. Nov 02. £600.*

Late Victorian inlaid rosewood nine piece drawing room suite. *W & H Peacock, Bedford. Mar 03. £600.*

George III inlaid and cross banded mahogany writing bureau. *W & H Peacock, Bedford. Dec 02. £600.*

Mid Victorian burr walnut foldover serpentine card table, 36in wide. *Tring Market Auctions, Herts. Nov 02. £600.*

Victorian giltwood framed wall mirror, c1880, 77cm wide. *Wintertons Ltd, Lichfield. Sep 02. £600.*

Victorian walnut sofa, upholstered and button back in brocade, 183cm. *Locke & England, Leamington Spa. Jan 03. £600.*

Late Regency rosewood card table, rotating foldover top, baize line surface, 36in wide. *Amersham Auction Rooms, Bucks. Nov 02. £600.*

Small late Victorian oval walnut sutherland table, 21in high. *Sworders, Stansted Mountfitchet. Apr 01. £600.*

19thC mahog.4 tier whatnot, 60cm wide. *Bristol Auction Rooms, Bristol. Apr 03. £600.*

Bouillotte table, 1880-1890, mahogany, marble top with brass rim, brushing slides. *Lots Road Auctions, Chelsea. Apr 03. £600.*

Edwardian mahogany, inlaid display cabinet, 29in. *Crows, Dorking. July 01. £600.*

Set of 6 early 20thC Carolean style oak dining chairs, with two similar chairs. (8). *Fellows & Sons, Hockley, Birmingham. July 03. £600.*

2190

Regency convex mirror, 11in dia. giltwood ball decorated frame, carved giltwood dolphin, pendant base, 18 x 33in. Woolley & Wallis, Salisbury. Aug 00. £600.

2191

19thC walnut breakfast table, quarter veneered, marquetry inlaid, tip top, 28in high, 53in wide. Amersham Auction Rooms, Bucks. Nov 03. £600.

Prices quoted are hammer and exclude the buyer's premium. Adding 15% will give approx. buying price.

2192

19thC Chinese hardwood display cabinet, c1890, 201 x 96cm. Sworders, Stansted Mountfitchet. Feb 04. £600.

2193

19thC papier mache work table, inlaid mother of pearl and painted flowers, 43cm wide. Lambert & Foster, Tenterden. Feb 04. £600.

2194

Late 19thC French walnut fauteuil, upholstered in pink dralon. Gorringes, Lewes. Jan 04. £600.

2195

Early 18thC oak coffer, 49.5in wide. Gorringes, Bexhill. Mar 04. £600.

2196

Rosewood and walnut work table, crossbanding and parquetry panels, sliding tray, late 19thC Continental, 23.75in wide. Andrew Hartley, Ilkley. Dec 03. £600.

2197

Regency burr yew Pembroke work table, 1ft 7in. Gorringes, Lewes. Sep 03. £600.

2198

Regency mahog. card table, folding top cross banded in maple, 35in wide. Gorringes, Bexhill. Sep 03. £600.

2199

Late 19thC George III satinwood and rosewood inlaid mahogany work table, 17.75in wide. Amersham Auction Rooms, Bucks. Mar 04. £600.

2200

William IV mahogany tea poy, fitted with 2 lidded caddies & 2 bowl apertures, 18.25in wide. Andrew Hartley, Ilkley. June 04. £600.

2201

Mahogany/walnut cabinet in Arts & Crafts style, stamped W Walker & Sons, Bunhill Row E.C., 47.75in wide. Andrew Hartley, Ilkley. Apr 04. £600.

2202

George III Irish mahogany dining chair, Chippendale style. Sworders, Stansted Mountfitchet. Feb 04. £600.

2203

Edwardian rosewood and inlaid envelope card table, 75 x 59cm. Rosebery's, London. June 04. £600.

2204

Cocktail cabinet, 1930s, burr walnut. Lots Road Auctions, Chelsea. Sep 03. £600.

2205

Victorian figured walnut and gilt metal mounted card table, floral marquetry panel, frieze drawer, 31in. Gorringes. Lewes. Apr 04. £600.

2206

18thC oak wardrobe, carved frame, 2 base drawers, 144 x 170cm. Sworders, Stansted Mountfitchet. Sep 03. £600.

2207

Oak six plank chest, hinged lid, 17thC, 52in wide. Andrew Hartley, Ilkley. Aug 01. £580.

135

Hammer Price £580

2208

Art Deco figured crossbanded blonde walnut dining table by Simpoles Ltd, Manchester, date 16.8.37, 60in x 111in. Morphets, Harrogate, N Yorks. Mar 01. £580.

2209

Edwardian bank of drawers with 3 columns of 10 drawers, 48in wide. Lots Road Auctions, Chelsea. July 01. £580.

2210

Early 19thC mahogany chest, 36 x 30.5in. David Duggleby, Scarborough. July 01. £580.

2211

19thC amboyna and ebonised credenza, 146cm. Cheffins, Cambridge. Sep 01. £580.

2212

Set early Victorian mahog. dining chairs, five with drop in seats. Sworders, Stansted Mountfitchet. July 01. £580.

2213

Empire style mahogany stool. Rosebery's, London. Sep 01. £580.

2214

Mid Georgian mahog. small folding tea table. Bristol Auction Rooms. Nov 01. £580.

2215

George III mahog. pembroke table, 36in wide. Andrew Hartley, Ilkley. Oct 01. £580.

2216

Victorian walnut needlework table. Tring Market Auctions, Herts. Jan 02. £580.

2217

George IV mahog. washstand, c1825, probably Scottish, 100 x 110cm. Rosebery's, London. Sep 02. £580.

2218

George III oak lowboy, 30in wide. Sworders, Stansted Mountfitchet. Apr 01. £580.

2219

George III oak chest on chest, top section with 3 long drawers, base with two, 40in wide. Sworders, Stansted Mountfitchet. Apr 01. £580.

2220

19thC mahog. triple wardrobe, 75in wide. Sworders, Stansted Mountfitchet. Apr 01. £580.

2221

Edwardian walnut revolving bookstand, 19in wide. Sworders, Stansted Mountfitchet. July 01. £580.

2222

George III mahog. Pembroke table, 100cm open. Locke & England, Leamington Spa. Jan 03. £580.

2223

Regency mahogany work box, ebony inlay, on a later stand, 11in wide. Sworders, Stansted Mountfitchet. Apr 01. £580.

2224

Late Victorian breakfront mahogany side cabinet, 68in wide. Sworders, Stansted Mountfitchet. Apr 01. £580.

2225

Victorian mahogany bookcase cabinet of small proportions, 76 x 48 x 186cm. Hamptons, Godalming. July 02. £580.

2226

Victorian iron and brass book press by S Mordan & Co, on a mahogany drop flap table, two drawers, one lead lined, 23in. Denhams, Warnham. Oct 03. £580.

2227

19thC inlaid figured walnut occasional table, 4ft. *Gorringes, Lewes. July 03. £580.*

2228

George III oak lowboy. *Locke & England, Leamington Spa. Nov 02. £580.*

2229

Victorian octagonal trumpet shaped work table, top (later restored) inlaid with various woods, fitted interior, 48.5cm dia. *Lambert & Foster, Tenterden. Feb 04. £580.*

2230

19thC satin walnut davenport, gallery to back, leather cloth lined writing surface, 23in wide. *Canterbury Auction Galleries, Kent. Apr 04. £580.*

2231

Joined oak oval gateleg table, early 18thC, planked top, 114cm wide. *Bristol Auction Rooms, Bristol. Jan 04. £580.*

2232

Regency mahogany cellarette, hinged lid, 14in wide. *Andrew Hartley, Ilkley. Dec 03. £580.*

2233

Edwardian mahogany vitrine, Sheraton Revival style, 113cm wide. *R. Wintertons, Burton on Trent. Feb 04. £580.*

The numbering system acts as a reader reference as well as linking to the Analysis of each Section

2234

Georgian mahog. travelling chest, plain front over 2 small drawers, later brass swan neck handles, original brass carrying handles, 47.5in wide, *Dee, Atkinson & Harrison, Driffield. Mar 04. £580.*

2235

George III mahog. hanging quadrant cupboard, 29in wide. *Amersham Auction Rooms, Bucks. Aug 01. £570.*

Hammer Prices £580-£550

2236

Early 18thC walnut dressing chest, 35in high, 40in wide. *Amersham Auction Rooms, Bucks. Nov 01. £570.*

2237

Early 20thC reproduction of a Carolean oak side table, top having moulded edge over a frieze drawer, 29.5in high, 32in wide. *Amersham Auction Rooms, Bucks. May 02. £570.*

2238

Late 19thC walnut card table, foldover top, applied Vitruvian scrolled, ormolu edge, 37in wide. *Amersham Auction Rooms, Bucks. Oct 02. £570.*

2239

Late George III mahogany Canterbury, box drawer base, 20in wide. *Amersham Auction Rooms, Bucks. Feb 04. £570.*

2240

Regency carved mahogany and upholstered settee. 7ft 2in wide. *Sworders, Stansted Mountfitchet. July 01. £560.*

2241

Pair 19thC corner easy chairs, rose dralon. *Canterbury Auction Galleries, Kent. Aug 02. £560.*

2242

Edwardian mahog. envelope top card table, 47.75in square maximum. *David Duggleby, Scarborough. July 01. £560.*

2243

Edwardian mahog. revolving bookcase, crossbanded with stringing, castors. *Andrew Hartley, Ilkley. Apr 04. £560.*

2244

William IV rosewood chaise longue, 170cm wide. *Rosebery's, London. Sep 03. £550.*

2245

Late Georgian mahogany adjustable reading table. *W & H Peacock, Bedford. Dec 02. £550.*

Hammer Price £550

17thC oak blanket box, four panel top, split ring hinges. 54.75in. *David Duggleby, Scarborough. July 01. £550.*

17thC oak coffer, 42in wide. *Sworders, Stansted Mountfitchet. July 01. £550.*

George III mahog. occasional table, 20in wide. *Hamptons, Godalming. Sep 01. £550.*

Victorian rosewood and parquetry games table, 1ft 8.5in. *Gorringes, Bexhill. Dec 02. £550.*

2247

Victorian walnut foldover top card table, 34in. *Crows, Dorking. July 01. £550.*

Victorian mahogany two tier buffet, 115cm. *Henry Adams, Chichester. Sep 02. £550.*

Lady's 1920s walnut veneered oval writing table, 37in wide. *Amersham Auction Rooms, Bucks. June 01. £550.*

Mid 19thC carved mahogany sideboard pedestal, (adapted) 32in wide. *Sworders, Stansted Mountfitchet. July 01. £550.*

2248

Victorian mahogany crank wind extending dining table, one extra leaf, 118cm wide, 188cm extended. *Dockree's, Manchester. June 01. £550.*

Charles II oak chest, bun feet, 37.5in wide. *Clarke Gammon, Guildford. June 03. £550.*

Set of six Art Deco walnut chairs and a dressing stool. *Lots Road Auctions, Chelsea. July 01. £550.*

Georgian design mahog. frame settee, spirally fluted rails, arms carved with birds heads, stylised hoof feet, 170cm wide. *Thos Mawer & Son, Lincoln. June 04. £550.*

2249

Edwardian mahog. book stand, 36.5in long. *Sworders, Stansted Mountfitchet. Apr 01. £550.*

19thC mahogany secretaire. *Lambert & Foster, Tenterden. Dec 01. £550.*

2259

19thC rosewood library table, 4ft wide. *Gorringes, Bexhill. June 03. £550.*

George III mahogany tray top commode, 76cm high. *Mellors & Kirk, Nottingham. June 03. £550.*

George III country oak bureau cabinet, 89 x 177cm. *David Duggleby, Scarborough. June 01. £550.*

Robert Thomspon's Craftsmen Limited kidney shaped table, matching 3 leg stool, both carved with 'Mouse'. (original receipt for 1983 and leaflet. *Lambert & Foster, Tenterden, Kent. Apr 03. £550.*

Early 20thC duck egg blue lacquered, gilded, chinoiserie decorated, bow front display cabinet, 54in wide. *Amersham Auction Rooms, Bucks. Apr 02. £550.*

19thC ebonised china cabinet, Sevres type plaque in gilt brass mount, bevelled mirror, 120cm wide. *Thos Mawer & Son, Lincoln. Feb 03. £550.*

2266

19thC gentleman's spoonback carved mahogany easy chair, in later stained green hide. Sworders, Stansted Mountfitchet. Apr 01. £550.

2267

Geo. III giltwood wall mirror, ball/figural frieze, corinthian capped columns, 35in wide. Sworders, Stansted Mountfitchet. Apr 01. £550.

The illustrations are in descending price order. The price range is indicated at the top of each page.

2268

Early 18thC carved oak open armchair, with strapwork ornament above initials HF and date 1612, planked seat. Wintertons Ltd, Lichfield. Jan 04. £550.

2269

Set 6 mid Victorian mahog. balloon back dining chairs. Amersham Auction Rooms, Bucks. Feb 04. £550.

2270

19thC walnut chiffonier, spiral fluted columns, toupie feet, 37in. Gorringes, Lewes. Apr 04. £550.

2271

19thC mahog. chiffonier, 87cm wide. Lambert & Foster, Tenterden. Aug 03. £550.

2272

19thC gilt wood and gesso Venetian girandole oval wall mirror. Lambert & Foster, Tenterden. May 02. £550.

2273

Edwardian mahog. standing corner cabinet, 68in high. Dee, Atkinson & Harrison, Driffield. Mar 04. £550.

Hammer Prices £550-£520

2274

George III mahog. pembroke table, 30in wide. Andrew Hartley, Ilkley. Feb 03. £540.

2275

Georgian inlaid/crossbanded mahogany 'Channel Islands' chest, 34in. Denhams, Warnham. May 04. £540.

2276

19thC parquetry burr walnut loo table, 119cm wide. Bristol Auction Rooms. Jan 04. £540.

2277

19thC butler's mahogany oval tray, folding sides, 35 x 26.5in. Canterbury Auction Galleries, Kent. Feb 04. £540.

2278

19thC carved mahogany jardiniere. W & H Peacock, Bedford. June 03. £540.

2279

Regency style mahog. sofa table, 41.5cm wide. Bristol Auction Rooms. Nov 01. £540.

2280

Italianate style wall mirror, 28in wide. Sworders, Stansted Mountfitchet. Apr 01. £530.

2281

18thC oak gateleg table, barley twist supports, 36.5in wide x 39.5in open. Dee, Atkinson & Harrison, Driffield. Mar 04. £530.

2282

Victorian mahogany chiffonier. John Taylors, Louth. June 01. £530.

2283

Small 18thC oak chest. Richard Wintertons, Burton on Trent. Apr 02. £520.

Hammer Price £520

2284

George II pine mule chest, panelled ends, possibly North Wales, 48in wide. Hamptons, Godalming. Nov 01. £520.

2285

Pair of 19thC carved walnut salon chairs. Sworders, Stansted Mountfitchet. Apr 01. £520.

2286

Edwardian mahogany pier cabinet, stringing, moulded edged top, 24in wide. Andrew Hartley, Ilkley. Aug 02. £520.

2287

Edwardian mahogany display cabinet, astragal glazed doors, 133cm wide. Ambrose, Loughton. Mar 02. £520.

2288

Mid Victorian walnut centre table, brown leather scriber, 42in wide. Amersham Auction Rooms, Bucks. Feb 02. £520.

2289

George III mahogany bureau, fitted interior, (some damage) 42in wide. Sworders, Stansted Mountfitchet. July 01. £520.

2290

Victorian mahog. work table, 22in wide. Amersham Auc. Rooms, Bucks. Mar 02. £520.

2291

19thC mahog. pedestal desk, 4ft wide. Sworders, Stansted Mountfitchet. July 01. £520.

2292

George III elm and burr elm bergere arm chair. Sworders, Stansted Mountfitchet. Apr 01. £520.

2293

Regency mahogany 'Scotch' chest, central hat drawer, 124 x 124cm. Rosebery's, London. Mar 02. £520.

2294

Walnut display cabinet, by Maple & Co., 60in wide, 48in high. Sworders, Stansted Mountfitchet. Apr 01. £520.

2295

Mid 19thC mahogany bow fronted chest, 45.5in wide. Sworders, Stansted Mountfitchet. Apr 01. £520.

2296

George III oak mule chest, 54in wide. Amersham Auction Rooms, Bucks. Nov 02. £520.

2297

Carved and gilt wood wing armchair in damask cream covering, 19thC. Andrew Hartley, Ilkley. Feb 04. £520.

2298

Edwardian inlaid mahogany salon suite: 2 seat settee, 2 armchairs and 4 singles. Sworders, Stansted Mountfitchet. Apr 01. £520.

2299

Reproduction oak oval gateleg dining table, 5ft 5in x 5ft. Sworders, Stansted Mountfitchet. July 01. £520.

2300

19thC mahogany bow fronted chest of drawers, oak linings, 36in wide. Sworders, Stansted Mountfitchet. July 01. £520.

2301

Late Victorian mahog. coaching table, elliptical stretchers, 35.5in open. Amersham Auction Rooms, Bucks. Nov 03. £520.

2302

Pair of Regency rosewood and brass inlaid bar back chairs, seat rails stamped 'W'. Sworders, Stansted Mountfitchet. Apr 01. £520.

Hammer Prices £520-£500

2303

Early 19thC yew wood/elm high stick back windsor elbow chair, crinoline stretcher. *Hampton & Littlewood, Exeter. Apr 04. £520.*

2304

Victorian rosewood three tier whatnot. *W & H Peacock, Bedford. Jan 03. £520.*

Prices quoted are hammer and exclude the buyer's premium. Adding 15% will give approx. buying price.

2305

Late Victorian walnut music cabinet, 26in wide. *Andrew Hartley, Ilkley. Apr 04. £520.*

2306

Late 17thC oak side table, 26in wide. *Tring Market Auctions, Herts. Nov 02. £520.*

2307

Regency mahogany three seat settee, reeded frame, 182cm. *Sworders, Stansted Mountfitchet. Feb 03. £520.*

2308

19thC cast iron hall chair. *W & H Peacock, Bedford. Feb 03. £520.*

2309

Georgian style mahogany wardrobe, 43in wide. *Tring Market Auctions, Herts. Jan 03. £520.*

2310

Early 20thC mahogany flame veneered breakfront sideboard, 71.5cm long. *Fellows & Sons, Hockley, B'ham. July 03. £520.*

2311

19thC rosewood card table, D shaped folding top, shaped frieze, 37in wide. *Gorringes, Bexhill. July 03. £520.*

2312

Late 20thC Titchmarsh & Goodwin Jacobean style court cupboard, 35in wide. *Amersham Auction Rooms, Bucks. June 03. £520.*

2313

Embossed & coloured leather four fold screen, 209cm. *Locke & England, Leamington Spa. May 03. £520.*

2314

George II style walnut caddy top chest of drawers, brushing slide. *Thos Mawer & Son, Lincoln. Feb 03. £520.*

2315

George III mahogany chest on chest, 202 x 107cm. *Rosebery's, London. Sep 03. £520.*

2316

19thC mahogany Empire sofa, gilt brass mounts, scrolled arms, 170cm. *Sworders, Stansted Mountfitchet. Sep 03. £520.*

2317

Edwardian Chesterfield sofa, 63in wide. *David Duggleby, Scarborough. Apr 01. £500.*

2318

19thC bow fronted mahogany sideboard, 42in wide. (repair). *Dee, Atkinson & Harrison, Driffield. Apr 01. £500.*

2319

19thC Dutch fruitwood and ebonised wine cooler, 17in high. *Andrew Hartley, Ilkley. Apr 01. £500.*

2320

19thC wall mirror, giltwood and gesso, shaped scrolling leaf frame. *Lots Rd Auctions, Chelsea. Oct 02. £500.*

Hammer Price £500

2321

Tall chest, American maple of 18thC design, 42in wide. *Lots Road Auctions, Chelsea. Nov 01. £500.*

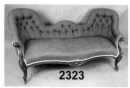

2322

Foot stool on turned mahog. legs. *Sworders, Stansted Mountfitchet. July 01. £500.*

2323

19thC double ended button back settee, carved walnut. *Sworders, Stansted Mountfitchet. July 01. £500.*

2324

19thC giltwood/gesso over-mantel mirror, 50in. *Gorringes, Bexhill. Sep 02. £500.*

2325

Edwardian strung mahogany display cabinet on table base, 37in wide. *Sworders, Stansted Mountfitchet. July 01. £500.*

142

2326

Victorian mahog. two drawer side table. *W & H Peacock, Bedford. Aug 02. £500.*

2327

George III inlaid mahogany secretaire chest, 46.5in. af. *Sworders, Stansted Mountfitchet. July 01. £500.*

2328

1920s walnut veneered cabinet bookcase, 52in wide. *Amersham Auction Rooms, Bucks. May 02. £500.*

2329

George III mahogany bureau, 106cm. *Locke & England, Leamington Spa. Feb 03. £500.*

2330

Duet stool with floral tapestry seat. *Sworders, Stansted Mountfitchet. Feb 03. £500.*

2331

19thC Continental rosewood veneered, serpentine front side cabinet, marble top, concealed frieze drawer, 51in wide. *Amersham Auction Rooms, Herts. May 02. £500.*

2332

George III inlaid mahogany chest. *W & H Peacock, Bedford. Mar 03. £500.*

2333

Set of 6 + 2 reproduction rush seat ladderback chairs. *Sworders, Stansted Mountfitchet. July 01. £500.*

2334

Art Nouveau mahogany occasional table, 24.25in wide. *Andrew Hartley, Ilkley. Aug 02. £500.*

2335

19thC brass frame three tier rosewood etagere, 37cm square. *Thos Mawer & Son, Lincoln. Nov 02. £500.*

2336

17thC single chair with open twist and block carved frame, 20.5in wide, 37in high. *Tring Market Auctions, Herts. Nov 02. £500.*

2337

Late 19thC French kingwood & floral marquetry occasional table, gilt metal and porcelain mounts, 1ft 2in. *Gorringes, Lewes. June 03. £500.*

2338

George III upholstered dining chair, serpentine back. *David Duggleby, Scarborough. Dec 01. £500.*

2339

George III mahogany corner cupboard, 31in wide. *Amersham Auction Rooms, Bucks. Oct 01. £500.*

Hammer Price £500

2340

Early 19thC mahog. drop leaf work table, two drawers, 77 x 42cm extended. *Thos Mawer & Son, Lincoln. Feb 03. £500.*

2341

19thC breakfront four door mahogany wardrobe with two hanging cupboards, 223cm wide, 190cm high. *Thos Mawer & Son, Lincoln. Feb 03. £500.*

> The numbering system acts as a reader reference as well as linking to the Analysis of each Section

2342

Georgian oak chest of drawers. *John Taylors, Louth. Sep 03. £500.*

2343

George III inlaid mahogany bowfront hanging corner cupboard, 2ft 7in. *Gorringes, Lewes. Jan 04. £500.*

2344

Victorian walnut spoon back open arm easy chair, upholstered in striped moquette. *Canterbury Auc. Galleries, Kent. Dec 03. £500.*

2345

Late Regency pollard oak sofa table, 37.5in wide closed. *Amersham Auction Rooms, Bucks. Nov 03. £500.*

2346

19thC mahog. twin pedestal kneehole desk, 122cm. *Locke & England, Leamington Spa. May 03. £500.*

2347

William IV mahog. D-shaped card table, 36in wide. *Canterbury Auc. Galleries, Kent. Dec 03. £500.*

2348

Matched set of 8 + 1 early 19thC ash, beech and elm framed Windsor chairs. *Amersham Auction Rooms, Bucks. Mar 03. £500.*

2349

Oak settle, panelled back, basically 18thC, now with upholstered seat, 1.87m long. *Sworders, Stansted Mountfitchet. Dec 03. £500.*

2350

Three panel leather screen, late 19th/early 20thC, with pelicans in a tropical landscape. *Lots Road Auctions, Chelsea. Mar 04. £500.*

2351

Victorian carved mahogany chaise longue. *Sworders, Stansted Mountfitchet. Feb 04. £500.*

2352

Set of 6 George III mahogany dining chairs. *Rosebery's, London. June 03. £500.*

2353

19thC gilt wood and ebonised overmantel mirror, 64in wide, 69.5in high. *Andrew Hartley, Ilkley. Feb 01. £500.*

2354

Continental mahog. writing table, 19thC, 39in. *Denhams, Warnham. Feb 04. £500.*

2355

George III mahogany tray top bedside cabinet, 24 x 18 x 31in high. *Canterbury Auction Galleries, Kent. Feb 04. £500.*

2356

George IV mahog. secretaire chest, rosewood cross-banded and boxwood line inlaid, 3ft 7in wide. *Gorringes, Bexhill. June 03. £500.*

2357

William IV mahogany card table with D shaped folding top, 3ft wide. *Gorringes, Bexhill. Mar 03. £500.*

2358

19thC Continental bow fronted walnut four drawer commode. *Sworders, Stansted Mountfitchet. July 01. £500.*

Hammer Price £500

Mahog. inlaid quartetto nest of tables. Eastbourne Auction Rooms, Sussex. Mar 02. £500.

2359

Early 20thC walnut pedestal desk by Maple & Co., 138cm wide. Lots Road Auctions, Chelsea. Apr 04. £500.

2360

George III style mahog. bow front sideboard, late 19thC, 92 x 142cm. Rosebery's, London. June 04. £500.

2361

Victorian Scottish mahogany chest of drawers, 49in wide. Sworders, Stansted Mount-fitchet. Apr 01. £500.

2362

Early 19thC mahogany child's high chair with a table base. Sworders, Stansted Mount-fitchet. Feb 04. £500.

2363

Regency period mahogany dwarf chest, 18in x 23in. Tring Market Auctions, Herts. May 02. £500.

2364

Pair of 19thC gilt wall mirrors, 2ft 7in. Gorringes, Bexhill. Dec 02. £500.

2365

Victorian rosewood teapoy, moulded top enclosing four canisters. Gorringes, Bexhill. May 04. £500.

2366

19thC Burmese carved teak box settle, with flowers, foliage and entwined dragons and peacock, hinged seat, 51in. Hampton & Littlewood, Exeter. Apr 04. £500.

2367

Edwardian mahogany inlaid and satin banded wardrobe/chest, 82in wide, 82in high. Dee, Atkinson & Harrison, Driffield. Mar 04. £500.

2368

Set 19thC rosewood 5 tier graduated hanging shelves, 60 x 114cm. Henry Adams, Chichester. July 02. £500.

2369

17thC oak coffer, carved with stylised tulip shape flowers, 120cm wide. Lambert & Foster, Tenterden. Apr 04. £500.

2370

18thC walnut chest, top with quarter veneer and cross-banded edge, 99cm wide. af. Lambert & Foster, Tenterden. Apr 04. £500.

2371

Late 19thC Chinese padouk wood and mother of pearl inlaid side cabinet, 113cm wide. Lots Road Auctions, Chelsea. Apr 04. £500.

2372

19thC giltwood urn stand, later marble top, four ornate scroll legs, 20in. Gorringes, Lewes. Mar 04. £500.

2373

Victorian rosewood and ivory inlaid writing desk, c1870, 71cm wide. Wintertons Ltd, Lichfield. Mar 04. £500.

2374

Early 18thC walnut chest, brass loop handles, bracket feet, 3ft 4in. Gorringes, Lewes. Mar 04. £500.

2375

19thC Anglo Indian occasional table, inlaid with various woods, rosewood baluster stem, 30.5in. Gorringes, Lewes. Apr 04. £500.

2376

Georgian oak bow fronted wall hanging corner cupboard, 24in wide. Dee, Atkinson & Harrison, Driffield. Mar 04. £500.

2377

Section X <£500 to £250

Such items in the Editor's opinion offer fantastic bargains for young people setting up a home. Even Art Deco 3-piece suites from the 1930s, with their long rake seating and low arms and backs, can be found for under £500.

Here are about twenty five examples of seventeenth century furniture, many offering excellent value as do dozens of the Georgian lots. The Victorian period and the twentieth century now dominate. Firstly, let us look at the Delft rack, **2378**. Remember the expensive spoon and plate racks? Here a 72 inch example fetched £480, probably good value. A simple object is the cricket table at **2389**. Mid to late eighteenth century, this oak example fetched £480 in 2002. Remember the cricket table on page 115, which fetched £800 at the same auction? Compare the two. Can you see why? And now turn back to the cricket table on page 26. This was a seventeenth century example in elm, which sold in December 2002 at Kivell & Sons, Bude for £4,200. The cheaper examples are smaller, but what makes the difference between a £500 cricket table and a £5,000 specimen?

Look at the matched series of ten wheel-back Windsor chairs at **2412**, which fetched only £480 in April 2004 in Burton-on-Trent. Compare these with the late Georgian armchair Windsor on page 148, **2415**, which has everything! Yew, elm, fruitwood, hooped spindle-back, pierced vase splat and a crinoline stretcher, at a similar price. Check also on page 149 the Georgian child's stick-back, still with traces of original paint (don't ever remove it). Which is the best investment buy? Now for a different type of furniture altogether in the seating category, furniture built for comfort! The relevant illustrations are **2398**, **2450**, **2502**, **2512**, **2568** and **2671**. **2450** and **2412** are identical settees from the same sale fetching different prices. There were two of them. Such items in the Editor's opinion offer fantastic bargains for young people setting up a home. Even Art Deco 3-piece suites from the 1930s can be found for under £500. Many typify the period, with their long rake seats and their low arms and backs. Earlier versions can be deep-seated with high, sprung arms offering supreme comfort. They remind one of early twentieth century advertisements where Mum and Dad, sat listening to the radio, Dad with a pipe in his hand and immortalised in films like *Brief Encounter.*

Readers can look at many drop-leaf tables, both original and reproduction. How does the late seventeenth century examples at **2478** or at **2702** compare? For families with space problems these are incredible value for money. They can be pushed up against a wall when not in use and later when fortunes are made, they will sell on for at least as much or more than was paid. Hopefully, your investment in antiques will then help pay for that much grander extending, refectory, or farmhouse version which can take centre stage in a dining room, cavenous kitchen or conservatory.

Now for the promised discussion on pine. There are at least four examples and only two or three in *Section 11*. These can be found at **2626**, **2693**, **2705**, **2794** and later at **2885** and **2910**. **2626** is a very neat, again painted, George III, versatile, corner washstand for only £350. I am told that painted pine is the preserve mainly of the American market. If so then we should change our ways before these rarer legacies of our heritage are long gone. The same goes for **2693**, a Victorian pitch pine cupboard with pointed arch panelled doors, excellent value at only £320. Or even better and providing it is in original condition, the nineteenth century pine double fronted cupboard at **2705**, which sold at Crows, Dorking in July 2001 for only £300. See the early Victorian pitch pine Gothic Revival fire surround at **2794**, which fetched £260 in 2001. New fire surrounds are a racket! Avoid at all costs those melamine-coated chipboard reproductions with their stuck on neo-classical ornament! Fireplace shops will fit your new fireplace at an exhorbitant fee and suddenly you have been set back a £1,000 at least and that's without the fire! Better to visit the antique specialists in your area. Some warehouses carry huge stocks. Often for less than half the money you can buy the genuine item in a range of original materials and then get your own carpenter or handyman to install. You will never regret it. There are models that will fit the traditional older homes or even new ones.

At last a stripped pine chest appears on page 174 at £200. The reason there is little pine is because auctions rarely include it in fine art sales preferring to keep it for their non-catalogue general sales, as it really does not sell very well at all. In other words, it is rarely photographed so is only rarely submitted. This does of course show pine has had its day, excepting the pair of console table at £15,000 on page 10! Certainly much of the stock has been ruined by stripping and the scarcity of genuine, unadulterated pieces, along with the ghastly reproductions selling on High Streets will probably guarantee its demise for years to come. The fashion now in lighter woods is for limed or stripped oak. Perhaps we are seeing a return to the Edwardian cottage mood.

Hammer Price £480

2378

18thC oak delft rack, 72in wide. Sworders, Stansted Mountfitchet. July 01. £480.

2379

17th/18thC elm bureau, fall front, stepped interior, 2 short and 2 long drawers. Denhams, Warnham. Aug 03. £480.

2380

Early 19thC bow fronted mahogany chest of drawers. Hogben Auctioneers, Folkestone. Sept 01. £480.

2381

19thC colonial brass mounted blanket chest, studded top and internal candle box, 129cm. Sworders, Stansted Mountfitchet. Oct 02. £480.

2382

George III mahogany bow fronted chest, rosewood cross-banding and stringing, brass ring handles, later ogee feet, 39in x 33.5in high. Andrew Hartley, Ilkley. June 02. £480.

2383

American etagere c1850s. Locke & England, Leamington Spa. Nov 02. £480.

2384

17thC style black lacquered two door cabinet on stand. af. Sworders, Stansted Mountfitchet. July 01. £480.

2385

19thC Antler chair. Lots Road Auctions, Chelsea. July 02. £480.

2386

19thC mahog. bowfront chest of drawers, turned columns, 45in wide. Sworders, Stansted Mountfitchet. Apr 01. £480.

2387

George III mahogany tilt top table, 31.5in dia. Sworders, Stansted Mountfitchet. July 01. £480.

2388

19thC walnut spoonback armchair. Tring Market Auctions, Herts. Nov 02. £480.

2389

Mid/late 18thC oak cricket table, 25in high, 24in dia. Amersham Auction Rooms, Bucks. Oct 02. £480.

2390

6 Victorian mahogany single dining chairs. (condition poor). Sworders, Stansted Mountfitchet. July 01. £480.

2391

Late 17thC oak side table, 84cm wide. (repairs and restorations). Hamptons, Godalming. July 01. £480.

2392

Mid 18thC oak tripod table, two part top with primitive tilt mechanism, 19in dia x 23.5in high. Hamptons, Godalming. Nov 01. £480.

2393

George III inlaid and cross banded mahogany bow front chest. W & H Peacock, Bedford. Dec 02. £480.

2394

Early 20thC French oval three drawer side cabinet. W & H Peacock, Bedford. Dec 02. £480.

2395

Early Victorian partners pedestal desk in need of repair. Hogben Auctioneers, Folkestone. Aug 01. £480.

2396

Georgian mahogany bowfront chest. W & H Peacock, Bedford. July 03. £480.

2397

Edwardian inlaid mahogany and brass lined jardiniere. W & H Peacock, Bedford. Jan 03. £480.

Victorian mahogany framed armchair, upholstered buttoned material. *Denhams, Warnham. Aug 03. £480.*

19thC dark mahog. envelope card table united by undertier, 56cm wide. *Lambert & Foster, Tenterden. Aug 03. £480.*

> The illustrations are in descending price order. The price range is indicated at the top of each page.

Pair 19thC mahogany folding library steps with brass hinges. *Sworders, Stansted Mountfitchet. Feb 04. £480.*

3 piece walnut bedroom suite: wardrobe, 87in high, dressing table, marble top washstand. *Dee, Atkinson & Harrison, Driffield. Mar 04. £480.*

Cotswold School Peter Waals English oak bureau, 3ft 5in high, 3ft wide. *Gorringes, Bexhill. Nov 03. £480.*

Victorian figured walnut four tier corner whatnot, 69cm wide. *Bristol Auction Rooms, Bristol. Jan 04. £480.*

19thC mahogany bookcase, two glazed doors, scrolled foliate mouldings, 41in wide. *Fellows & Sons, Hockley, Birmingham. Oct 03. £480.*

Late 19thC Orkney child's chair, pine with rush and seagrass woven curved back, 32in high. *Canterbury Auction Galleries, Kent. Feb 04. £480.*

Hammer Prices £480-£470

Edwardian mahog. quartetto of occasional tables, 25.5in wide overall. *Tring Market Auctions, Herts. Nov 03. £480.*

Pair of Victorian black papier mache occasional chairs by Jennens & Betteridge, inlaid in mother of pearl, floral needlework. *Canterbury Auc. Galleries, Kent. Feb 04. £480.*

19thC Oriental bamboo glazed bookcase. *Kidson Trigg Auctions, Swindon. May 04. £480.*

Victorian dark oak davenport, carved with lions masks, leaf scroll ornament, classical urn and swags, leathered slope, 27in wide. *Canterbury Auc. Galleries, Kent. Apr 04. £480.*

Edwardian mahog. settee, red dralon upholstery, 43.5in wide. *Dee, Atkinson & Harrison, Driffield. Mar 04. £480.*

George I design walnut and mahogany banded serpentine card table,32in. *Gorringes, Lewes. Apr 04. £480.*

Matched series of 10 Windsor chairs, 19thC and later. (one an armchair) *R.Wintertons, Burton on Trent. Apr 04. £480.*

19thC mahogany stool, over-stuffed top, tapestry covering, 14.5in wide. *Andrew Hartley, Ilkley. Apr 01. £475.*

Elm curved back settle. *Crows, Dorking. May 01. £470.*

Hammer Prices £470-£450

Early 19thC Windsor yew, elm, fruitwood hooped spindle back arm-chair, pierced vase splat, crinoline stretcher. *Tring Market Auctions, Herts. Mar 02. £470.*

18thC style figured walnut reverse breakfront writing desk, 40in wide. *Dockree's, Manchester. Feb 01. £460.*

Early 18thC oak chair. *Hamptons, Godalming. Jan 02. £460.*

Pair of Victorian rosewood footstools of C scroll form, upholstered in turquoise velvet, 15in wide. *Andrew Hartley, Ilkley. Dec 03. £460.*

Oak panelled coffer, fascia carved with scrolling foliate frieze over 3 panels, leaf carved upright, moulded stiles, 46in wide. *A. Hartley, Ilkley. June 02. £460.*

Early 19thC mahog. cellarette of sarcophagus form, fitted as a work box, 24in. *A. Hartley, Ilkley. Aug 02. £460.*

Edwardian Sheraton revival painted satinwood boudoir armchair, 83cm. *Bristol Auction Rooms. Dec 01. £460.*

19thC mahog. chest of four drawers with brushing slide, 24in wide. *Sworders, Stansted Mountfitchet. July 01. £460.*

Victorian carved rosewood framed double ended sofa. *W & H Peacock, Bedford. Jan 03. £460.*

Edwardian strung mahogany two door cabinet, 30in wide x 39in high. *Sworders, Stansted Mountfitchet. Apr 01. £460.*

Edwardian inlaid mahogany drinks cabinet. *Henry Adams, Chichester. Sep 02. £460.*

Mid 17thC oak five plank coffer of small proportion, 36in wide. *Tring Market Auctions, Herts. Mar 03. £460.*

Edwardian ebony string inlaid, satinwood breakfront side cabinet, 39.5in wide. *Amersham Auction Rooms, Bucks. May 03. £460.*

17th/18thC oak coffer of panelled construction, hinged lid, interior fitted with a candle box, 41in. *Denhams, Warnham. Mar 04. £460.*

Cotswold School walnut armchair by Peter Waals, slip in seat. *Gorringes, Bexhill. Nov 03. £460.*

19thC mahog. bergere child's cradle, arched arabesque hood, 104cm long, 138cm high. *Sworders, Stansted Mountfitchet. Feb 04. £460.*

19thC figured mahog. chest, 120cm wide. *Bristol Auction Rooms, Bristol. Jan 04. £460.*

Carved oak box settle, three panelled back with stylized flowers, birds, mask heads etc. *Lambert & Foster, Tenterden. May 02. £460.*

17thC and later oak blanket box or coffer, scroll carved detail, 65in wide. *Wintertons Ltd, Lichfield. July 01. £450.*

Edwardian mahog. bow front chest of drawers, 30in wide. *Dee, Atkinson & Harrison, Driffield. Apr 01. £450.*

Hammer Prices £450-£440

2435

18thC Continental walnut occasional table, 19.5in sq., restorations. Hamptons, Godalming. Mar 02. £450.

2436

Austrian giltwood stand, carved with an amorini over an acanthus cartouche raised by bun feet, 22in. Gorringes, Lewes. Apr 01. £450.

Prices quoted are hammer and exclude the buyer's premium. Adding 15% will give approx. buying price.

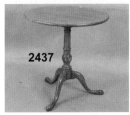

2437

Mahogany tripod table, with a spiral vase column, 27in dia. Sworders, Stansted Mountfitchet. July 01. £450.

2438

19thC mahog. bureau bookcase, a marriage, 39in wide. Dee, Atkinson & Harrison, Driffield. Apr 01. £450.

2439

William IV mahog. open armchair, buttoned leather upholstered seat. Clarke Gammon, Guildford. Sep 02. £450.

2440

19thC mahog. bow front chest of 2 short, 3 long drawers, 105cm wide. Lambert & Foster, Tenterden. Jan 03. £450.

2441

19thC mahog. writing table, 45in wide. Dee, Atkinson & Harrison, Driffield. Mar 04. £450.

2442

4 Victorian walnut balloon back chairs, paper furniture retailer's label underneath. Biddle & Webb, Birmingham. Apr 04. £450.

2443

George III mahogany bureau, stepped fitted interior, 106 x 91cm. Rosebery's, London. June 04. £450.

2444

Child's Georgian stick back windsor arm chair, hooped back, shaped seat, traces of original paint, 18thC, 28in high. Andrew Hartley, Ilkley. June 04. £450.

2445

George III inlaid mahogany secretaire chest, 42in wide. af. Sworders, Stansted Mountfitchet. July 01. £450.

2446

19thC French kingwood and veneered jardiniere, metal liner and bun feet, 17.5in wide. Andrew Hartley, Ilkley. Feb 01. £440.

2447

19thC mahogany bow fronted chest of drawers, 42in wide. (af) Sworders, Stansted Mountfitchet. Apr 01. £440.

2448

19thC rosewood centre table, 41.75 x 21.5in. A. Hartley, Ilkley. Dec 01. £440.

2449

Mahogany octagonal two-tier inlaid centre table, 102cm. attributable to Lambs, Manchester. Dockree's, Manchester. June 01. £440.

2450

Two seat Victorian drop end settee, 4ft 10in wide. Sworders, Stansted Mountfitchet. Apr 01. £440.

2451

Early Victorian rosewood cheval firescreen, Berlin woolwork panel, 113cm high. Locke & England, Leamington Spa. Jan 03. £440.

2452

Victorian oak settle with ornately carved decoration, 59in long. Sworders, Stansted Mountfitchet. July 01. £440.

2453

Late Victorian Maple & Co Ltd lady's inlaid rosewood writing table. W & H Peacock, Bedford. Aug 02. £440.

149

Hammer Prices £440-£430

2454

Early Victorian rosewood work table. Locke & England, Leamington Spa. Nov 02. £440.

2455

Carved mahog. Gainsborough chair, 19thC, upholstered in chinoiserie wool tapestry. D M Nesbit & Company, Southsea. June 03. £440.

2456

19thC ebonised and painted tilt top occasional table by Jennens and Bettridge, London, 62cm dia. Rosebery's, London. June 03. £440.

2457

Victorian mahog. Wellington chest, 20in wide. Denhams, Warnham. Jan 04. £440.

2458

Geo. III inlaid mahog. night table, shaped gallery tray top, 57cm wide. Bristol Auction Rooms, Bristol. Sep 03. £440.

2459

19thC walnut wood carved bergere chair, upholstered seat and back. Denhams, Warnham. Aug 03. £440.

2460

19thC George III design mahog. occasional table, pie crust top, 1ft 7in. Gorringes, Lewes. Jan 04. £440.

2461

Pr. Geo. III mahog. sideboard pedestals, incurved mouldings inlaid with rosewood bandings and boxwood stringings, 22in wide. Canterbury Auction Galleries, Kent. Feb 04. £440.

2462

17thC carved oak coffer, 48in wide. Tring Market Auctions, Herts. Oct 03. £440.

2463

19thC mahogany D shaped chest, 4 long drawers, turned handles, 37in. Denhams, Warnham. Feb 04. £440.

2464

5 late George III rosewood, brass inlaid dining chairs, cane seats. Canterbury Auc. Galleries, Kent. Feb 04. £440.

2465

Mid Victorian apprentice dressing chest, 11.25 x 12.5 x 12.5in. Amersham Auction Rooms, Bucks. Mar 03. £440.

2466

19thC mahog. frame spoon-back gentleman's armchair. Thos Mawer & Son, Lincoln. June 04. £440.

2467

Edwardian mahogany and marquetry writing table, line inlaid and crossbanded in satinwood, leather lined top, 42in wide. Gorringes, Bexhill. May 04. £440.

2468

Victorian mahogany spoon back easy chair in green dralon. Canterbury Auction Galleries, Kent. Aug 02. £440.

2469

19thC burr walnut lady's work table with single drawer, writing slide. Biddle & Webb, Birmingham. Apr 04. £440.

2470

Victorian figured walnut three division canterbury, 62cm wide. af. Bristol Auction Rooms, Bristol. Jan 04. £430.

2471

George III mahog. drop leaf dining table, supported upon Gillows style reeded legs, single detachable leaf, 169cm extended. Sworders, Stansted Mountfitchet. Feb 04. £430.

2472

1920s Queen Anne style walnut cabinet bookcase, 78in high, 36in wide. *Amersham Auction Rooms, Bucks. June 01. £420.*

2473

Pair of rosewood bedside cabinets in 19thC style. *Sworders, Stansted Mountfitchet. Apr 01. £420.*

The numbering system acts as a reader reference as well as linking to the Analysis of each Section.

2474

Edwardian mahogany framed settee, satinwood marquetry and boxwood string inlaid decoration. *Amersham Auction Rooms, Bucks. 01. £420.*

2475

Sheraton period mahogany elbow chair. *Sworders, Stansted Mountfitchet. Apr 01. £420.*

2476

Set of 4 Edwardian mahogany dining chairs. *Dee, Atkinson & Harrison, Driffield. Apr 01. £420.*

2477

Victorian mahog. showframe corner chair, label Edwards & Roberts, London. *Dockree's, Manchester. June 01. £420.*

2478

Late 17thC oval drop leaf table with turned under frame. *Sworders, Stansted Mountfitchet. July 01. £420.*

2479

Victorian walnut pier cabinet with tulipwood cross banding, 2ft 8in. *Gorringes, Lewes. July 02. £420.*

2480

19thC oak hanging corner cupboard. *Sworders, Stansted Mountfitchet. July 01. £420.*

Hammer Price £420

2481

19thC elm and ash Windsor rocking chair with crinolene stretcher. *W & H Peacock, Bedford. July 02. £420.*

2482

Repro oak dresser base with a pot board base, 5ft 4in wide. *Sworders, Stansted Mountfitchet. July 01. £420.*

2483

Regency mahogany chest of 2 short, 3 long drawers, ogee bracket feet, 45.5in wide. *Sworders, Stansted Mountfitchet. Apr 01. £420.*

2484

Oak Orkney chair. *Sworders, Stansted Mountfitchet. July 01. £420.*

2485

Victorian oval inlaid walnut lift-top work table. *W & H Peacock, Bedford. July 03. £420.*

2486

19thC mahog. and satinwood inlaid occasional table, 22in wide. *Amersham Auction Rooms, Bucks. June 01. £420.*

2487

Victorian walnut wine table quarter veneered, moulded edge, 18in wide. *Andrew Hartley, Ilkley. Aug 03. £420.*

2488

18thC oak bow front hanging corner cupboard, 100cm high. *Thos Mawer & Son, Lincoln. Feb 03. £420.*

2489

Yew Windsor armchair. *Andrew Hartley, Ilkley. Feb 03. £420.*

Hammer Prices £420-£400

2490

Victorian occasional table, parquetry/inlaid crossbanded top, 29.5in wide. A. Hartley, Ilkley. Oct 03. £420.

2491

Set of four Victorian inlaid salon chairs. John Taylors, Louth. Nov 03. £420.

2492

George III mahogany linen cabinet, panelled doors, three internal slides, long drawer, 129cm wide. Thos Mawer & Son, Lincoln. June 04. £420.

2493

Adzed oak coffee table, by Robert 'Mouseman' Thompson, 36 x 15in. Dee, Atkinson & Harrison, Driffield. Mar 04. £420.

2494

William IV rosewood centre table. Denhams, Warnham. Mar 04. £420.

2495

George III mahogany step commode, centre step opening. Sworders, Stansted Mountfitchet. Dec 03. £420.

2496

George III mahog. twinflap supper table, 36in wide. Tring Market Auctions, Herts. Nov 03. £420.

2497

George III mahogany sofa table, 5ft 1in extended. af. Sworders, Stansted Mount-fitchet. July 01. £420.

2498

19thC Continental walnut & marquetry four drawer chest, 53.5in wide. Sworders, Stansted Mountfitchet. Apr 01. £420.

2499

Victorian oval figured walnut wood loo table, top with crossbanding and satinwood stringing, 46in. Denhams, Warnham. June 04. £420.

2500

19thC walnut display cabinet, glazed door, foliate ormolu mounts, 30.5in wide. Dee, Atkinson & Harrison, Driffield. Mar 04. £420.

2501

Regency mahogany reading armchair, solid top rail with reeded edge, lozenge pierced vertical splats. Rosebery's, London. June 04. £420.

2502

Victorian 17thC design wing back armchair with 18thC floral tapestry back, seat and arm pads. Gorringes, Lewes. Apr 04. £420.

2503

Mid 19thC mahog. whatnot, 143 x 55cm. Rosebery's, London. Dec 03. £420.

2504

1920s feather banded figured walnut small chest of four graduate drawers, 75.5cm wide. Bristol Auction Rooms, Bristol. Jan 04. £410.

2505

19thC inlaid figured walnut sutherland table, D shaped flap top with foliate panels, 76cm wide. af. Bristol Auction Rooms. Jan 04. £410.

2506

Victorian carved & parquetry inlaid oak writing table, 113cm wide. af. Bristol Auction Rooms. Jan 04. £410.

2507

Carved walnut cassone, prob. North Italian late 17thC, 155cm wide. Bristol Auction Rooms, Bristol. Jan 04. £410.

2508

Writing table of interesting design in black exotic wood with shagreen drawers. Lots Road Auctions, Chelsea. Aug 01. £400.

2509

George III mahog. tea table, foldover top having foliate carved edge, 33in wide. *Amersham Auction Rooms, Bucks. June 01. £400.*

2510

Set 6 Victorian upholstered oak dining chairs. *Sworders, Stansted Mountfitchet. Mar 01. £400.*

> The illustrations are in descending price order. The price range is indicated at the top of each page.

2511

Victorian mahogany X framed stool, 19.75in wide. *Andrew Hartley, Ilkley. Oct 01. £400.*

2512

Two seat Victorian drop end settee, 58in wide. *Sworders, Stansted Mountfitchet. Apr 01. £400.*

2513

Old reproduction mahogany bureau, with a fitted interior, 30in wide. *Sworders, Stansted Mountfitchet. Apr 01. £400.*

2514

Mahog. tray topped commode raised on square tapering supports. *Biddle & Webb, Birmingham. Jan 02. £400.*

2515

Late Victorian mahogany show wood framed chair. *Amersham Auction Rooms, Bucks. Feb 02. £400.*

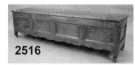

2516

19thC oak French provincial long chest, poss. Normandy, 6ft wide. *Sworders, Stansted Mountfitchet. Apr 01. £400.*

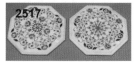

2517

Pair of inlaid marble table tops, 31cm dia. *Sworders, Stansted Mountfitchet. Apr 01. £400.*

2518

Regency giltwood mirror, ht. 31in, damaged. *Dockree's, Manchester. Nov 00. £400.*

Hammer Price £400

2519

Edwardian walnut linen press, 4ft 4in wide. (internal trays missing). *Sworders, Stansted Mountfitchet. Apr 01. £400.*

2520

Victorian 'Beaconsfield' satin walnut triple wardrobe, 6ft 2in wide. *Sworders, Stansted Mountfitchet. Apr 01. £400.*

2521

Regency giltwood overmantel mirror, carved frieze of Mars on his chariot, 101 x 79cm. *Sworders, Stansted Mountfitchet. Feb 04. £400.*

2522

Edwardian mahogany and inlaid display cabinet. *Crows, Dorking. Sep 01. £400.*

2523

Victorian walnut music canterbury with three divisions, 1ft 9in. *Gorringes, Bexhill. July 02. £400.*

2524

Mahogany/satinwood cross banded side table of neo classical design, 84cm wide. *Thos Mawer & Son, Lincoln. Apr 02. £400.*

2525

Victorian mahogany spoon back armchair. *Gorringes, Bexhill. May 02. £400.*

2526

Mahogany kneehole writing desk, 122cm. *Henry Adams, Chichester. July 02. £400.*

2527

Regency mahog. card table on ring-turned tapering legs, 34.25 x 34.5in overall. *Clarke Gammon, Guildford. Apr 01. £400.*

Hammer Price £400

2528

18thC oak lowboy, 34in wide. *Sworders, Stansted Mountfitchet. July 01. £400.*

2529

Geo. III mahog. bow fronted chest, 107cm. *Locke & England, Leamington Spa. Sep 02. £400.*

2530

Victorian carved oak parlour chair, tan hide upholstery. *Sworders, Stansted Mountfitchet. July 01. £400.*

2531

Victorian burr walnut and inlaid whatnot on Canterbury base, c1860, 51cm wide. *Wintertons Ltd, Lichfield. Mar 03. £400.*

2532

Late17th/18thC oak side table, plank top, single drawer, ring turned block legs, 46in wide. *Amersham Auction Rooms, Bucks. July 02. £400.*

2533

George III mahog. drop leaf table, square legs, 36in long. *Sworders, Stansted Mountfitchet. July 01. £400.*

2534

19thC mahogany Pembroke table with one real and one dummy drawer, 86cm wide. *Lambert & Foster, Tenterden. Jan 03. £400.*

2535

20thC sofa, 177cm wide. *Lots Road Auctions, Chelsea. Jan 03. £400.*

2536

William and Mary cabinet top chest of walnut faced drawers, 42in wide. af. *Sworders, Stansted Mountfitchet. July 01. £400.*

2537

Georgian cross banded mahogany bowfront chest. *W & H Peacock, Bedford. Feb 03. £400.*

2538

Antique elm plank coffer with internal candle box. *W & H Peacock, Bedford. Jan 03. £400.*

2539

Late Georgian mahog. twin flap supper table, 46in wide. *Tring Market Auctions, Herts. Mar 03. £400.*

2540

Regency mahogany Pembroke table. *W & H Peacock, Bedford. June 03. £400.*

2541

19thC mahogany chest, deep central hat drawer, 128cm wide. *Lambert & Foster, Tenterden. Jan 03. £400.*

2542

George II lacquered wood hanging corner cupboard, 23.75in wide. *Clarke Gammon, Guildford. Sep 02. £400.*

2543

Late 19thC Continental, Louis XV style floral marquetry inlaid, walnut and rosewood veneered bureau de dame, 26in wide. *Amersham Auction Rooms, Bucks. June 03. £400.*

2544

Victorian walnut Wellington chest. *W & H Peacock, Bedford. July 03. £400.*

2545

Yew and ash spindle back rocking chair, elm saddle seat, late 18th/19thC. *Andrew Hartley, Ilkley. Feb 04. £400.*

2546

19thC carved stained beech settee, 205cm wide. *Bristol Auction Rooms. Jan 04. £400.*

2547

Georgian mahog. bow front sideboard, 44in. *Denhams, Warnham. Dec 03. £400.*

2548

William IV mahogany cross framed stool with needlework seat. *Sworders, Stansted Mountfitchet. Feb 04. £400.*

> Prices quoted are hammer and exclude the buyer's premium. Adding 15% will give approx. buying price.

2549

Victorian walnut wood open bookcase, 48in. *Denhams, Warnham. Dec 03. £400.*

2550

Child's mahog. wing rocking chair, hinged commode seat, 19thC, 27.5in high. *A. Hartley, Ilkley. Aug 03. £400.*

2551

19thC bergere, black japanned. *Lots Road Auctions, Chelsea. Mar 04. £400.*

2552

17thC oak joint stool, 18 x 10 x 20in high. (split to top and 2 stretchers replaced). *Canterbury Auc. Galleries, Kent. Feb 04. £400.*

2553

Victorian rosewood, inlaid centre table, porcelain castors, 71 x 77cm. *Rosebery's, London. June 04. £400.*

2554

George III satinwood/ebony inlaid mahogany cabinet bookcase, glazed doors, 71in high. *Amersham Auction Rooms, Bucks. Oct 03. £400.*

Hammer Price £400

2555

Late George III mahogany and floral marquetry cellaret, 1ft 4in. (split top). *Gorringes, Lewes. Mar 04. £400.*

2556

Set of Regency style grained pine open dwarf shelves, 38in wide. *Sworders, Stansted Mountfitchet. Apr 01. £400.*

2557

Edwardian inlaid mahogany shield shaped box toilet mirror, 28in wide, 34.5in high. *Sworders, Stansted Mountfitchet. Apr 01. £400.*

2558

Japanned & bamboo writing table, c1890, raised gallery, 2 trinket drawers, leather gilt tooled surface, 2 drawer frieze, 100 x 93cm. *Rosebery's, London. June 04. £400.*

2559

Edwardian mahogany glass sided display cabinet with satinwood stringing. *John Taylors, Louth. Mar 04. £400.*

2560

Panelled oak hall seat, 60in wide. *Sworders, Stansted Mountfitchet. July 01. £400.*

2561

Early 18thC oak chest of 2 short and 3 long drawers (in two sections) block feet, 96cm wide. *Lambert & Foster, Tenterden. June 04. £400.*

2562

One of a pair of 19thC girandoles, 72cm high, af. *Lots Road Auctions, Chelsea. Mar 03. £400.*

Hammer Price £380

2563

Victorian papier mache pedestal table, 26in wide. Lots Road Auctions, Chelsea. Jan 02. £380.

2564

Late Regency mahogany tray top night table, 82 x 38cm. Rosebery's, London. June 03. £380.

2565

Late 17thC small oak chair. Sworders, Stansted Mountfitchet. July 01. £380.

2566

American ash/beech comb back windsor chair. Sworders, Stansted Mountfitchet. July 01. £380.

2567

Pair of Dutch marquetry elm dining chairs, 18thC and later. Clarke Gammon, Guildford. Sep 02. £380.

2568

Early 20thC three piece suite. Sworders, Stansted Mountfitchet. Dec 02. £380.

2569

Victorian walnut tub chair 'Goodall & Co Manchester'. Sworders, Stansted Mountfitchet. July 01. £380.

2570

Late 17thC oak coffer with lozenge carved panels, 42in wide. Sworders, Stansted Mountfitchet. Apr 01. £380.

2571

Set of four early 20thC Chippendale style dining chairs. W & H Peacock, Bedford. Mar 03. £380.

2572

Victorian walnut settee, spiral twist spindle back, serpentine seat, on twist legs, fitted brass castors. Gorringes, Lewes. Mar 01. £380.

2573

Victorian inlaid rosewood tub armchair. Sworders, Stansted Mountfitchet. Apr 01. £380.

2574

5 + 2 19thC elm/beechwood Windsor chairs. (some damage). Sworders, Stansted Mountfitchet. Apr 01. £380.

2575

Edwardian inlaid mahogany settee, old gold damask, 98cm wide. Lambert & Foster, Tenterden. Aug 03. £380.

2576

Oak side cabinet, bevelled glazed doors and panels on a table base, 76in wide. Sworders, Stansted Mountfitchet. Apr 01. £380.

2577

George III mahogany and oak tripod table, 34cm dia. Sworders, Stansted Mountfitchet. June 03. £380.

2578

William IV mahogany teapoy, 33in high, 17in wide. Amersham Auction Rooms, Bucks. June 03. £380.

2579

Early 19thC quadrant washstand, 22in wide. Andrew Hartley, Ilkley. Feb 01. £380.

2580

Edwardian mahog. bowfront writing table with leather inset, 107cm. Henry Adams, Chichester. July 02. £380.

2581

Anglo Indian hardwood military chest in 2 sections, recessed brass handles, 36in wide. Canterbury Auction Galleries, Kent. Feb 04. £380.

2582

18thC oak box settle, hinged seat, 72.5in wide. Dee, Atkinson & Harrison, Driffield. Mar 04. £380.

2583

Early 18thC elm/oak chest, 3ft 10in high. Gorringes, Bexhill. Sep 03. £380.

2584

Pair of late 19thC French walnut single beds, cast gilt mounts. Sworders, Stansted Mountfitchet. Dec 03. £380.

2585

Victorian walnut spoon back armchair, deep button back with roll arms. Rosebery's, London. June 04. £380.

2586

Pair of wall mirrors, carved gilt wood frames, each 37in x 32in. Sworders, Stansted Mountfitchet. Apr 01. £380.

2587

Pair of Georgian style octagonal inlaid rosewood and cross banded wine tables, 18in. Denhams, Warnham. Dec 03. £380.

The numbering system acts as a reader reference as well as linking to the Analysis of each Section.

2588

Early 20thC mahog. vitrine cabinet. Locke & England, Leamington Spa. Oct 03. £380.

2589

Set of 4 Victorian mahogany balloon back dining chairs, overstuffed seats. Dee, Atkinson & Harrison, Driffield. Mar 04. £380.

Hammer Prices £380-£360

2590

Art Nouveau oak smokers cabinet, fitted interior including a Brannem humidor, 46cm wide. Peter Wilson, Nantwich. July 02. £365.

2591

Late Regency mahog. stool, upholstered seat, tulip carved tapered legs. Gorringes, Lewes. Feb 01. £360.

2592

Mahogany chest, fitted for cutlery. Sworders, Stansted Mountfitchet. Apr 01. £360.

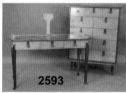

2593

Laslo Hoenig Hungarian maple bedroom suite: chest of drawers, dressing table, double headboard and wardrobe. (in pieces and incomplete). Sworders, Stansted Mountfitchet. Apr 01. £360.

2594

Georgian mahogany chest. W & H Peacock, Bedford. Feb 03. £360.

2595

19thC walnut framed nursing chair in needlework covering. Andrew Hartley, Ilkley. Oct 01. £360.

2596

18thC painted pine barrel back hanging corner cupboard. Thos Mawer & Son, Lincoln. Feb 03. £360.

2597

George III oak/mahogany linen press, 126cm. (altered to a wardrobe). Locke & England, Leamington Spa. May 03. £360.

2598

5 19thC elm tick and wheel back dining chairs. Denhams, Warnham. Aug 03. £360.

Hammer Price £360

2599

William IV mahog. sarco-
phagus shaped cellaret,
19.5in wide. Clarke Gammon,
Guildford. Feb 03. £360.

2600

George III mahog. corner two
tier washstand, line inlay,
61cm wide. Locke & England,
Leamington Spa. Jan 03. £360.

2601

19thC walnut glazed display
cabinet, 86.5cm. Locke &
England, Leamington Spa.
May 03. £360.

2602

Georgian style mahog. sofa
table, with ebony line inlay,
152cm fully open. Locke &
England, Leaming-ton Spa.
Jan 03. £360.

2603

18thC walnut chest of
drawers, (poor condition)
41in wide. Sworders, Stansted
Mountfitchet. July 01. £360.

2604

Set of four Victorian balloon
back dining chairs. Locke &
England, Leamington Spa.
May 03. £360.

2605

Aesthetic movement, ebonised
centre table, 41in dia.
Sworders, Stansted Mount-
fitchet. July 01. £360.

2606

Regency rosewood breakfast
table. W & H Peacock,
Bedford. July 03. £360.

2607

Late 17thC oak coffer, candle
box, carving possibly later,
128cm wide. Bristol Auction
Rooms, Bristol. Jan 04. £360.

2608

19thC walnut refectory table,
on turned legs, 12ft long,
47in wide. Sworders, Stansted
Mountfitchet. Apr 01. £360.

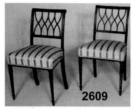

2609

Set 4 early 19thC Sheraton
style mahogany dining chairs,
reeded crests, latticed back,
overstuffed seats.
Amersham Auction Rooms,
Bucks. June 02. £360.

2610

Victorian burr walnut conical
workbox. Thos Mawer & Son,
Lincoln. Feb 03. £360.

2611

Art Nouveau bentwood
rocking chair.
Sworders, Stansted Mount-
fitchet. Apr 01. £360.

2612

George III fruitwood chest,
reeded planked top, 33in
wide. Gorringes, Bexhill.
Mar 04. £360.

2613

Anglo Indian hardwood
military chest in 2 sections,
36in wide. Canterbury Auc.
Galleries, Kent. Feb 04. £360.

2614

Early 18thC Japanese black
lacquer cabinet, 102.5cm.
Locke & England, Leaming-
ton Spa. Oct 03. £360.

2615

Victorian mahogany drop flap
Doctor's/work table, 19in.
Denhams, Warnham.
Dec 03. £360.

2616

Edwardian mahogany elbow
chair, woolwork upholstery.
Dee, Atkinson & Harrison,
Driffield. Mar 04. £360.

2617

Victorian mahog. music stool,
marquetry inlaid with lyre
and arabesques, canterbury
interior. Gorringes, Bexhill.
July 03. £360.

Hammer Prices £360-£340

2618

Geo. III mahog. carver chair, drop in seat. *Locke & England, Leamington Spa. Sep 03. £360.*

2619

Victorian child's mahogany high chair. *Lots Rd Auctions, Chelsea. Apr 03. £350.*

The illustrations are in descending price order. The price range is indicated at the top of each page.

2620

19thC walnut sewing cabinet. *Locke & England, Leamington Spa. Oct 03. £350.*

2621

Early 20thC walnut linen press. *Crows, Dorking. July 01. £350.*

2622

Bergere chair. *Lots Road Auctions, Chelsea. May 03. £350.*

2623

Set 4 19thC German mahog. dining chairs in the Gothic manner. *Canterbury Auction Galleries, Kent. Feb 04. £350.*

2624

Set of 2 + 2 George III style mahogany dining chairs, drop in seats. *Cheffins, Cambridge. Feb 04. £350.*

2625

Mid 18thC oak side table, 99 x 53 x 73cm. *Hamptons, Godalming. July 02. £350.*

2626

Geo. III painted pine corner washstand. *Sworders, Stansted Mountfitchet. Feb 04. £350.*

2627

Set of 4 19thC mahog. dining chairs, woolwork drop in seats. *Dee, Atkinson & Harrison, Driffield. Mar 04. £350.*

2628

George I walnut veneered wall mirror, 48in high. *Sworders, Stansted Mountfitchet. Apr 01. £350.*

2629

19thC mahog. chest, 36.5in wide. *Dee, Atkinson & Harrison, Driffield. Apr 01. £350.*

2630

Child's late 18thC fruitwood rocking commode chair. *Crows, Dorking. Jan 03. £350.*

2631

Set 4 19thC rosewood dining chairs. *Dee, Atkinson & Harrison, Driffield. Apr 01. £350.*

2632

George III mahog. Pembroke table, satinwood stringing, 53 (closed) x 57cm. *Locke & England, Leamington Spa. Sep 02. £350.*

2633

Victorian bamboo lacquered/painted single pedestal writing desk. Japanese manner, 90cm wide. *Marilyn Swain Auctions, Grantham. Dec 03. £340.*

2634

Steel/brass mounted adjustable stool, c1900, frame stamped Hare & Son. *Rosebery's, London. Sep 03. £340.*

2635

Late Regency mahog. pedestal table, tip top, rounded corners, 32in wide. *Amersham Auction Rooms, Bucks. June 03. £340.*

159

Hammer Prices £340-£330

2636

Pair of late 19thC children's chairs. Amersham Auction Rooms, Bucks. Mar 01. £340.

2637

Victorian mahogany corner chair, drop in seat. Andrew Hartley, Ilkley. Feb 04. £340.

2638

Regency style kingwood and satinwood etagere, 56 x 35cm. Rosebery's, London. Sep 03. £340.

2639

18thC oak cradle, 39in long. Sworders, Stansted Mountfitchet. Apr 01. £340.

2640

Tray top table, 19thC, painted tole, depicting interior scene with gamekeeper and family, 77cm wide. Lots Rd Auctions, Chelsea. Mar 04. £340.

160

2641

Oak bench with arcaded decoration, 48in. Denhams, Warnham. Feb 04. £340.

2642

Edwardian mahog. three tier etagere, removable 2-handled tray, 31in high. Canterbury Auction Galleries, Kent. Feb 04. £340.

2643

George III mahog. chest, large brass carrying handles, 49in wide. af. Sworders, Stansted Mountfitchet. July 01. £340.

2644

Early 19thC mahog. washstand inset with pottery bowl, 57cm dia. Sworders, Stansted Mountfitchet. Sep 03. £340.

2645

Set of four 19thC rosewood dining chairs, over-stuffed seats. Amersham Auction Rooms, Bucks. Apr 02. £340.

2646

19thC mahog. swivel top envelope games table, 20.5in, top distressed. Dockree's, Manchester. Feb 01. £340.

2647

Regency wall mirror with a convex plate, carved giltwood frame, 31.75 x 20in overall. Clarke Gammon, Guildford. June 03. £340.

2648

Victorian mahogany/stained collectors cabinet, glazed door revealing 9 drawers, 22 x 33in. David Duggleby, Scarborough. July 01. £340.

2649

19thC mahogany work table, drop leave, 2 frieze drawers, (restoration) 21in wide. Sworders, Stansted Mountfitchet. July 01. £340.

2650

Edwardian mahogany and crossbanded display cabinet, 22.5in wide. Wintertons Ltd, Lichfield. July 01. £340.

2651

Early 19thC mahogany/ebony string inlaid kneehole desk, 42in wide. Amersham Auction Rooms, Bucks. Aug 02. £340.

2652

Set 6 19thC walnut dining chairs by Gillows of Lancaster, each stamped 'Gillow 13551'. Sworders, Stansted Mountfitchet. Oct 02. £330.

2653

Edwardian mahogany bow front china display cabinet cross banded in satinwood, 60cm wide. Thos Mawer & Son, Lincoln. Apr 02. £330.

Hammer Prices £330-£320

2654

Maple & Co mahog. writing table, leather inset top, one drawer stamped, 36in square. Sworders, Stansted Mountfitchet. Apr 01. £330.

2655

Lot 371

19thC caddy top mahog. chest, 36.5in. Lambert & Foster, Tenterden. Feb 02. £330.

Prices quoted are hammer and exclude the buyer's premium. Adding 15% will give approx. buying price.

2656

Georgian mahog. bird cage table with pie crust border, 20in. Denhams, Warnham. May 04. £330.

2657

Late Victorian flame veneered mahog. pot cupboard, white marble top, shelved interior, 30in high, 14in dia. Amersham Auction Rooms, Bucks. June 03. £330.

2658

George III oak bureau, fitted interior, 92.5cm. Locke & England, Leamington Spa. May 03. £330.

2659

Regency rosewood fold over card table, 36in wide. af. Sworders, Stansted Mountfitchet. Apr 01. £320.

2660

Oak pedestal desk, top with red inset, fitted eight drawers, 48in. Lambert & Foster, Tenterden. Feb 02. £320.

2661

Pair of Edwardian mahogany and caned single bedsteads. Sworders, Stansted Mountfitchet. Apr 01. £320.

2662

William and Mary style high backed walnut chair. Wintertons Ltd, Lichfield. July 01. £320.

2663

18thC mahogany table top cabinet, ebony/holly inlaid, 13.5in wide. Tring Market Auctions, Herts. Sep 02. £320.

2664

Mahog. lamp table, oval top on a carved tripod base, 20in wide. Sworders, Stansted Mountfitchet. Apr 01. £320.

2665

George III mahogany corner cupboard, on a later stand, 48in high. Sworders, Stansted Mountfitchet. Apr 01. £320.

2666

Late 17thC walnut high back dining chair. Gorringes, Lewes. Apr 01. £320.

2667

2 similar Edwardian mahog. armchairs, floral gold fabric. Dee, Atkinson & Harrison, Driffield. Apr 01. £320.

2668

Victorian mahogany two drawer writing table, 48in wide. Sworders, Stansted Mountfitchet. Apr 01. £320.

2669

19thC wall mirror, moulded pediment above twin cluster column pilasters, overall 27.5 x 22in. Dockree's, Manchester. Feb 01. £320.

2670

George III mahogany elbow chair. Sworders, Stansted Mountfitchet. Apr 01. £320.

2671

1930s stained beech framed 4 piece suite: 3 person bergere settee, 3 matching armchairs. Amersham Auction Rooms, Bucks. Sep 02. £320.

Hammer Price £320

19thC mahog. chiffonier, plinth base, 107cm. Locke & England, Leamington Spa. May 03. £320.

George III mahogany pedestal tripod table, 30.5in wide. Tring Market Auctions, Herts. Mar 03. £320.

19thC mahogany tilt top breakfast table, 132 x 83cm. Thos Mawer & Son, Lincoln. Feb 03. £320.

19thC mahogany and bergere swinging cradle, 100cm long. Sworders, Stansted Mountfitchet. June 03. £320.

Early 18thC oak stool, 55cm high, 45cm wide. Wintertons Ltd, Lichfield. Mar 03. £320.

18thC style mahogany framed Bishop's chair, gros point upholstery. Fellows & Sons, Hockley, B'ham. July 03. £320.

Edwardian inlaid mahogany display table, crossbanded top, glazed cabinet base, 42.5cm wide. Bristol Auction Rooms, Bristol. Jan 04. £320.

Edwardian mahog. dressing table, mirror above 2 glove drawers, 42in. Denhams, Warnham. Mar 04. £320.

Early 19thC oak clerks desk on stand, fall front, fitted interior, 49cm. Sworders, Stansted Mountfitchet. Feb 04. £320.

19thC mahog. bow front chest, shaped apron, 39.5in wide. Dee, Atkinson & Harrison, Driffield. Mar 04. £320.

Pair of Regency style X-frame giltwood stools, padded tops, lotus leaf clasped spindle stretchers. Rosebery's, London. June 04. £320.

17thC oak coffer, later carving and top, 139cm wide. Sworders, Stansted Mountfitchet. Apr 01. £320.

Late 19thC Renaissance style walnut X framed armchair. (Reputedly the property of a former Duke of Norfolk). Gorringes, Bexhill. Mar 04. £320.

Edwardian inlaid and cross banded mahogany oval centre table. W & H Peacock, Bedford. Feb 03. £320.

Edwardian carved mahogany framed chaise longue. W & H Peacock, Bedford. Mar 03. £320.

Edwardian rosewood string inlaid sofa table, 39in wide closed. Amersham Auction Rooms, Bucks. Nov 02. £320.

19thC mahogany, satinwood marquetry inlaid settee. Amersham Auction Rooms, Bucks. May 02. £320.

Victorian rosewood three tier whatnot, 23in wide. Gorringes, Bexhill. Mar 03. £320.

Early 20thC mahog. display cabinet, glazed sides, inlaid central panel, 70.5in high. Dee, Atkinson & Harrison, Driffield. Mar 04. £320.

2691

Mid 19thC 2 drawer mahog. washstand, 42in wide. *Sworders, Stansted Mountfitchet. Apr 01. £320.*

2692

Mahog. fold over tea table, 36in wide. *Sworders, Stansted Mountfitchet. July 01. £320.*

2693

Victorian pitch pine cupboard, 2 pointed arch panelled doors, 50in wide. *Sworders, Stansted Mountfitchet. Apr 01. £320.*

2694

Regency rosewood lamp table, 22in long. *Sworders, Stansted Mountfitchet. July 01. £320.*

2695

19thC Louis XIV style oak framed open armchair. *Tring Market Auctions, Herts. Jan 02. £310.*

2696

19th carved oak hall table, fitted drawer each end, 54in wide. *Lambert & Foster, Tenterden. Feb 02. £310.*

2697

Victorian walnut wine table, twisted column, tripod legs, 22in dia. *Sworders, Stansted Mountfitchet. Apr 01. £310.*

2698

Leather hippopotamus footstool, 34in long. *Sworders, Stansted Mountfitchet. Oct 01. £310.*

2699

Georgian style mahog. ribbon back armchair, c1900, drop in seat, 109cm. *Bristol Auction Rooms. Nov 03. £310.*

2700

Art Deco walnut display cabinet, 51in high. *Sworders, Stansted Mountfitchet. July 01. £300.*

Hammer Prices £320-£300

2701

Pair 18thC American walnut dining chairs. *Gorringes, Lewes. Oct 01. £300.*

2702

Mid 18thC oak dining table, raised on baluster turned block legs, 27.5 x 42in open. *Amersham Auction Rooms, Bucks. Apr 01. £300.*

> The numbering system acts as a reader reference as well as linking to the Analysis of each Section.

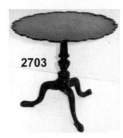

2703

George III mahog. piecrust tip-up tripod table, block with trade label, Wolf & O'Meara, Manchester, 74cm. *Dockree's, Manchester. June 01. £300.*

2704

Victorian oak Bishop's open armchair and footstool. *Clarke Gammon, Guildford. Sep 02. £300.*

2705

Late 19thC pine double fronted cupboard. *Crows, Dorking. July 01. £300.*

2706

17thC oak six plank coffer, 45in wide. *Sworders, Stansted Mountfitchet. July 01. £300.*

2707

19thC inlaid walnut nursing chair. *Sworders, Stansted Mountfitchet. July 01. £300.*

2708

George III mahog. pembroke table, end drawer (af) 33.5in wide. *Sworders, Stansted Mountfitchet. July 01. £300.*

2709

Late 17thC carved oak panel back armchair, some later carving to back and seat, af. *Lambert & Foster, Tenterden. Aug 01. £300.*

Hammer Price £300

2710

Victorian strung and inlaid walnut pier cabinet, 36in wide. Sworders, Stansted Mountfitchet. July 01. £300.

2711

George III mahogany swing toilet mirror, with a drawer, 15.5in wide. Clarke Gammon, Guildford. Feb 03. £300.

2712

Bergere walnut armchair with shaped back and unusual convex sides. Peter Wilson, Nantwich. Nov 01. £300.

2713

Edwardian mahogany tray top plant stand, 34cm high. W & H Peacock, Bedford. July 02. £300.

2714

Continental oak coffer, domed plank lid, iron strap hinges, 17thC, 48in wide. A. Hartley, Ilkley. June 02. £300.

2715

19thC stained beech button back chair upholstered in peppermint green fabric. Dee, Atkinson & Harrison, Driffield. Apr 01. £300.

2716

Continental walnut escritoire, fitted interior, no stand, 36in wide. Sworders, Stansted Mountfitchet. July 01. £300.

2717

18thC oak slope top bible box carved in deep relief, 65cm wide. Thos Mawer & Son, Lincoln. Apr 02. £300.

2718

Oak late 17thC style drop leaf table. Sworders, Stansted Mountfitchet. July 01. £300.

2719

Herman Miller aluminium framed swivel office chair, label and cast no. 938-138. Fellows & Sons, Hockley, Birmingham. Dec 02. £300.

2720

19thC oak bureau, 36in wide. af. Sworders, Stansted Mountfitchet. Apr 01. £300.

2721

Welsh oak coffor bach, drawer to base, c1780, 19in wide, (for restoration). Lambert & Foster, Tenterden. Oct 01. £300.

2722

Victorian ash triple wardrobe, 76in wide. Sworders, Stansted Mountfitchet. Apr 01. £300.

2723

Victorian ebonised and inlaid two door display cabinet. W & H Peacock, Bedford. Feb 03. £300.

2724

19thC pine chest of drawers with later painted decoration, 37in wide. Sworders, Stansted Mountfitchet. July 01. £300.

2725

Set 3 mahog. side chairs, drop in seats, early 18thC. Andrew Hartley, Ilkley. Feb 04. £300.

2726

Regency mahog. washstand in the manner of Gillow, 29.5in wide. Andrew Hartley, Ilkley. Oct 01. £300.

2727

Geo. III oak hanging corner cupboard, 32in wide. Gorringes, Bexhill. Mar 04. £300.

2728

Late 17thC carved oak four panel coffer, 50in wide, 20in high. Tring Market Auctions, Herts. Jan 03. £300.

2729

19thC oak chest, 37.5in wide. Sworders, Stansted Mount-fitchet. Apr 01. £300.

2730

Chinese hardwood elbow chair, crest rail carved with two birds. Sworders, Stansted Mountfitchet. Apr 01. £300.

The illustrations are in descending price order. The price range is indicated at the top of each page.

2731

Mid Victorian mahogany buffet, 43in high, 42in wide. Amersham Auction Rooms, Bucks. Oct 02. £300.

2732

19thC walnut corner whatnot, marquetry inlaid with pierced gallery, 2ft. Gorringes, Bexhill. Dec 02. £300.

2733

18thC oak bench of joined construction, 44in. Denhams, Warnham. Feb 04. £300.

2734

Pair of Victorian mahogany hall chairs on cabriole legs. Locke & England, Leamington Spa. May 03. £300.

2735

Edwardian mahog. tub chair with ornate openwork back, tapestry seat. Gorringes, Lewes. June 03. £300.

2736

William IV mahog. washstand in Gillows style, 94cm wide. (gallery split). Dreweatt Neate, Newbury. Nov 02. £300.

2737

Edwards & Roberts oak hall table, 3ft 6in wide. Gorringes, Bexhill. Sep 03. £300.

Hammer Price £300

2738

George III mahogany shield back armchair, Hepplewhite design, carved with Prince of Wales feathers, drapery swags. Canterbury Auction Galleries, Kent. Aug 03. £300.

2739

Edwardian mahogany two tier revolving bookcase. W & H Peacock, Bedford. July 03. £300.

2740

Georgian country oak hanging corner cabinet. Denhams, Warnham. Aug 03. £300.

2741

Edwardian mahog. two tier revolving bookcase, 49cm. Locke & England, Leamington Spa. July 03. £300.

2742

19thC Continental serpentine sided writing table, galleried undertier, 92cm wide. Thos Mawer & Son, Lincoln. Feb 03. £300.

2743

Pr. Geo. IV rosewood library chairs, close nailed backs and seats. Sworders, Stansted Mountfitchet. Feb 04. £300.

2744

Oak Art Nouveau hanging cabinet, 2ft 3in. Gorringes, Lewes. June 03. £300.

2745

George III mahogany chest of drawers, 110cm wide 54cm deep. Thos Mawer & Son Lincoln. June 04. £300.

2746

Edwardian lady's carved walnut writing table. W & H Peacock, Bedford. July 03. £300.

165

Hammer Prices £300-£280

2747

Late Victorian mahogany apprentice piece dress chest, drawers with glass handles, 19in wide. Amersham Auction Rooms, Bucks. Apr 04. £300.

2748

Victorian mahog. salon chair, pale green damask covering, padded shield back. Andrew Hartley, Ilkley. Feb 04. £300.

2749

Elm side chair, drop in upholstered seat. Andrew Hartley, Ilkley. Feb 04. £290.

2750

Late 19thC oval string inlaid and banded occasional table, 27in wide. Dockree's, Manchester. Feb 01. £280.

2751

Pair of Edwardian salon chairs, mahogany and satinwood banded. Lots Road Auctions, Chelsea. July 01. £280.

2752

Late Victorian oak framed hall stand, 80in high x 45in wide. Amersham Auction Rooms, Bucks. June 01. £280.

2753

American oak wing back arm chair, with squab cushions. Sworders, Stansted Mountfitchet. July 01. £280.

2754

French Louis XV style walnut finish corner display cabinet. Clarke Gammon, Guildford. Sep 01. £280.

2755

Robert Thompson of Kilburn mouseman oak saddle stool. Dee, Atkinson & Harrison, Driffield. Apr 01. £280.

2756

Arts and Crafts oak window seat, 36in long. Sworders, Stansted Mountfitchet. July 01. £280.

2757

George III mahog. washstand of serpentine outline, 55.5cm. Locke & England, Leamington Spa. Jan 03. £280.

2758

Three fold Victorian nursery screen, panel carved in relief with Noah's Ark. (distressed). Thos Mawer & Son, Lincoln. Feb 03. £280.

2759

Oak drop leaf dining table, two frieze drawers on turned legs, 50in wide. Sworders, Stansted Mountfitchet. Apr 01. £280.

2760

Victorian mahogany chaise longue. Thos Mawer & Son, Lincoln. Nov 02. £280.

2761

Edwardian settee, with inlaid Art Nouveau decoration. Sworders, Stansted Mountfitchet. Apr 01. £280.

2762

Set 5 matching 19thC ladder-back dining chairs, rush seats and one similar. Locke & England, Leamington Spa. May 03. £280.

2763

Edwardian inlaid two seater settee. John Taylors, Louth. Oct 03. £280.

2764

Set 4 + 1 salon chairs, early 20thC French carved giltwood showframes. Lots Rd Auctions, Chelsea. Aug 03. £280.

2765

19thC mahog. reclining chair, re-upholstered. Sworders, Stansted Mountfitchet. Dec 02. £280.

2766

Pair of gothic revival high back hall chairs upholstered in woolwork. *Thos Mawer & Son, Lincoln. Feb 03. £280.*

2767

19thC strung mahog. corner washstand with a folding top. *Sworders, Stansted Mount-fitchet. July 01. £280.*

Prices quoted are hammer and exclude the buyer's premium. Adding 15% will give approx. buying price.

2768

19thC Anglo Indian carved hardwood chair, cane seat. *Locke & England, Leamington Spa. May 03. £280.*

2769

Victorian rosewood prie-dieu, leaf carved crest rail, original woolwork, wrythen supports. *Dee, Atkinson & Harrison, Driffield. Mar 04. £280.*

2770

Victorian inlaid walnut settee. *Sworders, Stansted Mountfitchet. June 03. £280.*

2771

Early 20thC kneehole desk, serpentine form, line inlaid, metal loop handles, 54in wide. *Dee, Atkinson & Harrison, Driffield. Mar 04. £280.*

2772

Edwardian inlaid and cross-banded mahogany towel rail, 32in long. *Sworders, Stansted Mountfitchet. Apr 01. £280.*

2773

19thC inlaid rosewood side cabinet, glazed doors, 93cm wide. *Lambert & Foster, Tenterden. June 04. £280.*

2774

19thC walnut (?) elbow chair in Jacobean style. *Sworders, Stansted Mountfitchet. Apr 01. £280.*

Hammer Price £280

2775

Set four Victorian mahogany dining chairs. *Dee, Atkinson & Harrison, Driffield. Mar 04. £280.*

2776

Edwardian mahogany and inlaid two tier occasional table, 20in wide. *Fellows & Sons, Hockley, Birmingham. Oct 03. £280.*

2777

Victorian oak stool with upholstered top, monopodia legs, 2ft 4in. *Gorringes, Lewes. Jan 04. £280.*

2778

Early 20thC mahog. serpentine fronted writing table, leather insert top, 101.5cm. *Locke & England, Leamington Spa. July 03. £280.*

2779

Geo. III mahog. 'D' end table, 50in wide. *Sworders, Stansted Mountfitchet. July 01. £280.*

2780

George III mahog. bow front hanging corner cupboard, 122cm. *Locke & England, Leamington Spa. Sep 03. £280.*

2781

Wing armchair on carved claw and ball foot front legs. *Sworders, Stansted Mount-fitchet. July 01. £280.*

2782

19thC French lady's kingwood /marquetry dressing table, 23in wide. *Canterbury Auc. Galleries, Kent. Dec 03. £280.*

2783

Victorian walnut framed open arm easy chair, green dralon. *Canterbury Auc. Galleries, Kent. Apr 04. £280.*

Hammer Prices £280-£260

2784

Art Deco walnut coffee table, 24in dia., and a side cabinet. Sworders, Stansted Mountfitchet. July 01. £280.

2785

19thC Continental walnut and kingwood work table, top with burr walnut banding, 24in wide. Canterbury Auction Galleries, Kent. Feb 04. £280.

2786

George III oak two drawer side table, 30in wide, af. Sworders, Stansted Mountfitchet. July 01. £280.

2787

Victorian figured walnut coffee table, quarter veneered oval top, turned and carved end supports, 104cm long. (legs reduced). Ambrose, Loughton. Mar 02. £275.

2788

Mid Georgian style mahogany stool with drop in seat, 20in wide. Tring Market Auctions, Herts. May 02. £270.

2789

Art nouveau mahog. display cabinet, 2 glazed doors, 38in. Gorringes, Lewes. Sep 03. £270.

2790

George III mahogany bow fronted toilet mirror, 18in wide. Sworders, Stansted Mountfitchet. Apr 01. £270.

2791

Victorian mahog. pembroke table. Sworders, Stansted Mountfitchet. Apr 01. £260.

2792

Early 20thC three seat high backed wing sofa, upholstered in floral pattern fabric. Locke & England, Leamington Spa. Oct 03. £260.

2793

19thC maple upholstered stool. Sworders, Stansted Mountfitchet. July 01. £260.

2794

Early Victorian pitch pine gothic revival fire surround, 48in wide. Sworders, Stansted Mountfitchet. Apr 01. £260.

2795

Art Deco limed oak dome top bookcase, 36in. Crows, Dorking. July 01. £260.

2796

Art Deco oval olive wood occasional table on U shaped base, 57cm. Sworders, Stansted Mountfitchet. June 03. £260.

2797

Carved oak elbow chair. Sworders, Stansted Mountfitchet. July 01. £260.

2798

Primitive ash chopping block, 19thC, 27in dia, 28in high. Hamptons, Godalming. Nov 01. £260.

2799

19thC mahogany chiffonier, 31in wide. Amersham Auction Rooms, Bucks. Oct 02. £260.

2800

Pair of early 20thC leather armchairs, tub style. Ambrose, Loughton. Feb 02. £260.

2801

Georgian mahogany chest of 2 short and 3 long drawers, 41in. Denhams, Warnham. Oct 03. £260.

2802

19thC mahogany occasional table. W & H Peacock, Bedford. June 03. £260.

2803

Georgian mahogany tray top commode with fall front, 17in. Denhams, Warnham. Dec 03. £260.

2804

Pair of George III mahogany elbow chairs, serpentine crests, tapestry upholstered seats. Amersham Auction Rooms, Bucks. Nov 03. £260.

The numbering system acts as a reader reference as well as linking to the Analysis of each Section

2805

19thC folding rosewood and marquetry nursing chair, over-stuffed seat, folding frame. Dee, Atkinson & Harrison, Driffield. Mar 04. £260.

2806

19thC oak hanging quadrant corner cupboard, H brass hinges, moulded base, 37.5in. Dee, Atkinson & Harrison, Driffield. Mar 04. £260.

2807

Edwardian rosewood settee, upholstered arms and back rests. Thos Mawer & Son, Lincoln. June 04. £260.

2808

Finely carved Hepplewhite design mahogany elbow chair. Thos Mawer & Son, Lincoln. Feb 03. £260.

2809

19thC mahogany side table, two boxwood strung drawers, 90cm wide. Thos Mawer & Son, Lincoln. Apr 02. £250.

2810

Antique metal bound seaman's oak chest, 30 x 22in. Lambert & Foster, Tenterden. Apr 01. £250.

2811

Early 20thC mahogany tray top tripod table, Chippendale design, 26.5in dia. Canterbury Auc. Galleries, Kent. Feb 04\. £250.

Hammer Prices £260-£250

2812

18thC coopered yoke bucket, 13in dia., 23.5in high. Tring Market Auctions, Herts. Sep 02. £250.

2813

Victorian childs cot, iron and brass, brass makers plaque 'R W Winfield & Co', 48in long. Sworders, Stansted Mountfitchet. July 01. £250.

2814

George III mahog. inverted bowfront washstand, ebony inlay, 45cm wide. Rosebery's, London. Sep 03. £250.

2815

Victorian walnut conical workbox, interior fitted with compartments, standing on relief carved triple cabriole supports. Thos Mawer & Son, Lincoln. Apr 02. £250.

2816

18thC oak panelled coffer, 52in wide. Dee, Atkinson & Harrison, Driffield. Mar 04. £250.

2817

Pair of George III mahogany side chairs. Cheffins, Cambridge. Sep 01. £250.

2818

Late 18thC Windsor chair, probably Buckinghamshire. Thos Mawer & Son, Lincoln. Feb 03. £250.

2819

Display cabinet in the form of the bow of a clinker built rowing boat, applied with a shield crest and painted with the Royal Coat of Arms, 193cm. Cheffins, Cambridge. June 01. £250.

Section XI   Under £250

It is essential when buying twentieth century furniture to buy the very best quality you can find, preferably with a maker's label. Avoid at all costs the utility furniture of the period, which is fit only for 'shipping'.

This final Section, may well contain purchases that perhaps would have been best avoided. Alternatively, studying these pages indicate that this area can also be the bargain basement for those collectors operating on a low budget. Here you can still find at lease five seventeenth century examples commencing with the probably seventeenth century dough bin at **2831** which should be more money, but is probably not in the best of health! Here also there are about thirty five Georgian pieces but the majority are Victorian with about sixty from the twentieth century. On page 171 is a handsome pair of Arts & Crafts mirrors complete with sconces with copper frames for £240. A further, simple mirror appears on page 182 at **3029** for only £45. Antique brass and copper has been seriously affected by reproductions and at the same time are out of favour as they need regular cleaning and don't always fit into the modern home where more often than not both Mum and Dad work.

Elm and country style features well in this Section as does oak. At **2824** is an elm bench of uncertain date but there is a good Georgian hoop-back Windsor at **2834** for only £240. At this price expect problems. The cottage kitchen look can certainly be enhanced by the set of four eighteenth century provincial elm, Chippendale style dining chairs which sold for £240 at W & H Peacock, Bedford in July 2003. Such a purchase will always hold its value and could even offer the benefit of profit in several years when family needs or greater affluence allow you to move up market. These chairs are probably getting on for 250 years old and certainly do not look to have reached the end of their life yet.

At **2873** is a nineteenth century child's wing rocking chair in mahogany. This sold for £210 in August 2002. Interestingly, another example **2986**, sold in the same sale for only £110, probably with faults. The Charles Eames swivel chair, **2880**, with its burgundy leather fetched £200 in July 2001 at Lots Road Auctions in Chelsea. Remember the first Eames example on page 53 which fetched £2,200? Check out the *Index*. This could have been a good investment. Is it possible to buy an Eames chair today for £200? Notice now at **2896** more George III elm dining chairs. Those wishing to buy into the Art Deco period will obviously study the *Index* and could take an interest in the rather quirky walnut drinks table with a pop-up centre which sold for a mere £190 in December 2003. The final Art Deco example in these

pages occurs at **2989** on page 180, when a fairly standard and nondescript display cabinet fetched only £110 at Ambrose, Loughton, in March 2002. This is utility furniture of the period and of 'shipping' interest only. It is essential when buying twentieth century furniture to buy the very best quality you can find, preferably with a maker's label. We have recently bought for the office, a good quality solid oak six feet long, 4-door cupboard, with the Nottingham maker's ivory/bone label attached to the back. This will increase in value. The display cabinet will not.

At **2938** are a pair of Elizabeth II coronation stools. Whilst most of the 1953 event memorabilia is ubiquitous and best avoided, these stools were a good buy and in years to come will increase in value. Period toilet mirrors, even serpentine fronted, with a shield shape mirror, **2941**, are not uncommon and seem out of favour at present. However, this one looks well worth the £160 investment and is pretty enough to grace a period mahogany chest of draws which one should be able to buy starting at £300-£400. See previous Section.

I know people who would die for the oak Gothic chair, **2946**, which sold in February 2003 for only £150. They collect good twentieth century oak which is very affordable and knocks modern furniture into 'a cocked hat'! The yew/elm stick-back at **2963** can be restored, but only by experts. Alternatively, the ash and elm smoker's bow at **2969** at only £130 and dating from the mid-nineteenth century is well under what you would pay retail which would be nearer £200. Similarly, the pair of Georgian fruitwood wheel-back Windsors, **2979**, which sold at Richard Winterton in Burton-on-Trent for only £120 in 2004 were good value for those seeking to build up a harlequin set of period kitchen chairs. Alternatively, the Windsor, **2993**, at £110 looks to be a reproduction. The Georgian ladder-back, **3013**, can also serve an individual use or more examples may be found. The Windsor slat-back, **3015**, is a serious bargain. So also is **3026**. The early nineteenth century Georgian country elm elbow chair, which found only £30 at Dee, Atkinson & Harrison, Driffield in March 2004 is a snip. There is a pretty Georgian mahogany corner washstand, **2983**, at only £120 on page 180. And consider the decorative bonus, plus the added feeling of space one can achieve by setting the early twentieth century wall mirror, **2991**, above a fireplace in a main living room.

2820

19thC mahogany piano stool, 13.25in wide. *Andrew Hartley, Ilkley. Apr 01. £240.*

2821

19thC carved mahog. armchair upholstered in old gold silk. *Lambert & Foster, Tenterden. Aug 01. £240.*

The illustrations are in descending price order. The price range is indicated at the top of each page.

2822

Pair late 19thC Arts & Crafts influenced 2 branch mirror-back wall sconces, copper frame, 11in wide, 17in high. *Tring Market Auctions. Herts. Nov 02. £240.*

2823

Edwardian inlaid mahogany display cabinet, 94cm wide. *Lambert & Foster, Tenterden. Apr 02. £240.*

2824

Elm bench, 8ft 1in long. *Sworders, Stansted Mount-fitchet. Apr 01. £240.*

2825

Edwardian satinwood easy chair, white line inlay, upholstered in green and cream regency stripe. *Hamptons, Godalming. July 02. £240.*

2826

Victorian mahog. two drawer writing table, with later top, 52in wide. *Sworders, Stansted Mountfitchet. Apr 01. £240.*

2827

Pair Edwardian easy chairs, inlaid mahogany frames, pink upholstery. *Sworders, Stansted Mountfitchet. July 01. £240.*

2828

Mid Victorian mahog. pedestal table, 27in high, 23in dia. *Amersham Auction Rooms, Bucks. Oct 02. £240.*

Hammer Price £240

2829

19thC crossbanded/strung mahogany chest of drawers, (crossbanding missing) 40in wide. *Sworders, Stansted Mountfitchet. July 01. £240.*

2830

19thC mahogany occasional table, 28in high, 23in wide. *Amersham Auction Rooms, Bucks. Mar 02. £240.*

2831

Elm dough bin on turned legs, 45in long. *Sworders, Stansted Mount-fitchet. July 01. £240.*

2832

Pair of Victorian button back armchairs. *Sworders, Stansted Mountfitchet. July 01. £240.*

2833

19thC mahog. corner wash-stand with blue/white basin, two Copeland bowls and a vase. *Sworders, Stansted Mountfitchet. July 01. £240.*

2834

Early 19thC ash/elm framed high hoop back Windsor chair. *Amersham Auction Rooms, Bucks. Mar 03. £240.*

2835

Geo. III mahog. elbow chair and a shield back elbow chair. *Sworders, Stansted Mountfitchet. Apr 01. £240.*

2836

Set of four 18thC provincial elm Chippendale-style dining chairs. *W & H Peacock, Bedford. July 03. £240.*

2837

Pair Georgian mahogany D-end tables. *W & H Peacock, Bedford. Feb 03. £240.*

2838

17thC oak table, with later top, 24in wide. *Sworders, Stansted Mountfitchet. Apr 01. £240.*

Hammer Prices £240-£220

Victorian walnut inlaid music cabinet, glazed door, 61cm. *Locke & England, Leamington Spa. May 03. £240.*

19thC walnut nursing chair, buttoned back and seat in velvet. *Lambert & Foster, Tenterden. Apr 03. £240.*

18thC mahog. hanging corner cupboard, 102cm high. *Thos Mawer & Son, Lincoln. Feb 03. £240.*

Early Victorian mahogany side table. *W & H Peacock, Bedford. July 03. £240.*

French walnut double bed, carved, panelled ends, 138cm wide. *Sworders, Stansted Mountfitchet. July 03. £240.*

Edwardian mahog. bow front display cabinet, inlaid with boxwood stringings, 34in wide. *Canterbury Auction Galleries, Kent. Feb 04. £240.*

Edwardian mahog. hanging corner cabinet, blind fret frieze, 30in high. *Sworders, Stansted Mountfitchet. July 01. £240.*

Child's Victorian rosewood spoon back revolving chair, triform base. *Denhams, Warnham. Oct 03. £240.*

Pair 19thC French gilt gesso upholstered single chairs. *Locke & England, Leamington Spa. July 03. £240.*

Edwardian inlaid mahogany revolving bookcase, two tiers, 50cm. *Locke & England, Leamington Spa. Sep 03. £240.*

19thC mahogany chest, shaped apron, 107cm wide. *Lambert & Foster, Tenterden. June 04. £230.*

19thC mahog. toilet mirror, twist turned supports, 36in high. *Sworders, Stansted Mountfitchet. July 01. £230.*

George III mahog. washstand /bidet. (interior converted). *Sworders, Stansted Mountfitchet. Apr 01. £220.*

Pair late 18thC Chippendale style, poss. Portuguese parcel gilt, walnut framed dining chairs. *Amersham Auction Rooms, Bucks. Dec 01. £220.*

Antique style oak side cabinet, two frieze drawers and 2 panelled doors, 46in wide. *Sworders, Stansted Mountfitchet. July 01. £220.*

George III mahog. Pembroke table, 98 x 104cm open. *Locke & England, Leamington Spa. Feb 03. £220.*

Pair 1930s upholstered and oak framed sprung rocking chairs. *Sworders, Stansted Mountfitchet. Apr 01. £220.*

Georgian style mahogany extending dining table, an extra leaf, 182cm. *Locke & England, Leamington Spa. Feb 03. £220.*

Edwardian mahogany telegram stand, by J C Vickery, brass tablet engraved 'Telegrams', 13.5in wide. *Tring Market Auctions, Herts. Sep 02. £220.*

Carolean style stool 61cm. *Sworders, Stansted Mountfitchet. Dec 02. £220.*

Prices quoted are hammer and exclude the buyer's premium. Adding 15% will give approx. buying price.

Early 20thC mahogany corner wall cupboard. *W & H Peacock, Bedford. Dec 02. £220.*

Edwardian inlaid mahogany display cabinet. *W & H Peacock, Bedford. Mar 03. £220.*

Victorian walnut three section Canterbury. *W & H Peacock, Bedford. July 03. £220.*

Geo. III mahog. fold over card table, rosewood crossbanding, ebony and boxwood inlay, 35in wide. af. *Sworders, Stansted Mountfitchet. July 01. £220.*

Set of six walnut Victorian balloon back chairs. *Locke & England, Leamington Spa. May 03. £220.*

Early Victorian rosewood X framed stool. (repaired). *Sworders, Stansted Mountfitchet. July 01. £220.*

Georgian oak chest, brass drop handles, 41.25in wide. *Dee, Atkinson & Harrison, Driffield. Mar 04. £220.*

Set of four Victorian balloon back chairs, drop in seats. *Lambert & Foster, Tenterden. Aug 03. £220.*

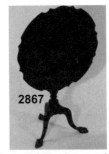

Early 20thC mahogany tilt top table. *W & H Peacock, Bedford. Feb 03. £220.*

Georgian mahogany tray top commode, tambour front above the commode drawer, 48 x 43cm. *Thos Mawer & Son, Lincoln. Feb 03. £220.*

19thC mahog. framed armchair upholstered mushroom buttoned material. *Denhams, Warnham. Mar 04. £220.*

Carved gilt wood pedestal table, inlaid specimen marble chessboard, 24in. *Denhams, Warnham. Dec 03. £220.*

19thC mahog. bureau, slope with 4 short, one long drawer, over 4 long drawers, 91.5cm wide, af. *Lambert & Foster, Tenterden. June 04. £220.*

Victorian ebonised occasional table, ivory inlaid amboyna banded top, 2ft. *Gorringes, Lewes. Mar 04. £220.*

Child's mahog. wing rocking chair, with pierced circular handle, shaped and pierced arms and waved apron, 19thC, 26.5in high. *Andrew Hartley, Ilkley. Aug 02. £210.*

173

Hammer Prices £210-£200

Set of four Victorian balloon back chairs. *Lambert & Foster, Tenterden. Apr 02. £210.*

Victorian inlaid walnut side cabinet, glazed panel door, 71cm wide. *Lambert & Foster, Tenterden. Feb 04. £210.*

Oak and inlaid hall table and matching stool. *Crows, Dorking. May 01. £210.*

'Mouseman' oak stool. (Top in poor condition). *Sworders, Stansted Mountfitchet. Apr 01. £210.*

17thC oak plank coffer, later carving, loose top, 3ft 3in. *Gorringes, Lewes. Sep 03. £210.*

Edwardian mahogany butler's tray and stand. *Crows, Dorking. Apr 01. £210.*

Charles Eames swivel chair in burgundy leather back and seat. *Lots Road Auctions, Chelsea. July 01. £200.*

19thC mahogany pedestal desk, 46in wide. *Sworders, Stansted Mountfitchet. Apr 01. £200.*

Edwardian mahogany envelope card table. *Crows, Dorking. May 01. £200.*

Victorian mahog. chiffonier, (replaced top). *Crows, Dorking. Aug 01. £200.*

American bow back writing chair. *Sworders, Stansted Mountfitchet. July 01. £200.*

Late Victorian stripped pine chest, on plinth base, 107cm wide. *Lambert & Foster, Tenterden. Sep 02. £200.*

Gilt framed oval wall mirror, rococo style, 25.5in high. *Fellows & Sons, Hockley, Birmingham. Dec 02. £200.*

Victorian mahog. side table, single frieze drawer, 26in wide. *Sworders, Stansted Mountfitchet. Apr 01. £200.*

Geo. III mahog. two plateau corner washstand. *Locke & England, Leamington Spa. Nov 02. £200.*

Victorian rosewood chiffonier, carved, moulded decoration, 102cm. af. *Lambert & Foster, Tenterden. Apr 02. £200.*

Mahogany bergere three piece suite. *Ambrose, Loughton. Mar 02. £200.*

Well carved Victorian gothic revival oak hall stand, 92cm wide. *Thos Mawer & Son, Lincoln. Apr 02. £200.*

2892

19thC mahog. hanging corner cupboard, 82cm wide. *Dreweatt Neate, Newbury. Nov 02. £200.*

2893

19thC Country made oak settle of pegged construction. 178cm. *Locke & England, Leamington Spa. Feb 03. £200.*

> The numbering system acts as a reader reference as well as linking to the Analysis of the Section.

2894

Late 18thC oak hanging corner cupboard, 90cm high. *Thos Mawer & Son, Lincoln. Feb 03. £200.*

2895

Edwardian mahog. Sheraton Revival design pedestal, simulated drawer, 62cm wide. *Thos Mawer & Son, Lincoln. June 04. £200.*

2896

Pair of George III elm elbow chairs, and a pair of similar single chairs to match. (4). *Andrew Hartley, Ilkley. Feb 03. £200.*

2897

Bamboo framed adjustable steamer chair, woven coloured cane decoration. *Sworders, Stansted Mountfitchet. June 03. £200.*

2898

18thC oak coffer, 138cm. *Locke & England, Leamington Spa. Feb 03. £200.*

2899

19thC Dutch marquetry mahogany elbow chair. (cut down). *Gorringes, Lewes. Jan 04. £200.*

2900

George III mahogany elbow chair, overstuffed seat. *Andrew Hartley, Ilkley. Feb 04. £200.*

Hammer Price £200-£180

2901

Late 19thC Continental walnut framed open armchair, padded blue dralon upholstered back and seat. *Amersham Auction Rooms, Bucks. May 03. £190.*

2902

Early 20thC Arts and Crafts inspired mahogany framed chair. *Amersham Auction Rooms, Bucks. June 01. £190.*

2903

Oak tripod table, 18.25in dia. *Lambert & Foster, Tenterden. Apr 03. £190.*

2904

George III oak wall mounting corner cupboard, 75cm. *Locke & England, Leamington Spa. Sep 02. £190.*

2905

19thC mahog. chest, 108cm wide. *Lambert & Foster, Tenterden. Aug 03. £190.*

2906

Art Deco walnut drinks table with a pop up centre, 78cm dia. *Sworders, Stansted Mountfitchet. Dec 03. £190.*

2907

Early 20thC pine framed Orkney chair. *Amersham Auction Rooms, Bucks. Nov 03. £190.*

2908

Oak storage cabinet, interior 9 sliding trays, tambour front, 21in wide. *Lambert & Foster, Tenterden. Apr 01. £180.*

Hammer Prices £190-£160

Pair early 19thC windsor chairs, yew cartwheel splats, spur stretchers. (one sd). *Richard Wintertons, Burton on Trent. Apr 04. £190.*

Victorian stained pine tavern table, on an X frame base, 54 x 30in. *Sworders, Stansted Mountfitchet. Apr 01. £180.*

Early 20thC walnut bergere three seater settee. *Ambrose, Loughton. Mar 02. £180.*

Edwardian oak shaving stand, adjustable mirror, 17.25in wide. *Dee, Atkinson & Harrison, Driffield. Mar 04. £180.*

Set of 3 Victorian mahogany balloon back dining chairs. *Dee, Atkinson & Harrison, Driffield. Mar 04. £180.*

Georgian mahog. bird cage tripod table, 77cm dia. *Thos Mawer & Son, Lincoln. June 04. £180.*

Oak bible box, 26in wide. *Sworders, Stansted Mountfitchet. July 01. £170.*

Victorian mahogany kneehole side table, 44in wide. *Sworders, Stansted Mountfitchet. July 01. £170.*

Victorian grained pine chest of drawers, 97cm wide. *Lambert & Foster, Tenterden. Aug 03. £170.*

Victorian mahogany chest with cross banded top, 99cm wide. *Lambert & Foster, Tenterden. Sep 02. £170.*

Spindle back rocking armchair. af. *Lambert & Foster, Tenterden. May 02. £170.*

19thC nursing chair, stained beech supports, front legs replaced. *Dee, Atkinson & Harrison, Driffield. Mar 04. £170.*

Victorian turned/carved rosewood piano stool, rising seat, gadrooned baluster column, claw feet. *Sworders, Stansted Mountfitchet. July 03. £170.*

Oak long stool, thumb carved frieze rail on spiral twist legs, 124cm. *Lambert & Foster, Tenterden. Apr 04. £170.*

19thC mahog. turned wood boot stand, 36.5in wide, 42in high. *Tring Market Auctions, Herts. Mar 03. £170.*

George III elm trunk, pair of sham base drawers, 45.5in wide. *Sworders, Stansted Mountfitchet. Apr 01. £160.*

17thC oak plank top coffer, 37in wide. af. *Lambert & Foster, Tenterden. Apr 03. £160.*

19thC walnut stool, on twist turned legs. *Sworders, Stansted Mountfitchet. Apr 01. £160.*

Continental mahog. plate rack, 120cm wide. (splits). *Dreweatt Neate, Newbury. Nov 02. £160.*

176

2928

19thC mahog. canteen box, 27in wide. Sworders, Stansted Mountfitchet. July 01. £160.

2929

Edwardian inlaid mahogany display cabinet, astragal glazed doors, squat cabriole legs, 90cm wide. Ambrose, Loughton. Mar 02. £160.

The illustrations are in descending price order. The price range is indicated at the top of each page.

2930

Edwardian mahog. serving/ butlers table, 37cm, af. Lambert & Foster, Tenterden. Feb 04. £160.

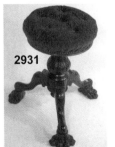

2931

19thC rosewood piano stool, rising top, stamped H Brooks & Co Ltd. Thos Mawer & Son, Lincoln. Feb 03. £160.

2932

19thC ship's surgeon's oak chest. W & H Peacock, Bedford. Dec 02. £160.

2933

Pair mahogany stools, tops require re-upholstering. Lambert & Foster, Tenterden. Jan 03. £160.

2934

Pair 19thC oak parlour chairs. (leather upholstery af). Sworders, Stansted Mountfitchet. Apr 01. £160.

2935

Victorian walnut open arm hall chair. W & H Peacock, Bedford. July 03. £160.

2936

Edwardian honey oak pedestal filing chest, top with hinged reading slope, tambour shutter, 19in. Denhams, Warnham. June 04. £160.

Hammer Prices £160-£150

2937

Reproduction carved oak monks seat/table, 42in wide. Lambert & Foster, Tenterden. Apr 03. £160.

2938

Pair Elizabeth II Coronation stools. W & H Peacock, Bedford. July 03. £160.

2939

Japanese Meiji period lacquer multi drawer work cabinet. Locke & England, Leamington Spa. Sep 02. £160.

2940

Edwardian mahogany fold over card table, 36in wide. Dee, Atkinson & Harrison, Driffield. Mar 04. £160.

2941

Hepplewhite period strung mahogany toilet mirror, 24in wide. Sworders, Stansted Mountfitchet. July 01. £160.

2942

19thC walnut prie dieu side chair, upholstered back, padded seat, 97cm. Bristol Auction Rooms. Jan 04. £155.

2943

Mahog. tripod table, original old top now fixed on pedestal base, 30in dia. (reduced in height). Lambert & Foster, Tenterden. Aug 01. £150.

2944

Victorian walnut framed spoonback chair. Sworders, Stansted Mountfitchet. July 01. £150.

2945

Late Victorian nursing chair, deeply buttoned back, seat upholstered in olive green dralon. Lambert & Foster, Tenterden. Apr 02. £150.

Hammer Prices £150-£140

2946

Solid oak Gothic inspired carver chair, panelled seat. Locke & England, Leamington Spa. Feb 03. £150.

2947

'Arts & Crafts' copper framed mirror, 21.5 x 17.5in. Sworders, Stansted Mountfitchet. Apr 01. £150.

2948

Victorian oval mahog. toilet mirror on spiral supports, 25in wide. Lambert & Foster, Tenterden. Feb 02. £150.

2949

Early 20thC Moorish occasional table, parquetry paua shell and ebony inlaid decoration, 18.5in. Gorringes, Lewes. June 03. £150.

2950

Ebonised three division Canterbury. Lambert & Foster, Tenterden. May 02. £150.

2951

18thC style walnut stool. Sworders, Stansted Mountfitchet. Apr 01. £150.

2952

Early 19thC mahogany toilet mirror, 18.5in wide. Dockree's, Manchester. Sep 00. £150.

2953

Period design oak joint stool, 45.5cm. Locke & England, Leamington Spa. Jan 03. £140.

2954

Geo. III mahog./yew wood stool frame. Sworders, Stansted Mountfitchet. Apr 01. £140.

2955

Walnut fender stool, tapestry top. Sworders, Stansted Mountfitchet. Apr 01. £140.

2956

Late Victorian mahogany, Duchess style dressing table, 46in wide. Amersham Auction Rooms, Bucks. June 02. £140.

2957

Strung mahog. book trough, 18in long. Sworders, Stansted Mountfitchet. July 01. £140.

2958

19thC elm dough bin, 37in wide. Sworders, Stansted Mountfitchet. July 01. £140.

2959

Victorian rosewood and brass inlaid writing slope, 50cm wide. Lambert & Foster, Tenterden. Apr 03. £140.

2960

Pair of 19thC mahogany tub chairs, gold dralon upholstery. Sworders, Stansted Mountfitchet. Apr 01. £140.

2961

Edwardian inlaid display cabinet. W & H Peacock, Bedford. Mar 03. £140.

2962

Victorian walnut salon chair. Lambert & Foster, Tenterden. Feb 04. £140.

2963

Late 18th/early19thC yew-wood/elm stick back Windsor armchair. (Thames Valley - reduced in height, damaged). Canterbury Auc. Galleries, Kent. Feb 04. £140.

2964

Edwardian inlaid mahogany collectors cabinet, 39cm wide. Lambert & Foster, Tenterden. Feb 04. £140.

2965

Late Victorian oak side table with a parquetry top, 114 x 79cm. Thos Mawer & Son, Lincoln. Feb 03. £140.

2966

Edwardian mahog. revolving piano/cellist stool, pad back and seat. Lambert & Foster, Tenterden. Feb 04. £140.

Prices quoted are hammer and exclude the buyer's premium. Adding 15% will give approx. buying price.

2967

Mahogany toilet mirror, 36in high. Sworders, Stansted Mountfitchet. Apr 01. £140.

2968

Mid Georgian mahogany fretwork wall mirror, 38cm wide. Bristol Auction Rooms, Bristol. Jan 04. £135.

2969

Ash and elm smokers bow chair. Sworders, Stansted Mountfitchet. July 01. £130.

2970

Regency carved mahogany carver chair. W & H Peacock, Bedford. July 03. £130.

2971

Late 19thC mahogany tilt top table, 60cm wide. Ambrose, Loughton. Feb 02. £130.

2972

Early 19thC rosewood pole-screen, 138.5cm. Locke & England, Leamington Spa. Sep 03. £130.

Hammer Prices £140-£120

2973

Period design oak joint stool, 45.5cm. Locke & England, Leamington Spa. Jan 03. £130.

2974

Edwardian mahogany tub chair, deep padded back. Dee, Atkinson & Harrison, Driffield. Mar 04. £130.

2975

Carved oak armchair, solid seat, baluster turned legs. Lambert & Foster, Tenterden. Apr 04. £130.

2976

Empire style mahog. torchere, veined marble top, gilt metal mounts, decorated with reefs and masks, 77cm. Rosebery's, London. June 04. £120.

2977

Late Georgian oak pedestal table, tripod sabre leg base. Richard Wintertons, Burton on Trent. Dec 01. £120.

2978

Victorian oak dresser base, 66in wide. Sworders, Stansted Mountfitchet. Apr 01. £120.

2979

Pair of fruitwood windsor chairs, early 19thC, hooped backs. Richard Wintertons, Burton on Trent. Apr 04. £120.

2980

Late 18thC fruitwood table top linen press. Sworders, Stansted Mountfitchet. July 01. £120.

2981

Mahogany occasional table, 1st half 20thC, Georgian style, 98cm wide. R. Wintertons, Burton on Trent. Feb 04. £120.

Hammer Prices £120-£100

19thC mahogany bow front chest of 3 drawers, 106cm wide, distressed. *Thos Mawer & Son, Lincoln. June 04. £120.*

George III mahogany corner washstand. *W & H Peacock, Bedford. Dec 02. £120.*

Sheraton Revival mahogany satinwood banded and ebony strung fold over card table, 68cm wide. *Thos Mawer & Son, Lincoln. Apr 02. £120.*

19thC armchair, Hepplewhite design, drop in seat, af. *Lambert & Foster, Tenterden. May 02. £120.*

Child's mahog. wing rocking chair, heart shaped handle, 19thC, 24.75in high. *Andrew Hartley, Ilkley. Aug 02. £110.*

Cast brass dressing mirror, pierced in renaissance style with masks, candle sconce to each side, 25in. *Gorringes, Lewes. Apr 02. £110.*

Oak bedside cupboard, fitted with one shelf, 21in. *Lambert & Foster, Tenterden. Feb 02. £110.*

Art Deco walnut display cabinet, shaped bar glazed doors, 104cm wide. *Ambrose, Loughton. Mar 02. £110.*

Edwardian mahogany corner armchair, inlaid marquetry, original corduroy seat. *Locke & England, Leamington Spa. Feb 03. £110.*

Early 20thC wall mirror with sheaf decoration, 140cm high. *Ambrose, Loughton. Feb 02. £110.*

Edwardian tub chair, splats pierced/carved with fleur-de-lys. *Dee, Atkinson & Harrison, Driffield. Mar 04. £110.*

Elm stick and wheel back Windsor chair on turned supports. *Denhams, Warnham. Mar 04. £110.*

Edwardian folding travelling beech rocking crib, spindle turned ends, 28in high. *Dee, Atkinson & Harrison, Driffield. Mar 04. £110.*

19th/20thC honey oak wine table, 19in. *Denhams, Warnham. Feb 04. £110.*

19thC mahog. commode chest, 64cm wide. *Lambert & Foster, Tenterden. Aug 03. £110.*

Antique mahogany chest, 43in. af. *Lambert & Foster, Tenterden. Apr 02. £100.*

Inlaid mahogany kidney shaped occasional table. *Lambert & Foster, Tenterden. May 02. £100.*

Hammer Prices £100-£90

2999

19thC American style spindle rocking chair. W & H Peacock, Bedford. Mar 03. £100.

3000

Victorian mahogany chaise longue, having green button back upholstery with fluted frieze, 119cm long. Ambrose, Loughton. Feb 02. £100.

> The numbering system acts as a reader reference as well as linking to the Analysis of the Section

3001

Edwardian mahogany and inlaid armchair. Dee, Atkinson & Harrison, Driffield. Mar 04. £100.

3002

19thC mahog. pot cupboard, 16.75in wide, 30.25in high. Dee, Atkinson & Harrison, Driffield. Mar 04. £100.

3003

Late 19thC domed pine trunk, wooden and metal slats, 92cm wide. Locke & England, Leamington Spa. Oct 03. £100.

3004

1930s walnut footstool, embroidered seat. Sworders, Stansted Mountfitchet. Sep 03. £100.

3005

Regency mahogany carver chair. W & H Peacock, Bedford. Feb 03. £100.

3006

Footstool with a floral tapestry seat, brass ring handles. Sworders, Stansted-Mountfitchet. Feb 03. £100.

3007

Victorian walnut and ebonised stool, woolwork upholstered square top, 23in high. Dee, Atkinson & Harrison, Driffield. Mar 04. £100.

3008

19thC maple single drawer side table. Sworders, Stansted Mountfitchet. July 01. £95.

3009

19thC mahogany chest commode. Sworders, Stansted Mountfitchet. July 01. £95.

3010

Victorian mahogany folding cake stand, 34in high. Dee, Atkinson & Harrison, Driffield. Mar 04. £95.

3011

Early 20thC turned mahog. 3 tier stand. W & H Peacock, Bedford. Mar 03. £90.

3012

2 open armchairs of similar design. Lambert & Foster, Tenterden. Dec 02. £90.

3013

Early 19thC mahog. ladder back carver, with rush seat. Dee, Atkinson & Harrison, Driffield. Mar 04. £90.

3014

Late Victorian mahogany armchair. Lambert & Foster, Tenterden. May 02. £90.

3015

Windsor slat back armchair, solid saddle seat on turned legs & stretchers. Lambert & Foster, Tenterden. Apr 02. £90.

181

Hammer Prices £85-£20

3016

20thC occasional table of French design, 107.5cm. *Locke & England, Leamington Spa. May 03. £85.*

3017

Inlaid walnut games table on bobbin turned twin end supports, centre stretcher, 34.25 x 16.5in. *Lambert & Foster, Tenterden. Feb 02. £85.*

3018

19thC child's oak and bergere caned chair. *W & H Peacock, Bedford. Dec 02. £85.*

3019

Oak collectors cabinet, fitted nine small drawers, 15 x 6.5in. *Lambert & Foster, Tenterden. Apr 01. £80.*

3020

Early 19thC mahogany elbow chair, overstuffed seat. *Dee, Atkinson & Harrison, Driffield. Mar 04. £80.*

3021

19thC stained beech campaign chair, caned seat. *Dee, Atkinson & Harrison, Driffield. Mar 04. £75.*

3022

19thC Continental satin birch and gesso armchair, lacks castors. *Gorringes, Lewes. Sep 03. £75.*

3023

Victorian ebonised adjustable piano stool. *Denhams, Warnham. Oct 03. £75.*

3024

Mid 19thC mahogany hall chair, shaped back with carved rosettes and painted with coat of arms, solid seat. *Rosebery's, London. June 04. £75.*

3025

Victorian upholstered stool, carved walnut legs. *Sworders, Stansted Mountfitchet. Apr 01. £75.*

3026

Victorian beech/elm seated smokers bow armchair. *Locke & England, Leamington Spa. Oct 03. £70.*

3027

Late 19thC rosewood pedestal table, 18in dia. *Amersham Auction Rooms, Bucks. Sep 02. £65.*

3028

Edwardian mahog. side table, two frieze drawers, 94cm wide. *Ambrose, Loughton. Mar 02. £60.*

3029

Arts & Crafts style copper mirror, 25in long. *Sworders, Stansted Mountfitchet. July 01. £45.*

3030

Victorian mahogany/inlaid jardiniere stand, 24.5in high. *Dee, Atkinson & Harrison, Driffield. Mar 04. £35.*

3031

19thC elm country elbow chair, curved crest rail on line incised uprights and pierced bar back, panel seat. *Dee, Atkinson & Harrison, Driffield. Mar 04. £30.*

3032

Mahogany occasional table, moulded top, platform undertier, 65cm wide. *Ambrose, Loughton. Mar 02. £20.*

3033

Edwardian mahogany occasional table. *Ambrose, Loughton. Feb 02. £20.*

A

Abbotswood furniture After Sir Walter Scott's house. Furnishings in Romantic-Gothic mood imitating Tudor and Jacobean work.

Acacia wood Yellowish with dark veining. Used for marquetry.

adze marks Ridges and hollows on furniture smoothed with an adze.

Aesthetic Movement c1865-1890. See also *art furniture*.

alder wood Found in 18thC country furniture. A brown wood with figured grain.

amboyna wood Golden brown with bird's eye curls.

amorini Plump little naked boys found in Baroque furniture.

anthemion Stylised honeysuckle on Neo-Classical furniture.

apple wood Long used for country furniture. Hard, pink to light brown.

ark Northern England term for a sloping lidded chest.

armada chest Iron strong box of the 17thC and 18thC.

armoire Continental term for a clothes cupboard.

art furniture In good taste, in contrast to much commercial manufacture. See *aesthetic*.

art nouveau Late 19th/early 20thC. A break-away from academic styles in favour of asymmetrical shapes, ethereal figures, sinuous plants, hair, flames, waves, etc.

arts and crafts Late 19thC artist-craftsmen movement.

ash wood Much used in country furniture. White, tough and springy, hence its use in tool handles.

astragal Small convex moulding concealing a join.

B

bachelor's chest Chest of drawers with folding top that opens as a writing table.

backstool Stool with four legs and an attached back.

ball and claw Claw grasping a flattened ball as foot on a cabriole.

baluster Swelling vase shape.

banding Strips of veneer edging furniture. Includes **straight banding** cut with the wood's grain; **crossbanding** cut across the grain; **feather banding** cut at the slant and **herringbone banding** - two narrow strips of feather banding.

baroque Massive, complex, vigorous, symmetrical style of the 1660s to 1730s. In revolt against Renaissance Classicism.

beechwood Light coloured close grained with small satin-like markings. Used for cheap painted and upholstered furniture/chairs.

bended-back chair. (fiddleback) Early 18thC chair with a baluster splat curved to fit the back.

bentwood furniture Beech often black stained, curved by pressure and steam.

bergère Strictly a French armchair but a caned version revived by Victorians.

berlin wool work Embroidery on squared mesh canvas in soft Marino wools.

birchwood White to pale close grained wood used for mass produced furniture and plywood.

birdcage The hinge device on tilt topped tables.

bird's-eye maple wood Yellowish brown with dark spots linked by wavy lines.

bobbin turning Repetitive turning in swell and ring outline.

bog wood Black timber, often buried deliberately in peat bogs.

bombé The French term for the swelling outline in case furniture.

bonheur du jour Lady's light, elegant writing table.

boule boulle buhl Delicate marquetry of tortoiseshell, horn or ebony inset with brass or silver.

boxwood Grainless pale wood used for inlay and marquetry.

broken pediment A break in the continuity of line or surface.

buffet Usually now-a-days an open shelved stand for dining room use.

bulb Turned egg-shaped swelling on furniture.

bun foot From the late 17thC, a flattened sphere foot.

bureau Literally, a sloping fronted desk which opens up to provide horizontal writing support.

burr or burl Attractive grain from densely knotted growth.

butler's tray, supper tray Sometimes with folding sides and on a folding stand.

C

cabriole leg Curves out at the knee, tapers and curves in above the foot.

campaign furniture Modern term for small, portable furniture associated with military use.

canterbury Small stand on casters with vertical gallery.

caqueteuse Gossip chair. Triangular seat, narrow raked back and curved arms to accommodate wide skirts.

carcase In furniture the basic box like structure.

Carlton House writing table Basically a desk with a D shaped superstructure of small drawers and cupboards.

case furniture Storage furniture as distinct from tables, chairs etc.

cellaret Lockable wine container kept in the dining room.

chaise longue A couch with one end in chair-back form.

chesterfield Double-ended overstuffed couch.

cheval glass Full length mirror swinging between tall supports.

cheveret Narrow table with writing space backed by a set of drawers or pigeon holes.

chiffonier Low cupboard.

Chippendale style Furniture resembling designs by Thomas Chippendale. (1718-79)

club foot, pad foot Rounded projection at the base of a leg, frequently on cabrioles.

coach table Top with central hinges closing up like a book.

coffer Chest with handles and without feet.

commode From the early 1700s French chest of drawers for the salon. In England from the 1750s, a low cupboard with or without drawers. Also associated with night use for the chamber pot.

console table A table supported at the back as a wall fixture, usually with ornate, scrolling incurving front legs.

court cupboard 16th/17thC side table shortened (court) into two or three tiers linked by corner pillars.

cresting Carved ornament surmounting furniture.

cricket stool, table With three turned legs to stand steady on hearthstones.

D

davenport desk A small slant topped desk mounted on a stack of side facing drawers.

day-bed (See *chaise longue*).

deal Pine or other coniferous woods in plank form.

dentils Cornice moulding of small rectangular blocks protruding downwards like teeth.

draw table Extending table with two leaves under a central section supported by bearers which when drawn out provide an extended table service. Popular from 1930s. Made in England from 16thC.

dresser Side table for displaying plate, often with a rack of shelves fixed above.

Dresser, Christopher Pioneer of modern design using severely functional forms.

drum table A round-topped four footed table, drawers in the frieze.

dumb waiter Two or three circular tiers on a central pillar.

dust boards Between drawers as part of the chest of drawers carcase.

E

egg-and-dart Classical architectural ornament consisting of a series of alternate ovals and points.

Egyptian ornament Sphinxes, scarabs, lotus etc. on English

furnishings in the 18thC. More widely popular during the Regency.

elm wood Tough hard wearing wood much used for the seats of Windsor chairs, country furniture.

envelope table Square topped with hinged triangular leaves folding over to the centre.

F

footman Four footed variant of the trivet.

forgery A deliberate fraudulent imitation.

four-poster Differing from a standing bedstead by having a low headboard thus requiring four posts to support the tester.

G

gallery Miniature railing in wood or metal on furniture.

games table Has a reversible top marked out for chess, draughts, backgammon etc.

gate-leg table Falling flaps are raised on additional legs hinged to swing out from the table framing.

Gillow Firm founded in Lancaster in 1695 with London showrooms from 1760s.

girandole In mirrors, has added branching candleholders. Usually in Rococo or Neo-Classical designs.

Gothic taste, Neo-Gothic Associated with Germanic tribes who plundered Rome in AD410. Prevalent in Europe c12th-16thC. Expressed in pointed arch and pinnacle, church window quarte-foils, galleries etc. Gothic revival e.g. Pugin 1812-52.

gueridon Small table or stand for a candlestick or lamp.

H

half-tester bed The tester and curtains extend over only the upper half of the bed and are not supported by posts.

Heal, Sir Ambrose (1872-1959) Furniture designer influenced by William Morris and the Arts and Crafts Movement.

Hepplewhite, George (d1786) Influential furniture designer. Restrained light Neo-Classicism. Grace, delicacy, gentility.

Hope, Thomas (1768-1831) Encouraged a revival of Grecian and Egyptian furnishings.

J

japanning Glossy, rich colours and black surfaces decorated in gold and colours in the style of Oriental resinous gum lacquers.

jardinière 19thC stand for a pot plant or flowers.

K

Kent, William (1686-1748) Architect and pioneer in reviving the Palladian style of heavily scrolled and pedimented furnitures.

L

laburnum wood Hard, heavy greenish yellow with pinkish brown shading. The slices from branches showing marked concentric growth rings were widely used from the 17thC onwards in oyster parquetry.

lacquer Ancient Chinese craft from the Chou dynasty, using the sap of the tree *rhus vernicifera*. Developed by the Japanese and the inspiration for European japanning.

ladder-back A chair with a tall back composed of horizontal rails.

Lancashire chair Name given to a heavy style of hoop-back Windsor. Often yew with turned decoration.

lignum vitae Immensely strong wood of contrasting dark brown and greenish black.

limed oak Wood treated with lime leaving it speckled white and unpolished.

loo table A circular table on a central pillar.

lunettes Half moon or semi-circular shapes found on 17thC furniture (1868-1928).

M

Mackintosh, C R Remembered for his tall austere furniture, designed for a specific setting.

mahogany Warm, brown wood from the West Indies and Central and South America. Cuban from the 1750s, Honduras later.

Manx table Tripod table with carved legs resembling those in the arms of the Isle of Man.

marquetry Elaborate patterns of flowers, birds, etc. in veneer.

Mendlesham chair Suffolk variant of the Windsor.

mouldings Wood cut in decorative section for cabinet making.

mule chest A chest with one or two drawers in the base. Forerunner of the chest of drawers.

N

Neo-classical style From 1760s, reaction to Rococo. Simple curves, vase/urn, reeded legs, low relief anthemion, patera, husk, swag, etc.

P

parquetry Wood veneers cut in symmetrical patterns.

pedestal A solid furniture support in contrast to legs.

pediment A frontal structure above the cornice.

pembroke table Light table with a draw and falling flaps.

piecrust table The rim is shaped in a series of curves.

pilasters Architectural ornaments as flattened columns attached to the corners of cased furniture.

pine wood, Scots pine A pale wood sometimes known as yellow deal, or red deal or pine.

plinth Base of a classical column.

Q

quartetto tables Three or four small tables in graduated sizes and fitting into each other.

R

Regency period Strictly 1811-20 but stylistically c1795-1825.

rent table Octagonal table with drawers all round the frieze.

Restoration period 1660s following the Restoration of the Monarchy under Charles II.

Rococo c1730-80. Asymmetrical, anti-classical. Cartouches, opposing C-scrolls, fantasies, rocks, shells waterfalls. Decoration at expense of form. Escape from heavy Baroque. Late Georgian and early Victorian revival, (2nd Rococo).

rosewood Heavy, dense, purplish brown with black figuring.

S

saddle seat Windsor chair seat of solid wood, usually elm, shaped with depressions to sides of a ridge.

satinwood A golden colour with a satin sheen fashionable in the late 18thC and the mid Victorian period.

scratch carving Simple lines incised into the wood.

Seddon, George (1727-1801) Cabinet maker in Aldersgate Street, London, from 1750.

settle Forerunner of the settee, shaped as a bench with panelled back and arms.

Sheraton, Thomas (1751-1806) Light Neo-Classical furniture. Emphasis on vertical straight lines, sensibility, delicacy.

sheveret See *cheveret*

smoker's bow chair Low back farmhouse kitchen Windsor with back and arms forming a continuous horizontal hoop.

splat Central vertical member of a chair back in baluster outline.

squab seat Chair seat with a low rim to hold a cushion.

steamer chair Victorian folding chair for reclining.

stretchers The horizontal rails linking a chair or table.

stringing Very narrow, square section strips of wood for inlay or veneer patterns.

stuffed-over Furniture framework completely covered by upholstery.

Sutherland table Small gate-leg with narrow top on trestle supports and wide, deep flaps.

swag In Neo-Classical ornament, a festoon of drapery, flowers or husks between two end supports.

swan-neck pediment Broken pediment of two opposing S-scrolls.

T

tabouret Round-topped upholstered stool.

tallboy Double chest of drawers.

tambour, reed-top A flexible desk lid or cupboard door sliding in grooved runners.

tester Wooden canopy of standing bedstead supported by a headboard and two posts, or by four posts.

trestle Vertical end support for table or bench.

tridarn, Cwpwrdd tridarn Traditional Welsh cupboard with the customary two tiers topped by a third stage of shelving.

V

Vitrine Glazed display cabinet.

W

wainscot From the Middle Ages oak quarter-cut and adze-trimmed into boards 8-10in wide. Deal wainscot billets were imported by the 18thC.

walnut wood Finely marked golden brown and usually English. Used for high quality furniture from 16thC.

Wellington chest A small chest of drawers about two feet wide secured by a single lock.

Welsh dresser Generic term from the late 19thC for this type of furniture. See also *Tridarn*.

whatnot, etagère, omnium Moveable stand for displaying treasures. Three or four open shelves supported by spindles resting on casters.

Windsor chair Strictly a chair where a solid saddle seat is bored to receive the back, arms and legs.

wine cooler, wine cistern To hold ice and water to keep wine bottles cool in hot, candle-lit dining rooms.

Y

yew wood Hard, close grained reddish brown native wood.

Furniture Index

This is an integral part of this book and contains approximately 4,500 references to the main sections. The colour coding of the alphabetic lettering system will enable the reader to complete faster searches. Furniture categories have been emboldened and colour-coded to avoid tedious searches through all entries. References to foreign styles have been included such as 'Irish' or 'Louis XV' but references to English styles such as 'Georgian' and 'Victorian' have been excluded on the basis of their frequent usage.